WOMEN AND THE FRENCH ARMY
DURING THE WORLD WARS,
1914–1940

WOMEN

and the

FRENCH ARMY

DURING

THE WORLD WARS,

1914–1940

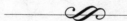

ANDREW ORR

INDIANA UNIVERSITY PRESS

This book is a publication of

Indiana University Press
Office of Scholarly Publishing
Herman B Wells Library 350
1320 East 10th Street
Bloomington, Indiana 47405 USA

iupress.indiana.edu

♾ The paper used in this publication
meets the minimum requirements of the
American National Standard for Informa-
tion Sciences—Permanence of Paper for
Printed Library Materials, ANSI
Z39.48–1992.

Manufactured in the United States of
America

Cataloging information is available from
the Library of Congress.
ISBN 978-0-253-02630-9 (cloth)
ISBN 978-0-253-02677-4 (paperback)
ISBN 978-0-253-02678-1 (ebook)

1 2 3 4 5   22 21 20 19 18 17

CONTENTS

ACKNOWLEDGMENTS

I AM DEEPLY indebted to the professors who trained and encouraged me both as a graduate student and an undergraduate. Most of all I am grateful to Tom Kselman, my doctoral advisor, for his patience, encouragement, and sage advice. Without fear of exaggeration, I can say that he always knew the right advice to give me and the most tactful way to do it.

During my time in graduate school at the University of Notre Dame I was lucky enough to acquire debts to a number of committed and talented professors, including Doris Bergen, who took the time to teach me how to apply for graduate school successfully and whose friendship and support I still value. Laura Crago invested an inordinate amount of time in improving my writing and teaching me to analyze sources with greater rigor. Gary Hamburg's aggressive questioning forced me to learn to articulate my arguments with greater precision and encouraged me to radically recast my project. I am also grateful to Emily Osborne, Semion Lyandres, and Jim Turner for their assistance. In addition, I am cognizant of the debts I owe to Gaines Post Jr. and Harold Rood, my advisors at Claremont McKenna College. Their teaching methods and research interests continue to shape my work.

I have been fortunate to receive financial support at several critical junctures while researching and writing this book. I am grateful to the Nanovic Institute for European Studies at the University of Notre Dame for helping to fund my initial research and to L'Institut de hautes études internationales et du développement in Geneva for providing funding through an Albert Gallatin Fellowship. An Edward Sorin Postdoctoral Fellowship at the University of Notre Dame gave me the time to reevaluate my work and begin the long process of turning it into this book. I am also grateful to Kansas State University's College of Arts and Sciences for generously supporting the final stages of my research with a Faculty Enhancement Program grant and a University Small Research Grant.

I would like to thank the editors at Indiana University Press. Gary Dunham's support for this project has been steadfast, and I appreciate his help. I am also grateful to the anonymous reviewers whose careful reading of my manuscript and judicious advice have helped to make this a better book. Brian Bendlin's copyediting had greatly improved the quality of this book and I am thankful for his invaluable assistance.

In my time as a graduate student and professor I have been especially blessed to work with a large number of colleagues whose friendship and professional expertise have helped me to develop, refine, and complete this book. I am grateful to Marc DeVore for his comradeship going back to our undergraduate days. I also want to thank Sean Brennan, with whom I spent many hours exchanging ideas. In addition, I am grateful to the Euro Lunch crew from Notre Dame, including Neil Dhingra, Troy Feay, Kari Foster, Mark McCarthy, Miriam Rainbird, Wendy Shrank, Nichole Thompson, and Samy Zaka.

Tina Pham has always been generous with her time and has helped me talk through the problems I have run into while working on this project. I would also like to thank my former flatmate in Geneva, Hebatullah Selim, whose friendship helped me enormously when I was writing far from my family and the rest of my friends. I am also grateful to Meggan and Jamie Keith and William and Zandra Towns, whose friendship in graduate school I have not forgotten.

Since becoming a professor I have been fortunate to continue to accumulate debts of gratitude. In particular I would like to thank Rachel Chrastil, whose advice on how to improve and shape my work has been unerringly wise. Jeff Crane, George Diaz, and Lila Rakoczy have helped me to improve my scholarship even as they have enriched my life with their friendship. I am also grateful to many of my colleagues at Kansas State University for their encouragement and friendship. In different ways David Defries, Al Hampshire, Michael Krysko, Heather McCrea, Bonnie

Lynn-Sherow, and Jim Sherow have all gone out of their way to help me and my family both professionally and personally.

Most of all I would like to thank my family for their encouragement and support. My wife Suzanne Orr helped me to conceptualize this book as a project focused on women in the French Army and assisted me as I grappled with European women's history, a field in which I had not originally intended to work. She has lived through this process with me and her encouragement has helped me to keep working even when I wanted to despair. Without her expertise and encouragement I would not have written this book.

I also want to thank my parents Cynthia Bemis and William Orr for everything they have done for me. Their love and sacrifices have helped me throughout my life, and I am deeply grateful to them. Nothing I have accomplished would have been possible without their support.

INTRODUCTION

JEANNE D'ARC'S memory hangs over any study of women and the French military. The fifteenth-century peasant girl from Lorraine who, despite being wounded by an arrow, led French soldiers to victory at Orleans and went on to take Jargeau after suffering a head wound has captivated women and men for nearly six hundred years. Her improbable string of victories turned a dynastic conflict into a holy war that reached its zenith when her army allowed the dauphin to be crowned King Charles VII of France in Reims on July 17, 1429. Even being burned at the stake in Rouen by her English enemies for allegedly practicing witchcraft added to Jeanne's romantic appeal by making her a martyr, and later a saint of the Catholic Church. Unfortunately, the heroic image associated with St. Jeanne d'Arc has, too often, obscured the contributions other women have made to France's national defense. For all of her prominence, Jeanne's story was ordinary in its extraordinariness. Rather than a unique figure, Jeanne d'Arc was merely the most prominent example of the many individual women who took up arms during the Middle Ages. Other examples included Isabel of Conche, Jeanne de Flandre (Jeanne la Flamme), and Jeanne Florquet (Jeanne Hachette). Although few women fought in field armies, let alone commanded them, like Jeanne d'Arc, many helped defend cities and castles. In individual instances their contributions were significant, but they were limited and remained extraordinary exceptions to the male preserve of combat. Focusing on the small number of women who either impersonated men or, like Jeanne, fought openly as women in an otherwise male force obscures the broad contributions women have made to national defense and reinforces the faulty assumption that until the twentieth century the military had always been a masculine preserve.

By studying the experiences of women who worked for the French Army from 1914 until 1940, this book challenges the conceptual barriers that separate scholarly studies of the military and civilian worlds by integrating the elements of political, women's, and social history with the military history of the French Army. The women who worked inside the army were officially civilians, and thus have been ignored by military historians, but they have also been overlooked by historians who have examined France's home front because they were part of the army. In addition, historians of the home front have accepted military history's convention of privileging wartime over peacetime and focusing only on periods of active warfare. This book studies the entire time period from 1914 until the fall of the Third Republic in 1940 as a cohesive whole by placing the interwar era at the center of its narrative as opposed to treating it as an interlude between more important events or a prologue to the Second World War. The result is a history of women and the French Army that shows that women and civilian men were much more involved in national defense than scholars have realized and provides a new way to explore the political evolution of the army's senior leaders, the men who created the Vichy Regime in 1940.

The First World War reversed the progressive exclusion of women from France's military community that had begun in the 1870s, and initiated a long redefinition of women's place within the armed forces. During World War I, civilian women provided vital labor inside the French Army by serving as civilian employees. They performed jobs previously done by soldiers, freed between 200,000 and 300,000 men for the front lines, and freed other men for work in civilian industries that supported the war effort. The established historiography has claimed that almost all of women's wartime gains within the army were erased during the demobilization process, but this study shows that thousands of women continued working within the French Army and, over the course of the 1920s, established a respected—though subordinate—place within the military community. This formed part of a larger redefinition of military identity and a reshuffling of respect within the army as a whole. This redefinition reflected military leaders' concern over the army's postwar contraction, the French Communist Party's efforts to propagandize conscripts and civilian men working for the army, and political debates about giving soldiers the right to vote.

Since the emergence of women's history as a field of study, scholars in the field have argued that placing women at the center of the historical narrative would do more than simply add missing voices to our understanding of the past; it would also force us to redefine periodization. Using women working in the French military as a lens with which to study the French Army and French politics during the late Third Republic challenges the standard periodization of the era.

Placing women at the center of this study reveals that the years 1926–28 were far more important to the French Army and French politics than scholars have previously realized. It was not until Raymond Poincaré returned to the premiership in 1926 that the government was able to finally organize the post–World War I French Army. In many ways the 1927 and 1928 Army Laws marked the point when the French government finally brought its army out of the Great War by beginning a transition to a postwar army. The 1927 and 1928 Army Laws were passed at the same time Poincaré stabilized the franc and restored France's diplomatic position after years of instability. Taken together, these achievements emphasize the importance of Poincaré's final premiership and the reality that it took almost a decade for France to finish demobilizing from the Great War. Unfortunately, the Great Depression soon mitigated many of Poincaré's achievements and instead of ushering in a period of stability within the country and the army, the postwar settlement was soon reopened during contentious budget negotiations.

Studying how military leaders reacted to women's return to the military community and debated their potential value to the army reveals the previously unrecognized importance of officers' fear of politicized conscripts and communism. During the 1920s, debates about hiring more women often fused with discussions about extending voting rights to soldiers and the French Communist Party's attempt to infiltrate the army through propagandizing conscripts and male civilian employees. These debates, which come into focus because of this study's attention to how women's military identity evolved, reveal a deep-seated and growing fear of the republican political system during the 1920s. That fear was rooted in prewar divisions, but it was magnified by wartime and postwar events, including the Trench Mutiny of 1917, the Black Sea Mutiny of 1919, and the French Communist Party's subversion campaigns during the Rif War of 1925–26.

Officers manifested their mistrust of the Third Republic's political system through their steadfast hostility to allowing soldiers, including themselves, to vote. In 1872 the National Assembly had removed soldiers' right to vote, but in the 1920s left-of-center politicians debated enfranchising soldiers. Officers resisted those efforts and argued that because the right to vote would need to be linked with other political rights, including free speech and the right to read any party's political literature, it would open the army to subversion by Far Left-wing political movements. These debates helped to reinforce women's perceived suitability as military workers because they too were disenfranchised and thus on the military side of the newly relevant civil-military voting divide.

This book draws heavily on previously unused sources in the French Defense Historical Service's archive in Vincennes. These sources, contained in a supplement to Series N, also known as Series NN, cover the 1919–40 period, but were unavailable to scholars for decades after Series N, covering 1871–1940, was opened. The supplement contains papers captured by the Germans in 1940 and then the Soviets in 1945. They remained in Russia until Boris Yeltsin returned them to France in the late 1990s. The supplement contains a treasure trove of military records from the level of the Army General Staff down to individual units that previous historians of women in World War I–era France have not had access to. This book also makes extensive use of the original Series N, women's service records in Series YG, and studies the military reform movement through the police and political surveillance files in the French National Archive's F/7 series.

As a matter of necessity, this study relies on the French Army's archival records and is limited by the paucity of sources that allow the women who worked inside the French Army to speak for themselves. This reflects the nature of military records and the lack of oral histories rather than an overall lack of sources about women inside the army. Unfortunately, the archival records reflect the viewpoints of male officers and officials, and even when the files contain women's own words, they are from women who were writing to their male military supervisors instead of describing their experiences on their own terms. Yet given the lack of firsthand accounts left behind by women who worked for the French Army during World War I or the interwar era, military documents remain the best available sources with which to study women's integration into the French armed forces.[1] In spite of—and sometimes because of—their limits, these records are useful for examining the changing relationship between military identity and women in the interwar French Army as well as the evolution of the army's relationship to the civilian world.

CHAPTER ORGANIZATION

Chapter 1 explores the return of women to France's military community during the First World War. Unlike the leaders of most other belligerent powers, France's politicians and generals refused to let women officially enlist, but they did allow them to work as civilian employees of the French Army. Coming after a forty-year period in which officers and politicians had tried to build a wall separating the army from the civilian world, this process was traumatic and produced strong internal resistance that was eventually overcome because of the intervention of senior military leaders, including the generals who served as ministers of war. They created a hiring preference and benefit system that favored women who had family connections to the military. The chapter demonstrates the diversity of women's civilian service inside the army and emphasizes their critical contributions to the army's war effort while exposing the strong undercurrent of opposition to their presence among career officers.

Chapter 2 studies the end of the war and the process of demobilization. During the war, most officers tolerated their dependence on women because they had few other options and expected that the end of the war would see a return to prewar conditions. This chapter demonstrates that although the November 1918 armistice initially led to a rapid contraction of the army's female workforce, that process was soon reversed because the army could no longer function without its civilian employees, including women. In the five months after the armistice, the army fired more than half its women employees, but by April 1919 the demobilization was creating unexpected administrative demands that led many offices to begin rehiring women. This new wave of hiring focused heavily on secretarial, accounting, and other types of office work; As a result it narrowed the scope of women's contributions to the army when compared to their work during the war. It was still, however, governed by a preference system that favored the widows and orphans of French soldiers, so many of the remaining women had blood ties to the army.

The revival of hiring triggered official opposition from some senior officers and male functionaries, but despite blisteringly hostile reports from senior administrators, officers' shortage of trained personnel led them to keep thousands of women on the payroll. By 1920 the fact that postwar cabinets wanted major cuts in the term of conscript service and the overall size of the army led France's most senior generals to explicitly endorse keeping thousands of women as civilian employees of the army without admitting that those women had become a permanent part of the army.

Chapter 3 examines the role of women in senior officers' responses to the military reform movement and the possibility of the French Communist Party infiltrating of the military. Faced with these perceived threats to their communal identity and institution, senior generals began contemplating radical measures in order to safeguard France's national security and their own vision of the army. This reaction opened new opportunities for women within the army and strengthened their claim to a form of military identity. Rather than prioritizing protecting force structure (i.e., weapons and manpower) Marshal Philippe Pétain and other military leaders focused on minimizing potential changes to the military's culture. While negotiating with the cabinet, Pétain drew heavily on the report of General George-Henri Brissaud-Desmaillet's Commission on Civil Employees, which called for hiring tens of thousands of new peacetime civilian employees, many of whom would be women, and using these employees to insulate the professional elements of the army from social, cultural, and political change. In 1926 Marshal Pétain agreed to a compromise with the Poincaré cabinet, and he and his senior generals promised to support a one-third reduction in the number of conscripts in exchange for the army being allowed to hire twenty thousand more civilian employees, most of whom would be women. Pétain also demanded and received a promise from the minister of war that the cabinet would block bills giving soldiers the right to vote or making fundamental changes to the military justice system. In the context of the generals' increasing fear of voting rights, civilian women's disenfranchisement made officers more comfortable with them taking over responsibilities from conscripted men.

Chapter 4 focuses on the role on women in the French Army as it prepared to fight another world war. Military leaders had hoped that the 1927 and 1928 Army Laws would stabilize the army's organization and provide a period of political peace for military leaders, but the Great Depression and the rise of Adolf Hitler prevented this. The army's female workforce grew slowly and unevenly during the 1930s until preparations for war led to a wave of new hiring in 1938. The consolidation of women's membership in the military community and increased acceptance of their military identity led to a dramatic decline in the number of officers willing to openly challenge women's value to the army.

At the same time that officers accepted women within the military community, they resisted efforts to improve women's job security and pay if it would reduce their control over their employees. Army leaders alternately opposed and ignored proposals to recognize long-term employees, some of whom had twenty years of service, as permanent employees. They also resisted all efforts to allow women to enlist in the army as soldiers, even though by the late 1930s women were already doing most of the jobs they would be expected to do as uniformed soldiers. When the Second World War began in 1939, civilian employees of the army were vital to its ability to mobilize and fight, but women still could not be soldiers. In addition, half of the army's female employees were officially only temporary employees, even though some of them had been working in the army since the previous war.

Chapter 5 traces women's involvement in the French Army into the Second World War and through the fall of the Third Republic in the summer of 1940. During the 1939 mobilization, women's enhanced status and expanded national defense roles were on display. From the very beginning army leaders sought to integrate women into the war effort as war workers and as civilian employees of the army itself. The chapter studies the roles women played in the French Army before the German invasion of May 1940, including their finally gaining the right to enlist, and charts their experiences as they advanced and then retreated with their units. Although a comprehensive account of women's roles within the Free French Forces and the Vichy Regime's military is outside the scope of this study, the chapter concludes by tracing prewar trends' continuing influence on the trajectories of women on both sides of the wartime divide and their reunification after Allied forces liberated France in 1944.

HISTORIOGRAPHY

Despite the voluminous scholarship on the world wars, scholars have struggled to integrate the home and battle fronts because of the disciplinary boundaries that separate military history from social, political, and women's history. For too long, military historians have cocooned themselves within the limits of military operations and defined their subjects based on combat units and uniformed personnel; as a result, they have perpetuated an overly narrow definition of the military that limits our understanding of the world wars and hampers attempts to contextualize contemporary conflicts in which civilian contractors and government operatives play critical roles.

Before the 1970s, historians of the world wars paid little attention to women's contributions to fighting beyond token recognition of their roles in uniformed auxiliary corps and in nursing. In the 1970s and 1980s, a rising generation of feminist scholars expanded the history of the world wars to cover women's roles in the civilian economy, the uniformed armed forces, and resistance movements. These scholars built on the work of earlier economic and labor historians to show that women's labor was critical to the success of the total war economies in belligerent countries. Leila Rupp's 1978 *Mobilizing Women for War* focused on the Second World War, but her description of the ephemeral nature of women's wartime employment gains became the standard scholarly interpretation of the effect of both world wars on women's roles and opportunities.[2]

During the late 1980s, historians of women and warfare experienced an important shift in how they studied women when theory and language, particularly the study of gender, emerged as central to the subfield. In her 1987 book *Women and War*, Jean Bethke Elshtain explored the role of myths, and their gendered language, in shaping how contemporary Americans understood and related to war.[3] As important as Elshtain's work was, Margaret Higonnet and Patrice Higonnet's introduction to *Behind the Line* has provided the theoretical underpinnings for the study of gender and armed conflict for the past thirty years; they employed the metaphor of DNA's double helix to argue that women's gains during the world wars were ephemeral because they never changed women's relative position compared to men, and by extension the relationship of femininity to masculinity.[4] Higonnet and Higonnet argued that although women appeared to advance in traditionally male-dominated fields during the wars by entering new professions, their position relative to men never changed because men also advanced to the hypermasculine role of soldier. As a result, men and women's relative positions remained constant and linked, like the two strands of DNA's double helix. When the war ended and men stepped back from their hypermasculine roles, women were pushed back into their prewar roles because they were still locked into an inferior position defined by their relationship to men.[5] Later scholars like Margaret Darrow, Susan Grayzel, Steven Hause, and Kimberly Jensen all showed the qualified and temporary nature of civilian women's gains.[6]

In her 1995 book *Manufacturing Inequality*, Laura Lee Downs showed that certain women factory workers retained some of their wartime gains, but even those gains took place within a gendered framework built on the assumption that biologically defined differences between the sexes were a natural foundation on which to build an internal hierarchy. Downs's close attention to the way women fit into the hierarchies of individual factories reminded scholars that internal hierarchies could be just as important as national hierarchies in accommodating and limiting changes in how gender was constructed and used within a society.[7] That insight informs the present study's investigation of how women fit into the French Army between 1914 and 1940.

In *Breadwinners and Citizens*, Laura Frader has shown the continuing importance of paternal authority in interwar French politics even amid debates about how to deal with war widows. The same concern for paternal authority that Frader found in the construction of the welfare state also shaped the way women were integrated into the interwar French Army. Frader's successful integration of race into her analysis was critical in showing that the French state consistently sought to reinforce white male power through welfare policy, marginalizing and disadvantaging both women and nonwhite men. Similar pressures existed within the French military, where officers also tended to balk at integrating both white women and men of color in the same work environment and, as in welfare policy, prioritized white women over nonwhite men while trying to protect white men's prestige and power.[8]

Social and political historians, including those who study women's history, have typically focused their studies on the home front and maintained the artificial division between the military and civilian society. This has produced some excellent work showing the effects of home fronts on the course of wars, such as Belinda Davis's *Home Fires Burning*, but it has reinforced the sense that women, and civilians in general, were outside actors and forces interacting with a separate military institution.[9] This is especially unfortunate for the study of World War I because it was the war's dissolution of the barriers between the military and the civilian worlds that made contemporaries see it as a total war. Some scholars have recognized this. In particular, Margaret Darrow's work on women as spies and military drivers has shown that even in France—which, unlike Britain and the United States, did not allow women to enlist in the military during World War I—small numbers of women acted as quasi soldiers. Meanwhile other scholars, including Catherine Lacour-Astol, have shown that women played important roles in the resistance during World War II.[10] In addition, Martha Hanna's work has shown that links between soldiers at the front and civilians at home were closer than previously realized and that the experiences of people at home and at the front shaped each other's view of the war.[11] Janet Watson's *Fighting Different Wars* provided some coverage of civilian women who worked for the British military during the war, but the fact of the existence of a uniformed women's auxiliary corps within the British Army pushed civilian employees to the margins of the study, and the book's focus on wartime experiences and postwar memory means that it is unable to explore how the arrival of women reshaped the British military over the long term.[12] Military historians have largely ignored civilian women's roles inside the French Army and other militaries during both the First World War and the interwar era because they were not legally soldiers.

Thankfully it is no longer novel to assert that women have played important roles in national defense in France and in other countries; yet as recently as 1993, prominent military historians could claim otherwise. As Frader laments, in *A History of Warfare* John Keegan, one of the most widely read military historians in the Anglophone world, asserted that although "women may be both the cause or the pretext of warmaking" and "positively messianic war leaders," it was nonetheless the case that warfare was "the one human activity from which women, with the most insignificant exceptions, have always and everywhere stood apart"; he went on to claim that warfare was "an entirely masculine activity."[13] Keegan's claim was already dubious in 1993, and any defense of his position required drawing the definition of warmaking very narrowly. The present study seeks to do the opposite: to show the centrality of women to even an all-male military by expanding the scope of military history to include civilians who worked inside the French Army.

This book seeks to expand the pale of military history by examining the hundreds of thousands women who worked as civilian employees of the French Army during World War I and the tens of thousands who worked for the army in the interwar era. It thus takes seriously John Lynn's exhortation that historians should focus "not on the few women who assumed male identities and served as soldiers but on the tens of thousands who inhabited the military community as women."[14] Moving beyond the traditional bounds of women's military history (which has focused on women passing as men), a few traditional bastions of women's activity (such as the field of nursing), and women's indirect contributions to the war as factory workers and fund raisers allows historians to explore the internal world of the military in wartime and peacetime and to recognize women's vital, prolonged, and diverse contributions to national defense.[15]

The history of women and the armed forces in France is an especially fruitful subfield because of an emerging historiography that pays special attention to their roles in national defense. In *Women, Armies, and Warfare in Early Modern Europe*, John Lynn argued that historians have asserted too rigid a division between soldiers and civilians and calls on scholars to integrate civilians into military history. Although Lynn's book dealt with Europe as a whole, he drew heavily on French examples because of France's importance during his time period.[16] Thomas Cardoza's *Intrepid Women*, a history of *cantinières* (women sutlers) in the French Army, continued the shift that Lynn called for and picked up where Lynn's story ended. Whereas Lynn's book looked broadly at European armies in the pre-absolutist period, Cardoza followed one group of women who worked for and within the French Army from the ancien régime until the Great War and showed that although *cantinières* were legally civilians, they performed tasks that were essential to the ability of the French Army to conduct military operations and were accepted as effectively part of the army. Cardoza has also demonstrated that between 1871 and 1914, French military and political authorities consciously pushed the *cantinières* out of the army.[17] The combination of Lynn and Cardoza's works and this book provide a history of women's continuous service within the French Army as civilians from the early modern period until the point at which women were accepted as legal soldiers in 1940.Cardoza has shown that *cantinières* became cultural symbols in France because of the way they crossed traditional gender boundaries. Because so many people associated them with the army, companies used images of *cantinières* to advertise and brand products. Images of *cantinières* were marketable because they represented something exotic: both the sensuality of women breaking the normal rules of society and the foreignness associated with the army's campaigns in Africa, East Asia, Latin America, and the Middle East. By contrast, the much more numerous civilian employees of 1914–40 were ignored by the French media and thus were absent from popular culture. Instead of focusing on the hundreds of thousands of women who spent time working as civilians inside the French Army, public attention focused on images of transgressive women dressed as male soldiers and essentially ignored the reality that the army depended on a mass of civilian women to function. Just as the reality of total war drained the sense of gallantry and romance out of the public's image of war, it also rendered an entire group of female workers culturally invisible because instead of wearing brightly colored uniforms these civilian women workers were indistinguishable from the rest of society the moment they left their army jobs. This shift from a small romanticized group to a mass force that blurred the lines between the military and civilian worlds was a microcosm of a similar, but larger, shift that encompassed the entire societies of the countries that waged the world wars.

In *Women in the British Army*, Lucy Noakes drew on Margaret Higonnet and Patrice Higonnet's double helix anaology to argue that despite women serving as soldiers in both wars, British officers never fully accepted them as legitimate parts of the army because of how strongly officers identified war as a masculine activity. Noakes depicted male military leaders as fighting a long—and, at least, culturally successful—rear-guard action against women's periodic gains. Men's resistance to women's progress and wartime service meant that women remained marginalized within the British Army during the world wars and in the more contemporary period as well. Noakes highlighted women's marginalization within the armed forces and the problems associated with the highly masculine-gendered construction of war.[18]

Despite the insights that scholars have gained by focusing on women's marginalization within military forces and the dangers of a highly masculinized concept of war, it is time to move beyond them. The field's focus on women's inferior position within belligerent societies and their inability to make lasting gains as a result of armed conflicts was emphasized early in the field's history through the analogy to DNA's double helix. That theory has proven enormously useful in guiding the field, but it is increasingly becoming obsolete.

Margaret Higonnet and Patrice Higonnet's classic essay on the double helix theory has helped shape the field of women, gender, and warfare for the last thirty years, but the time has come to examine other angles. For the last twenty years, scholars such as Downs have shown that the world wars did lead to some gender change in combatant countries, and scholars of race and gender, including Frader, have shown the double helix's exclusive focus on gender is outdated. Geoff Read's *The Republic of Men* was a critical contribution to this trend despite not directly addressing either world war. By reading the gendered language of political parties next to their racial ideas and class appeals, Read was able to reinvigorate political history by obtaining new insights from a seemingly traditional topic, the history of interwar French political parties.[19]

In addition, the double helix theory's rarefication of wartime and peacetime as distinct from each other, a binary pair, makes the theory a problematic tool with which to understand the effects of the world wars; modern total wars blur the war-peace distinction. This study shows that the French Army's demobilization process continued well into the 1920s and it began transitioning from a peacetime to a wartime army in the late 1930s. This blurring of the barrier between war and peace is especially evident when looking at women's roles, opportunities, and identity. Within the French Army, women continued making gains into the late 1920s as a result of the prolonged process of demobilizing the army.

An attempt to move beyond the double helix should recognize the complexity of human societies and the fact that people's daily lives are rooted in specific places and contexts. The differences among contexts within a country, and even more so across national borders, mean that it is likely impossible to reconstruct a master narrative for how the world wars affected women that is valid in the preponderant majority of contexts. Any effort to comprehensively understand the wars' effect on women and the construction of gender would be greatly aided by more research on women in non-Western societies and even nonbelligerent European states. Studies of war and the colonial state abound, but applying a broader framework that recognizes the multiplicity of ways women contributed to the war effort would give scholars a better view of the effects of the world wars from African, Asian, and Latin American perspectives.

Explaining how the world wars shaped the construction of gender and the gendered division of power and privilege in Western societies requires understanding both how race and class interacted with gender in society as a whole and a realization that a society is really a collection of related and overlapping groups more than a cohesive homogeneous entity. As a result, gender, class, and race are often constructed differently within different segments of society. This was certainly the case in France during the era of the world wars because the French Army had a political culture in which class functioned differently than it did in society as a whole and coexisted with officers' belief that they constituted a class within the military and a distinctive caste in regard to the rest of French society. Thus, women civilian employees experienced gains in prestige and increased acceptance within the military community relative to the male conscripts who made up the majority of men in the military workplace, but only minor gains relative to male officers.

NOTES

1. Bonnie Smith's biography of Lucie Brun includes one of the very few firsthand accounts from a female civil employee. Brun, however, worked for a medical unit in Caen only briefly during the war, and did not continue into the interwar era. See Bonnie Smith, *Confessions of a Concierge: Madam Lucie's History of Twentieth-Century France* (New Haven, CT: Yale University Press, 1985), 37–39.

2. Leila Rupp, *Mobilizing Women for War: German and American Propaganda, 1939–1945* (Princeton, NJ: Princeton University Press, 1978).

3. Jean Bethke Elshtain, *Women and War* (Chicago: University of Chicago Press, 1987).

4. Margaret Higonnet and Patrice Higonnet, "The Double Helix," in *Behind the Line: Gender and the Two World Wars*, ed. Margaret Higonnet, Jene Jackson, Sonya Muchel, and Margaret Weitz (New Haven, CT: Yale University Press, 1987), 34.

5. Higonnet and Higonnet argue that although women appeared to "move forward" by taking jobs previously reserved for men, men also "move[d] forward" into the even more masculine and prestigious role of wartime soldier, thus preserving the relative hierarchy of prestige and power based on gender until the end of the war when demobilization returned soldiers to their prewar stations and pushed women back with them. Ibid.

6. Susan Grayzel, *Women's Identities at War: Gender, Motherhood, and Politics in Britain and France during the First World War* (Chapel Hill: University of North Carolina Press, 1999); Kimberly Jensen, *Mobilizing Minerva: American Women in the First World War* (Urbana: University of Illinois Press, 2007); Margaret Darrow, French *Women and the First World War: War Stories of the Home Front* (New York: Berg, 2002), 8, 230.

7. Laura Lee Downs, *Manufacturing Inequality: Gender Division in the British and French Metalworking Industries, 1914–1939* (Ithaca, NY: Cornell University Press, 1995).

8. Laura Frader, *Breadwinners and Citizens: Gender in the Making of the French Social Model* (Durham, NC: Duke University Press, 2008).

9. For an outstanding example, see Belinda Davis, *Home Fires Burning: Food, Politics, and Everyday Life in World War I Berlin* (Chapel Hill: University of North Carolina Press, 2000).

10. Catherine Lacour-Astol, *Le genre de la Résistance: La Résistance féminine dans le Nord de la France* (Paris: Presses de Sciences Po, 2015).

11. Martha Hanna, *Your Death Would Be Mine: Paul and Marie Pireaud in the Great War* (Cambridge, MA: Harvard University Press, 2006).

12. Janet Watson, *Fighting Different Wars: Experience, Memory, and the First World War in Britain* (New York: Cambridge University Press, 2004).

13. John Keegan, *A History of Warfare* (New York: Random House, 1993), 75–76

14. John A. Lynn II, review of Thomas Cardoza, *Intrepid Women: Cantinières and Vivandières of the French Army, American Historical Review* 116, no. 3 (2011): 879–80.

15. See, for example, De Ann Blanton and Lauren Cook, *They Fought Like Demons: Women Soldiers in the Civil War* (New York: Vintage, 2003); Sarah Rosetta Wakeham, *An Uncommon Soldier: The Civil War Letters of Sarah Rosetta Wakeman, alias Pvt. Lyons Wakeman, 153rd Regiment, New York State Volunteers, 1862–1864*, ed. Lauren Cook Burgess (New York: Vintage, 1996); and Carol Berkin, *Revolutionary Mothers: Women in the Struggle for America's Independence* (New York: Oxford, 2003). There is still useful research being done in these fields; see, for example, Chantal Antier, *Les Femmes dans la Grande Guerre*

(Paris: Payot, 2011) on women in wartime France; and Fabrice Virgili and Danièle Voldman, *La Garçonne et l'assassin: Histoire de Louise et de Paul, déserteur travesti, dans le Paris des années folles* (Paris: Payot, 2011) on desertion and cross-dressing.

16. John A. Lynn II, *Women, Armies, and Warfare in Early Modern Europe* (New York: Cambridge University Press, 2008).

17. Thomas Cardoza, *Intrepid Women: Cantinières and Vivandières of the French Army* (Bloomington: Indiana University Press, 2010).

18. Lucy Noakes, *Women in the British Army: War and the Gentler Sex, 1907–1948* (New York: Routledge, 2006).

19. Geoff Read, *The Republic of Men: Gender and the Political Parties in Interwar France* (Baton Rouge: Louisiana State University Press, 2014).

WOMEN AND THE FRENCH ARMY
DURING THE WORLD WARS,
1914–1940

1

―――― ✌ ――――

Weapons of Total War, 1914–1918

The First World War had a profound effect on the French Army and led to changes in how officers defined military identity and whom they accepted as being part of the military community. Those changes revered a long-term process of masculinizing the military community that originated with the French Revolution and accelerated during the early Third Republic. Just as the crisis of 1914 and the advent of modern total war during World War I forced French commanders to change their combat tactics and adapt their force structure, it also led them to change the army's relationship to women. Unlike many other belligerent powers such as Russia, the United Kingdom, and the United States, France did not recruit women as soldiers or sailors. Instead, the French Army hired women as temporary civilian employees to take over rear-area functions and free men for combat duty.

These women were not recognized as soldiers, but they performed a wide variety of vital functions, and senior military leaders devoted a considerable amount of time and resources to recruiting them and debating their futures within the army. Their arrival in the military community was unexpected, and it challenged established assumptions that self-discipline was a uniquely male trait and the cornerstone of military professionalism. Many officers objected to women's sudden return to the military community, but senior generals and most ministers of war strongly supported hiring women to deal with the army's critical personnel shortage during the war. This pressure from the top led to the creation of a set of hiring preferences that favored the widows and orphans of fallen soldiers, but otherwise hiring was decentralized to allow officers to respond to changes in their workload quickly. Despite significant opposition to women being part of the military community, by the end of the war there were nearly 200,000 women working inside the French Army.

THE MASCULINIZATION OF THE ARMY

The fact that women as a group were not permitted to be warriors did not mean that they played no role in France's many wars before 1914. As John Lynn has shown, women played important roles in early modern European armies as essential members of seventeenth- and eighteenth-century mixed military-civilian "campaign communities." When King Gustavus Adolphus of Sweden led a campaign in Germany during the Thirty Years War, he had more civilians than soldiers in his forces.[1]

Civilians were crucial to the period's aggregate contract armies' ability to feed and supply themselves. Merchants recognized a campaigning army as a lucrative market. The French Army tolerated the presence of regular merchants, but it also institutionalized specific civilians' roles in providing soldiers with supplies. Some civilians worked for the army as sutlers, or *vivandiers*.[2]

Many of the sutlers were women (*vivandières*), and other women also followed the armies and worked as laundresses, seamstresses, and cooks. During the period of aggregate contract armies, the wives and children of the soldiers traveled and served with the forces. Indeed, soldiers' sons were the French Army's main source of voluntary recruits before the French Revolution. Although most enlisted men were single, and aristocratic officers almost never brought their wives or young children with them, French armies still contained thousands of civilians. Many wives and children added to the army's labor pool, but they drained its supplies and slowed it down because it was effectively impossible for a commander to order his soldiers to abandon the slower-moving civilians or deny them a share of the army's food when so many of them were from the soldiers' families. While hampering an army's mobility, women helped to feed the army through a combination of foraging, trading, and food preparation.[3]

As Thomas Cardoza has shown, in the late 1600s the French state began to officially license certain individual soldiers to be *vivandiers*. These soldiers continued to fulfill their normal military obligations, but had a special license to sell supplies to their comrades. In theory they were expected to run their businesses themselves, but in practice they could not fulfill their contracts without help because they also remained soldiers. Among other things, they could not leave camp or depart from the column, which meant it would have been almost impossible for them to procure new supplies while on campaign. As a result, *vivandiers* were always allowed to marry. *Vivandiers'* wives were called *vivandières* and did most of the work, but the contracts technically belonged to their husbands. Because *vivandières* were not soldiers, they were permitted to depart from the army while it was campaigning to scavenge for extra food or to purchase alcohol and tobacco. Women's ability to go places their husbands could not meant that they, and not their husbands who held the contacts, were the people actually providing the additional supplies the army needed and individual soldiers demanded. Some women even sold their wares, especially alcohol, to soldiers on the battlefield.[4]

Although *vivandières* were vital to the French Army's functioning and morale, they were not initially given much control over their own destinies. Because the contracts were officially held by their husbands, if a *vivandière's* husband died, whether of natural causes or in battle, she lost the right to sell her goods. In practice, most *vivandières* were allowed to immediately remarry another soldier to continue to act as a *vivandière*, but that still left them with a choice between an immediate remarriage or losing their livelihood and community. Between the late seventeenth and early twentieth centuries, *vivandières* were a constant presence in the French Army. They marched with the king's armies in the cabinet wars of the eighteenth century, and became a normal and expected source of supplies.[5]

During the French Revolution, military and political leaders feared that women were naturally dangerous to military discipline and tried, often unsuccessfully, to minimize their military roles. This fit with the French Revolution's gendered ideology, which recognized men alone as true citizens. The masculinization of the revolutionary state affected the *vivandières*, but military commanders found that they could not do without the women. Despite the new regime's success in expanding the power of the state and the resources available to the armed forces, *vivandières* continued to provide vitally needed supplies, and officers recognized their important role in maintaining solders' morale. During the revolutionary era *vivandières* also gained important new rights, including the legal right to hold their government contracts in their own names instead of through their husbands. The new national army depended on living off the land to allow it to move quickly, which placed a premium on foraging and local trade. *Vivandières* took the lead in both activities and contributed to Napoleon's armies' ability to move rapidly around Europe and repeatedly surprise opposing armies.[6]

Vivandières, who became increasingly known as *cantinières* over the course of the nineteenth century, continued to serve with the army after the Bourbon Restoration. *Cantinières* followed their units to Algeria in 1830 and stayed on with the French forces in North Africa. Starting in 1830 they were permitted to wear a modified form of the French Army's uniform that included both a skirt and pants. Over time, uniformed *cantinières* became central to the public's image of the army. *Cantinières* experienced their golden age during the Second Empire; much like the Zouaves, they were widely depicted in advertising and became romantic symbols of Napoleon III's exotic foreign campaigns. They served, and sometimes died, in Napoleon III's war in Italy and in the Franco-Prussian War that saw the end of the emperor's reign and the fall of the Second Empire.[7]

Despite being the face of the Napoleon III's army, *cantinières* were not officially recognized as soldiers. They worked for and lived with the army, and they were vital to its ability to operate, but legally they remained civilians. As such, their position was often vague, even to themselves. Many honestly believed that they were in the army and would be entitled to a pension when they retired. The Ministry of War's regulations clearly stated that they were not entitled to pensions of their own, though they might be entitled to a widow's pension through their husbands. Their confusion was not unique: most civilians seem to also have assumed that *cantinières* were soldiers.[8]

The fall of Napoleon III and his Second Empire in September 1870 marked the beginning of the end for the *cantinières*, though that was far from obvious at the time. *Cantinières* followed their units into battle, and many were trapped with Marshal Achilles Bazaine's force in the besieged city of Metz after the French defeats at the battles of Mars-la-Tour and Gravelotte–St. Privat in August 1870. Others were captured along with Marshal Patrice MacMahon and their emperor when the rest of the Imperial Army was surrounded at Sedan in September. Although they were not legally recognized as soldiers, many *cantinières* shared the same experiences that soldiers did: they fought with their units, were killed or wounded by enemy fire and, in some cases, endured captivity when their units surrendered to the invading Germans. *Cantinières* also served units raised by the Government of National Defense. Despite their sometimes heroic service during the war, the postwar government began a forty-year process of removing women from the military community.[9]

The 1872 Army Organization Law established a conscription system in which a minority of men who drew bad draft numbers served five years while others served only one. This created a gross inequity that was controversial from the time it was adopted by the monarchist-dominated assembly. The division of the conscript class into long- and short-service conscripts meant that most of the men in the peacetime infantry companies would be long-service troops and a large proportion of reservists would be former short-service conscripts. This system limited the French Army's available manpower in peacetime because up to half of all short-service conscripts were being trained at any given time. Such a shortage meant that military leaders continued to rely on civilians to staff support services. In addition, the law banned all members of the armed forces from voting.[10] By excluding soldiers, who were all men and almost all of voting age, the National Assembly added them to the list of citizens deemed unable to exercise universal suffrage responsibly, a list that included minors, convicted criminals, and women.[11]

The Third Republic's leaders believed women and male minors lacked the maturity, independence, and faculties of reason required to vote responsibly, and criminals had forfeited their political rights through antisocial behavior, but soldiers and sailors were different. A military man was an otherwise qualified voter, whom parliamentarians judged to be too dangerous to be allowed to exercise the basic right of his citizenship because of his profession. The Paris Commune had begun when politicized national guardsmen had revolted when the government tried to disarm them, which reinforced military and political leaders' fears that politics could infect the military. Many political leaders also feared that officers could use their control over their men to control their votes (much as priests had used their influence to influence villagers' votes in the 1848 parliamentary elections), and this would give the military too much control over the political system.[12] The ban included career officers and noncommissioned officers, conscripts, and even recalled reservists. The Ministry of War claimed to be sensitive to the potential conflicts this provision created between civil and military power and promised to avoid scheduling reserve convocations during elections.[13]

At the end of the Franco-Prussian War, *cantinières* performed the same duties they had before the war, but in the late nineteenth century, republican politicians and reformist military leaders increasingly questioned the need to tolerate them. After wresting control of the government away from the monarchists in the late 1870s, moderate republican leaders maintained the monarchists' prohibition on women and soldiers voting and emphasized a gendered conception of citizenship that privileged men's alleged superiority in self-discipline and emotional control to justify excluding women from voting rights.[14]

The presence of many quasi-uniformed women with the army challenged anti-suffrage politicians' claims that women lacked the capacity to exercise full citizenship. The fact that *cantinières* were not legally soldiers did not change the fact that they were uniformed and integrated into the army's structure and contributed to its combat effectiveness. From the outside they looked a lot like soldiers and as such were a living challenge to the gendered construction of citizenship under the Third Republic. The expansion in the size of the army that resulted from the 1872 Amy Organization Law allowed commanders to use conscripts to displace civilian service personnel. In 1875 and 1879, new laws reduced the number of *cantinières* in the service by restricting new hiring so that attrition would slowly shrink their numbers. In addition, the legislation allowed men to serve as *cantiniers*, which created a form of competition that further reduced the number of new *cantinières* in the late nineteenth century.[15]

By 1889 the military elite recognized that it was politically impossible for the government to maintain the gross inequalities of service created by the 1872 Army Organization Law; Minister of War Charles de Freycinet, in cooperation with senior generals, brought forward the 1889 Recruitment Law, which eliminated the bifurcated conscription system and set the term of conscript service at three years. It reduced, but did not eliminate, the inequalities of obligation among French conscripts. Young men training to be teachers, for a religious ministry, studying at selected schools, or holding or studying for certain specialized diplomas were allowed to serve only one year.[16]

The advent of something closer to true universal male military service contributed to the elimination of the *cantinières*. The 1889 Army Law significantly increased the army's available manpower. Instead of relying on quasi-militarized women to help supply the army, French generals and political leaders expanded the army's supply services to provide enough food and personal supplies to meet soldiers' basic needs.

By the 1880s the Ministry of War was imposing increasingly demanding regulations that aimed to create a more homogenous army that included new rules for *cantinières*. When unit commanders proved unwilling to fully apply the rules against women who had lived and worked with their units for years, the ministry transferred supervision of *cantinières* from commanding officers to the gendarmes. In 1890, new regulations banned *cantinières* from wearing modified uniforms and instead issued them simple badges. The new regulation removed the *cantinières'* marker of military identity and was an important step on the way to their official suppression. In 1888 and again in 1892, the Conseil Supérieur de la Guerre (which included France's most senior generals as well as the president of the republic and the minister of war) debated eliminating *cantinières*; in the first case the minister of war decided that the narrow favorable vote was too close to act on, and in the second a conservative majority voted against elimination.[17]

In the wake of the Dreyfus affair, new regulations squeezed the *cantinières'* profits and attacked their positions. In 1900 the Ministry of War, motivated by public concerns about heavy drinking and alcoholism among conscripts, banned hard alcohol sales on military posts; the effect was to devastate many *cantinières'* profits. Although they could still sell beer, wine, and other beverages like coffee and tea, hard alcohol was their largest source of profit and had been their signature product for two hundred years. Shortly afterward, Minister of War General Louis André, a republican and a Dreyfusard, ordered the army to open soldiers' cooperatives and mess circles for noncommissioned officers.[18] These two instructions effectively eliminated *cantinières'* main reason for existing in peacetime by providing places for enlisted men to congregate and purchase nonregulation food and drink.

In 1905 the Two-Year Service Law prompted the final crisis for the *cantinière* system; it eliminated almost all remaining exemptions and was passed amid a strong Dreyfusard reaction against the professional army with its conservative traditions, monarchism, Catholicism, and antisemitism. The cabinets of Émile Combes and then Maurice Rouvier secured the passage of the new law, which emphasized equality of military service and uniformity within the army; the 72,000 men privileged under the 1889 law lost their draft exemption.[19]

The Two-Year Service Law brought a new wave of concern for the physical and moral health of conscripts and focused attention on the aging *cantinière* corps. The law was a death warrant for the *cantinières* because it required that in the future, only veterans would be hired to run canteens. The law effectively banned the hiring of any more *cantinières* because women could not be soldiers and thus could not be veterans. The remaining *cantinières* were soon stripped of the right to sell alcohol at all and lost the right to accompany their units on maneuvers and campaigns, effectively severing them from their historical purpose. The final blow came in October 1906, when the Ministry of War issued new instructions that accelerated the process of closing canteens and increased pressure on commanders to purge the ranks of women.[20] Over the following years almost all of the remaining *cantinières* gave up; some found other employment, but many probably simply retired. The long process of choking off recruitment helped this process along. As a result of the army's refusal to license new *cantinières*, the average age of surviving *cantinières* drifted steadily upward as their numbers continued to dwindle.

WOMEN AND THE EXPECTED WAR

As European tensions escalated before 1914, some voices called for women to directly contribute to national defense. After years of lobbying from the Red Cross, the French military finally consented to integrate Red

Cross personnel, including women working as nurses, into its mobilization plans in 1910. In 1913 Jane Dieulafoy responded to a report in *Les Temps* that the Austrians were considering hiring women as civilian employees to re-place soldiers doing rear-area work if a war broke out. Writing in *Les Temps* on March 22, and later in public speeches, she called on the French gov-ernment to emulate Austria by creating a force of women who would be trained in peacetime so that if war came, they could immediately take over a wide array of noncombat duties from men, who would then be free to go to the front.[21]

Some commentators, including the *Figaro* writer Louis Chevreuse, sup-ported Dieulafoy's proposal, but others ridiculed the idea. Writing in *Le Matin*, Clément Vartel exploited Dieuladoy's defiance of traditional gen-der markers to undermine her idea; he reminded his readers that Dieula-foy had lived an atypical life and dressed as a man—implying though not actually claiming that she was a lesbian. He urged French women to con-centrate on being the mothers of sons who would serve France rather than take on military responsibilities. Although there is no reason to believe that Dieualofoy influenced the government's decision to hire women to supplement male military manpower during the First World War, the press did remind readers about her plan when the Ministry of War began recruiting women in 1915.[22]

When the French Army marched to war in August 1914 the last handful of *cantinières* were forbidden to follow; For the first time ever, French troops marched to war in Europe without women accompanying the col-umns. In a victory for the exclusionary gender ideology of the Third Re-public, the 1914 army was the most masculine France had ever deployed in Europe and likely the most masculine French army ever. It may not have been solidly republican (especially among its senior commanders), but it was a people's army made of conscripts and, above all, they were men. Following Louis Loyzeau de Grandmaison's doctrine of the *offensive à outrance*, which taught that aggression was the key to winning battle, the army was expected to relentlessly attack the Germans in an act of retrib-utive violence that would restore France's honor, lost as a result of the defeat of 1870–71 and the consequent violation of French nationhood sym-bolized by Germany's annexation of Alsace and upper Lorraine. That violence was intended to validate the continued existence of the Third

Republic by showing that it had renewed France's power and virility. As Frenchmen collectively struggled to redeem their country's honor, they were supposed to do so in a purely masculine zone; but this male army was a thoroughly new republican creation which did not survive the war.

THE GREAT WAR AND THE RETURN
OF THE WOMEN

The mobilization of French forces in August 1914 initially failed to create many new opportunities for women. French leaders quickly accepted women as nurses in military hospitals far from the front, but resisted giving them other opportunities. Margaret Darrow and Chantal Antier have shown that as the army's demand for soldiers and munitions workers depleted France's male labor pool in 1915, first civilian weapons makers and then government and military leaders reluctantly accepted women's labor as essential to winning the war. But still the French government refused to follow the British—and later American—example of enlisting women.[23]

Instead the French Army hired women as civilian employees to free soldiers for the front lines. These women worked in a variety of jobs, ranging from clerical and bookkeeping work to manual labor, and some even worked as quasi-uniformed military drivers near the front. But none of them were recognized as soldiers. Because of the decentralized system of hiring and paying women, it is difficult to determine exactly how many worked for the army over the course of the war, but by 1917 at least 150,000 women, excluding nurses, worked directly for the army in nonfactory positions, and more worked for private companies or other agencies supporting the war effort. Although these women were officially only civilian employees, they effectively increased the combat power of the French Army by freeing hundreds of thousands of soldiers for combat duty.[24]

Germany's invasion of France on August 3, 1914, triggered frantic preparations in the army's medical corps, civilian hospitals, and government departments responsible for public health. Before the war, France's military hospitals had been staffed by enlisted men who had been trained and certified as military nurses, but the demands of the war almost instantly overwhelmed their ability to care for the sick and wounded. As a result the army and government appealed for aid from any quarter able to give it, and that included women and the Catholic Church, despite many political leaders' anticlericalism. Until 1905 many of France's nurses had been women in Catholic religious orders, but the 1905 Law on Associations had dissolved many orders and drove others out of providing public services, such as nursing. Many of the women remained in France or neighboring countries, however, and the call to war led to a moment of reconciliation in which anticlerical politicians welcomed the voluntary service of Catholic women, including laywomen and women from the religious orders.

During the Great War, approximately four thousand hospitals supported the French war effort. Some of the hospitals were organized by religious and secular nongovernmental organizations, and others were taken over by private concerns later in the war. Despite private participation in medical care, the government was not able to rely on prewar staff to manage the military medical centers and almost immediately began accepting offers from individual women and from nongovernmental organizations to help, including ten thousand male and female members of Catholic religious orders. Despite the legal imposition of *laïcité*, military and governmental leaders allowed nuns in government hospitals to wear their full habit, and by 1916 many laywomen working as nurses were wearing a modified habit as their uniform. The October 1916 issue of *L'Illustration* depicted a civilian nurse wearing a white habit and described her has having "taken the laic habit in wartime."[25]

At their peak strength, ninety thousand women were working as nurses in military hospitals—twenty thousand as paid nurses and seventy thousand as volunteers. They came from diverse backgrounds, ranging from aristocrats to the working class. Many were individual volunteers, but ten thousand were religious, and others were organized through various French Red Cross organizations, including the Union des Femmes de France, the Association des Dames Française, and the Société de Secours aux Blessés Militaires. Formal nursing was usually restricted to adults, but young women from the age of sixteen served as auxiliaries, preparing dressings, organizing supplies, reading to patients, and accompanying wounded men on walks in hospital gardens.[26]

The complexity of France's wartime medical system helped to reduce concerns that bringing ninety thousand women and teenage girls into it would challenge established gender roles or constitute the militarization of women. Because only a minority of nurses received pay, their labor could be easily dismissed as temporary and secondary. Few could doubt that when the war ended, volunteer nurses would leave military hospitals; they would receive the army's thanks, but they would not be invited to remain in their positions after the war and so would not have a long-term influence on the character and development of the postwar army. Moreover, many of them were not even officially volunteering for the army. Red Cross volunteers were officially working for their associations, which were only cooperating with the military.[27] Thus the women themselves had only an indirect and theoretical claim to be working in the French Army.

Nursing itself was seen as a safe occupation for women because the public's perception of it emphasized many of the traits associated with middle-class femininity—especially nurturing and maternal love. The pseudoparental way in which men constructed women's identity as nurses sanitized the activity, making it respectable for upper-class women and mitigating many of the prejudices associated with women performing other kinds of war work. This process was not accidental, and was the by-product of efforts by private and public organizations associated with nursing to create a space for women that would not challenge gender roles. The return of thousands of nuns helped to desexualize the way the public and officers saw the wartime nursing profession. The combination of the complexity of nurses' chain of command rendering them remote from the army, the fact that most nurses were volunteers, and the conscious construction of a traditional and widely accepted gendered identity led to nurses being seen as safe employees, in no small part because their roles were assumed to be temporary.

FEMALE CIVIL EMPLOYEES: WAR WIDOWS AND WORKING MOTHERS

As the war dragged on, military and political leaders slowly realized that the growing need of the army for soldiers and factories for workers was exhausting France's male workforce. Over the course of 1915, first civilian weapons makers and then military and political leaders accepted that women's labor was necessary to sustain the war effort, and this led to discussions within the army about how to recruit and use women. Initially, political and military leaders assumed that it would be easy to recruit qualified women to replace soldiers in rear-area positions; as a result, they sought to prioritize applicants so that those whom they considered most deserving received the best positions. In June 1915, Minister of War Alexandre Millerand established a system of hiring preferences for female civil employees, which revealed the military's view of what made a woman deserving of a job.[28] Millerand's system was based on advice from his military and civil cabinets and thus reflected the opinion of military leaders; it gave the highest preference "to the widows of servicemen killed by the enemy or who died of their wounds or from illnesses contracted in the army."[29] It also gave progressively less preference to the wives of wounded soldiers, the widows of civilian workers killed in military installations, and the daughters of dead or wounded veterans.[30]

During early 1915, some units began to hire women in growing numbers as civilian employees. On November 10, 1915, Minister of War General Joseph Gallieni ordered army officers and civilian administrators to begin hiring women to replace civilian men and soldiers in rear-area positions. Brushing aside concerns that women were too undisciplined to be trusted, Gallieni told his officers that they had a "duty" to hire women to perform any job they were capable of doing; he ordered them to hire women to replace men doing office work in order to free men for the front, where the French Army was suffering terrible losses. This hiring of women was part of an efficiency drive that also urged increased use of telephones to save labor and time and called on officers to reorganize offices to reduce the amount of time and labor dedicated to administration and planning during wartime.[31] In the written order Gallieni concluded, "I am sure that, understanding the necessities of present time, every echelon of the hierarchy will carry out [this order] to the extreme limit of its abilities and means." He concluded by promising his subordinates that if the army dedicated itself to implementing the hiring of civilians, including women, with "all the activity and energy of which it is able," it would be able to carry on "fighting without truce or respite, until the definitive hour of final victory."[32]

As part of Gallieni's push to hire women, his cabinet's Second Bureau hired Georgine Blanchet on December 15, 1915. Blanchet was exactly the kind of woman Millerand's preference system was intended to bring into military employment. In December 1915 she was a twenty-five-year-old war widow looking for a job to support herself. Her superiors were pleased with her performance and she remained in her position until the war ended and she remarried.[33]

Not all of the women hired in the wake of Gallieni's appeal so clearly conformed to Millerand's preferences. Mélanie Marie Bareil was the twenty-two-year-old wife of enlisted man Paul Bareil. In December 1915 she began working as an auxiliary civil employee doing office work in Paris. She did not fit into any of the categories of privileged employment the army had identified, though in 1918 she would trade on her status as the wife of a mobilized soldier to petition for a need-based raise. Although her position was intended to be a temporary one, Bareil would eventually make a career out of her temporary employment by remaining with the army for more than twenty-two years. In May 1919 she was assigned to work for Georges Clemenceau's military staff, and after his resignation the army transferred her to the Infantry Directory. She finally left her job in May 1938 when she was declared disabled and granted a pension.[34]

Gallieni's order to hire women involved identifying positions that could be opened to them. One of the first fields the Ministry of War identified was nursing, a field in which individual women and women's organizations had already made huge contributions.[35] In December 1915 the ministry ordered hospitals to replace any remaining male military nurses with civilian women as part of a process of "systematically organizing the employment of more and more feminine labor in the establishments of the Health Service." The ministry repeated its orders in August 1916 and criticized hospital directors for continuing to use too many male military personnel.[36]

In May 1916 the ministry instructed all commanders to begin hiring large numbers of women and advised them, "The principle must be that any work able to be done by a woman and currently confided to a soldier must from now on be executed by female workers." The Underdirectory of Personnel and Mobilization circulated a list of positions that were open to women for the duration of the war. Although warning the list was not exhaustive, the report specifically included orderlies, accountants, telephone operators, mail workers, typists, stenographers, cooks, and secretaries for unit staffs, intelligence bureaus, and other services. The ministry set wage ceilings for all positions, but delegated the power to set exact wages to the generals commanding France's military regions and to the commanders of the specific posts hiring civilian employees.[37] Women also worked as maintenance workers, and as cyclists for the headquarters and bases of territorial divisions in European France, Algeria, and Tunisia. By early 1917, 36 percent of soldiers assigned to these tasks in North African units had been replaced by civilian women.[38]

Over the course of 1916, the Ministry of War expanded its drive to include fields that had not already been feminized and began to institutionalize the 1915 call to bring women into the army's employment. A June 1916 ministry circular instructed officers and civilian administrators to replace as many soldiers doing support work with civilians as possible. The ministry explicitly instructed commanders and administrators to replace soldiers with women whenever possible and only to replace soldiers with civilian men if it was absolutely essential for the job to be done by a man.[39] Despite the drive to expand women's roles, the army command and the ministry remained opposed to putting women in uniform or placing them in the combat zones.

In June 1916 Minister of War General Pierre Roques reiterated his support for Millerand's system of hiring preferences and for women as civil employees. In response to a letter from the Fédération Nationale de Personnel Civil de Établissements de la Guerre he affirmed his commitment to his predecessors' hiring policy.[40] By that time, however, it was becoming clear that the system rested on the naive assumption that the supply of available French women workers exceeded the army's labor needs. It also reflected officers and politicians' belief that the nation and the army owed a debt to fallen soldiers' families. This policy defined women by their relationship to men, and in this case to military men, marking them as dependents and de facto family members. In military leaders' eyes, it was the manly sacrifice of wartime soldiers and the suffering that brought to their family members that justified hiring widows and daughters rather than the women's skills or desire to support the war effort.[41] The army's regulations thus categorized women based on their relationships to military men in ways that were similar to Margaret Higonnet and Patrice Higonnet's double helix theory's abstract descriptions of how wartime gender roles evolved.[42]

The summer hiring campaign produced immediate results and brought a new influx of women into the army. On August 17, 1916, Marie-Louise Mercier began working as a secretary in the Central Administration of the Ministry of War. She was exactly the kind of woman that Millerand and Roques thought the army should be hiring: a thirty-year-old war widow and the mother of a son born during the war. Her family home was in Wignehies in the German-occupied Département du Nord. For Mercier, and many women like her, the army offered the prospect of stable and respectable employment and perhaps even the chance to help avenge their fallen family members by working as directly as possible to ensure that France won the war.[43]

THE 1916 REGIME

Over the course of 1915 and 1916, local military administrators hired women like Mercier based on individual or regional arrangements. The French government classed all the women the army was hiring as temporary auxiliary employees, a classification that allowed them to be hired quickly but denied them job security. The terms of employment varied greatly among the different military regions, and sometimes within the same unit or office. Yet as the number of women working for the army grew, the ad hoc system started to break down. As units or offices moved, officers soon found that they needed a system to maintain temporary auxiliary employees' positions without burdensome paperwork. Military leaders also recognized that a more systematized process would make the army a more attractive employer by allowing hiring officers to spell out predictable pay and benefits.

In December 1916 General Roques solidified women's positions within the army by establishing the 1916 Regime, which laid out rules for hiring women as auxiliary employees, regulated their working conditions, and dealt with issues of pay and discipline. The regime mandated security checks on all applicants, including their families and their personal morality, though in practice those checks were rarely more than perfunctory. It also banned the hiring of women already employed by the government and reaffirmed the established system of hiring preferences. The decree fixed the normal workday at seven hours and granted a half day of leave for every two weeks an employee worked, set rules for advancement, and regulated employees' eligibility for government pensions.[44] By December 1916 the French labor market was already badly overburdened, but Roques stood by the preferential system Millerand had created. His decision reflected the army's almost willful refusal to recognize the limits of France's economic potential and the officer corps' sense of duty to the families of dead soldiers.

Despite the new regulations, many officers still resisted giving women any role in the military or recognizing the value of their contribution to the war effort. Roques acknowledged that many officers opposed hiring women, and he tried to shame dissenters into obedience, even writing, "I regret to say that certain service chiefs have failed in their duty, some through negligence or by not changing their habits."[45] Roques's language questioned recalcitrant officers' professionalism by implying that they lacked the self-discipline to obey orders they disagreed with. He praised women's wartime work and predicted that many would remain with the army after the war. He advised his officers that the "maximum effort should be made with the view of substituting women, except where it is absolutely impossible, for the numerous soldiers still employed in the support services" Roques authorized officers to imply the possibility of permanent employment to women, though he never promised that all, or even most, would be able to keep their jobs after the war.[46] This shows that as early as December 1916 some generals believed the war had made women a permanent part of the army.

OPPOSITION TO WOMEN EMPLOYEES

Many senior officers, including the commanders of several French military regions, objected to hiring women despite pressure from the Ministry of War to do so.[47] General Pierre Dubois warned the ministry against relying on women's labor, but General Pierre Ruffey, the commander of the Eleventh Military Region (Nantes), was the most vocal critic of the policy.[48] Ruffey, the former commander of the Third Army who had been relieved of command after losing the Battle of the Ardennes in August 1914, conceded that women might be useful in some posts, such as depot workers, but that they needed to be kept away from staff officers and important posts. He argued that women were only useful if they were assigned "purely material" work that did not involve creativity, independent initiative, or discretion. In a report to the Ministry of War, Ruffey argued that women were lazy and hard to supervise, lied to get out of work, and were inherently destructive to military professionalism. He cited women's "maternal complications" and their "frequent unavailability" to justify his claim that they were poor employees.[49]

Ruffey implicitly questioned male soldiers' professionalism by presenting their self-discipline as tenuous and liable to collapse in the face of sexually available women. He explained that women brought immorality into military life and that their "inevitable promiscuity" created "the obligation for officers and chiefs of staff to exercise surveillance like that of a parent and a vice cop." He also warned that because women's lack of self-control extended beyond their sexuality, hiring them would lead to "inevitable gossip" that would assure "indiscretions" on the part of women working in sensitive posts.[50] General Ruffey repeatedly denounced women's lack of self-discipline, but his warning exposed a deeper fear that male soldiers' sexuality would overwhelm their military professionalism. His attacks against female civil employees revealed his concern that French soldiers lacked enough self-discipline to meet the challenges of modern warfare and thus his fear that French soldiers' ability to engage in manly self-restraint was inadequate for modern war.[51]

French officers' understanding of military professionalism was broadly similar to nineteenth-century American conceptions of manliness. Gail Bederman has shown that in the early twentieth century, American men changed the way they constructed their gender from a concept of manliness based on self-mastery and self-restraint to an idea of masculinity that focused on vigor and potency.[52] During and after the Great War, France's professional army officers linked their professional and gender identity through manly self-discipline; officers like Ruffey assumed that military virtue required such restraint, and that as a result only men could possess military virtue and thus be of value to the military. In effect they believed only men could be self-disciplined because only men could be manly; by extension, women were deemed undisciplined because they were unmanly and thus inherently dangerous to the army and its mission.

Ruffey was not alone in his criticism, though he was the most violent critic of women's roles as civilian employees. General Baptiste Faurie, commander of the Fourth Military Region (Le Mans), expressed a more nuanced concern about women inside the army. In his report to the First Bureau of the General Staff (Personnel and Administration), Faurie affirmed that women were generally performing well in his region but that there were some significant problems. He complained that many women were underqualified for their positions, and emphasized the need to quickly and comprehensively train them in the skills needed for their jobs and to familiarize them with working for the army before they became useful employees.[53]

In his December announcement of the 1916 Regime, Minister of War Roques replied directly to Ruffey and Faurie's criticisms. He acknowledged Faurie's concern that many newly hired women were inexperienced and agreed that they arrived with a "complete ignorance of military terminology," but retorted that if post commanders made energetic efforts to teach and acculturate them, the women rapidly became good employees. He asserted that "the results achieved after a few months of effort are plainly satisfactory" and praised women as good workers who, when given the chance to learn their jobs, were every bit as hardworking and desirous of helping the war effort as the soldiers they replaced.[54]

Yet even when commanders supported hiring women, they often encountered problems recruiting enough applicants. One such officer was A. M. B. Drude, the commanding general of the Third Military Region (Rouen). Like Ruffey, Drude had an unhappy history with commander in chief of the French forces, Marshal Joseph Joffre, who had removed Drude from his combat command in 1915 and had exiled him to a rear-area garrison. On January 14, 1917, Drude complained that although he had replaced the majority of his office staff with women in Caen, La Havre, and Rouen he had not been able to find enough women to do the same in Bernay, Falaise, Lisieux, and St. Adresse. General Drude explained that the post at St. Adresse was isolated and he had to recruit women in La

Havre, but that the journey was time-consuming for women to make; he called for greater efforts to help posts like St. Adresse overcome such problems.[55]

Although Drude achieved impressive results in replacing soldiers with civilian women, he insisted that the transition could never be total. He argued that his female employees retained family obligations that could interfere with their work, including their mobilized husbands' periodic return on leave. He warned that without keeping a cadre of soldiers at hand, women's family obligations could bring the unit's work to a standstill with little or no warning, though he offered no examples or other evidence to substantiate his claims.[56]

In an attempt to rebut some officers' criticisms of women, the Ministry of War conducted a work study to determine how efficient women workers were compared to the men they replaced. During 1915 and 1916, Ministers Gallieni and Roques had held out hope that women could perform some jobs better than men, thus justifying their hiring with a claim beyond just the shortage of male workers. In December 1917 a report prepared by the First Bureau of the General Staff refuted claims that women were more or less efficient than the men they had replaced, finding that the work value ratio of women to men was just under 1:1. Given that many of the female civil employees received on-the-job training, the slight reduction in efficiency was probably a result of new hires having to learn their jobs before reaching peak efficiency. The high command dismissed the small difference in productivity as insignificant and cited the study as proof that women were just as effective as men.[57]

Despite Ruffey's criticisms, the number of female civil employees rose rapidly in 1915 and 1916. The army's own figures for how many women it employed were incomplete, rarely compiled, and often contradictory, which makes it impossible to precisely determine the number of women working for the army at any given time. Based on wartime estimates, in January 1916, 53,000 women worked for the army in nonfactory and nonnursing positions and by January 1, 1917, this number had risen to 123,000.[58] In November 1916, army administrators estimated that hiring women in nonfactory and nonnursing positions had freed 210,000 men for combat duty.[59] This was a crucial contribution to a force that suffered

350,000 deaths during the battles of Verdun and the Somme between February and December 1916.[60]

AFTER THE 1916 REGIME

In 1917, French generals bowed to ministerial pressure and accepted that if the British could use women as drivers, so could the French. Margaret Darrow has shown that despite the British example and support for women drivers from Minister of War General Hubert-Louis Lyautey in early 1917, the French Army employed fewer than three hundred women as drivers for the Army Automobile Service (Direction de Service Automobile or DSA) during the war.[61] Because these women worked in the militarized area near the combat zones, they were eventually issued uniforms as a matter of convenience, to stop the military police from hindering them from performing their duties by constantly asking what they were doing in the war zone.[62] Although they remained civilians, they were the only women allowed to wear an officially sanctioned version of a military uniforms since 1890 and, like the case of *cantinières*, this blurred the line between soldiers and civilians working for the army. At the end of the war these women, who had been the most militarized during the war, were among the first to be released from the army's service.[63] The fact that Automobile Service drivers wore a form of military uniform and operated inside the military exclusion zone just behind the front marked them as special and drew more popular attention during the war than their meager number warranted, but that interest faded quickly when the war ended. Enid Bagnold's 1920 novel *The Happy Foreigner* followed a fictional British woman who became a driver for the French Army, though the book was written in English and thus made little impression in France.[64]

The pace at which the army hired women stagnated in 1917 because of France's growing labor shortage. Darrow has also demonstrated that officers' commitment to hiring women flagged in 1917 as pressure from senior generals and the Ministry of War to hire women slackened. As a result, the number of women working for the French Army leveled off because the rate at which it hired women slowed.[65] Despite the general backlash, the army continued to hire women, and the numbers of them working in some units or offices actually rose. Between May 1917 and April 1918 the number of women hired each month remained fairly level, with monthly totals ranging between a low of 2,627 and a high of 3,372 every month except October 1917, which saw the exceptionally low level of 2,198 new hires.[66] October 1917 was the month General Philippe Pétain abandoned plans for a spring offensive and began preparing to defend against an anticipated German attack; that decision disrupted normal hiring because it meant that many units had to be redeployed.

Officers' sexism limited the number of women hired by the army in 1917 and 1918, but economic and strategic factors were also at play. By early 1917, the French labor market was extremely tight because of the competing needs of the French Army for soldiers and civilian weapons makers. During 1917, French weapons manufacturers expanded production and their workforces in order to provide heavy weapons for the growing US Army and to keep to General Pétain's plan to dramatically expand the French Army's heavy artillery and tank forces. The expansion of the industrial workforce exacerbated France's labor shortage and made it harder for the army to recruit civilian employees; as a result, it had trouble finding enough employees of either gender to meet its needs. The French Army High Command's Labor Directory reported chronic labor shortages throughout 1917 and asked local governments to help with recruitment. Mayors all over France wrote back, apologizing for the problem, but explained that conscription and factory needs had already exhausted their local labor markets. Most promised to help in any way they could, but held out little hope of finding more workers. The mayor of Le Bourget reported that "the many factories working on national defense in Le Bourget absorb all available labor (male and female)" and that "for more than two years" he had been unable to hire enough people to meet the city government's needs.[67]

In addition to appealing to local government, military leaders tried to advertise their positions as widely as possible. Individual posts used word of mouth as an effective but limited way to recruit new staff, but they also advertised publically. Because each post hired women independently and based on a unique pay scale, potential employees applied directly to individual posts instead of a central hiring office. As a result, commanders found themselves competing against each other for the same candidates. The army's main form of advertising jobs was to put up posters in public areas specifying the available positions and sometimes pay and other employment policies. In March 1917 the evacuation hospital at the train station of La Courneuve–Aubervilliers, north of Paris, and the Intendance office in nearby Le Bourget simultaneously advertised similar positions, thus competing for staff in the area's depleted labor market.[68]

The two advertisements revealed that the post commanders were interpreting the Ministry of War's hiring preferences differently. Both posters indicated a hierarchical list of hiring preferences, but the lists were different: the hospital in La Courneuve–Aubervilliers preferred to hire men free of military obligations, followed by men too young for service, women, men disabled by illness or injury during the war, and then foreigners; the Le Bourget Intendance office preferred men free of military obligations, men disabled by illness or injury during the war, men too young of military service, foreign men, and then women of any age. This difference did not violate the army's official hiring preference for women, because that policy specified how to prioritize different groups of women. But it did not specify where women should fit within preferences for different groups of men. As a result, some commanders placed women last while others placed women above some groups of men. This inconsistency suggests that despite several orders calling for the wholesale replacement of men with women in rear-area support service, in actual practice post commanders retained significant autonomy and had a major influence on the number of women working for their commands.[69]

The preference for men free of military obligations over women in the hospital's poster may well have been a violation of previous orders to substitute women for men—including civilian men—whenever possible. The fact that both post commanders preferred male over female employees, despite repeated orders to favor women over men whenever possible, shows how inconsistently the policy of feminization was being applied. This also helps to explain why higher authorities issued so many seemingly redundant orders to hire more women.

Recruiting was sometimes successful, even in 1917; that year twenty-one-year-old Lucie Brun accepted a position with the Army Health Service office in Caen. Brun was not a war widow, but she had lost a fiancé, having become engaged to a soldier named Philippe in July 1914. When her fiancé went to war, she wrote letters to him every day until his death in October 1914.[70] Before working for the Health Service she had worked in her mother's store in Liseaux, but business was poor, and in 1916 Brun had met a soldier on his way to the nearby city of Caen. In 1917, with the support and advice of a Madame Norman, whose family were local notables, she convinced her mother to agree to her taking a job with the Health Service in Caen. Madame Norman had explained that "the regimental headquarters just a few streets over is looking for a young woman to do its paperwork" and promised Brun's mother that she would "go with her to inquire about a position." Given the French Army's acute labor shortage, and the support of a local notable, Brun easily secured a position.[71]

Brun's description of her stint as a civilian employee in the Health Service presented the job as financially useful, somewhat glamorous, and a bit scandalous. She noted that the money she earned was important both to her and to support her family because of the poor business at the family store. She enjoyed the freedom of working with other "girls my age" instead of with her mother, noting later "how different it was from working with Maman." The office was "in charge of provisioning troops in the area," and the officers in charge, whom she described as "very important men," had been businessmen before the war. According to Brun, they "joked with us, taught us how to forge their signatures on requisitions." She also provided some support for General Ruffey's charge that women employees were routinely involved in sexual liaisons with male officers: "each [officer] was separated from his family, and I soon discovered that each had his *petite amie* chosen from my fellow workers."[72]

Brun resigned from her position during the war after becoming engaged to Pierre Lemaire, the soldier she had taken the job to be near. When Lemaire was assigned to the Salonika Front, he asked Brun to quit her job with the Health Service despite the financial hardship it would create. Lemaire acknowledged the value of the job, but said, "I also know what goes on in those offices. Unprotected women shouldn't be working, and besides, you'll have enough to do getting ready for the marriage." At least in Lucie Brun's case, the army lost an employee because some people believed that its work environment was immoral and unfit for respectable women.[73]

Another factor that slowed the hiring of women in 1917 was senior commanders' need to deal with the mutinies that shook the army between April and June 1917. After General Robert Neville's offensive in Chemin-des-Dames failed in April 1917, many soldiers in the attacking armies had had enough; when Neville ordered the attacks renewed, some soldiers refused. The result was a widespread series of mutinies that included units throughout the army, and eventually forty-nine French divisions experienced some form of collective disobedience that manifested itself in actions ranging from refusing to return to the front to attacking officers, though no officers were killed. In some places mutineers' relations with their officers were cordial enough that they promised their officers that they would not fire on other French soldiers or civilians. In the wake of the mutiny, General Neville was replaced by General Pétain, who canceled the offensive and set about using a carrot-and-stick strategy to restore order.[74]

Inexplicably, the German Army did not realize the mutiny was happening, but it left a deep scar on the French officer corps. While commanding the 170th Division in May 1917, General Émile Taufflieb personally witnessed the 17th Infantry Regiment mutiny against its officers at Soissons. He reported hearing shots fired, including one that passed near his head. Mutineers cried "La paix," "À bas la guerre," and "À Paris!" Taufflieb reacted to the mutiny by speculating that he could have the five worst offenders in every company executed and was one of the senior officers least likely to reduce mutineers' sentences.[75] Although only a minority of officers had Taufflieb's experience, the 1917 French Army Mutinies shook the entire officer corps and were a major reason why interwar officers feared that conscripts were unreliable; it would later harden their opposition to giving soldiers the right to vote.

When Pétain's officers studied the causes of the mutinies, they recognized that many mutineers were reacting against the heavy losses they had suffered in failed offensives, but they also believed that they had been sparked by a wave of antiwar propaganda that had made it inside military units and complaints about soldiers' poor treatment at the hands of their officers; General Louis Franchet-d'Esperey commented that the mutiny was the result of "an organization coming from Paris under the instigation of the Germans." This further consolidated a belief that the conscripts had become politicized by outside forces.[76]

Pétain's carrot-and-stick approach combined attempts to solve the enlisted men's grievances and make clear that he would harshly punish future disobedience. The stick was provided by courts-martial, which tried many mutineers and sentenced 629 men to death, though only about forty-three were executed; the carrot included canceling any major offensives in the near future, improving living conditions at or near the front, and granting soldiers more leave to spend with their families.[77]

The mutiny did not directly involve women, but the high command's response affected them both directly and indirectly. Canceling offensives reduced the need to squeeze more men out of rear-area positions and replace them with women, thus slowing the hiring of women.

In an attempt to recruit and retain more women married to soldiers and to respond to soldiers' frustration at not being able to spend time with their employed wives while on leave, the army expanded its leave policies to allow women to spend more time with their husbands. A September 1917 press release detailed a new leave policy that allowed women married to soldiers up to thirty days of paid leave every year that would be coordinated with their husbands' leaves. If a female employee's husband received more leave, she would be entitled to the additional leave as well, but without pay.[78] This modified the 1916 Regime's leave policies, which allowed women to earn up to thirteen days of paid leave per year. In January 1918 the Ministry of War opened a school especially to teach women to be military typists and stenographers, which demonstrated the shortage of trained women and the Ministry of War's belief that the war was far from over. The school was important given the French Army and the Ministry of War's increasing use of skills tests to rank and hire candidates for clerical positions and the acute shortage of skilled workers the army faced by 1918.[79]

Despite the army's willingness to commit resources in the recruitment of women, officers' inconsistent willingness to accommodate female employees' needs complicated the army's efforts. Although the ministry granted generous leave packages to the wives of soldiers, it refused to allow women working in military facilities postal franking privileges to send mail to their families or to allow commanders to give women free military train passes to visit their family while on leave, even if the women had taken jobs far from home to meet the military's needs.[80]

Because of the challenging labor market and the army's inconsistent willingness to accommodate women's needs, it struggled to retain the employees it hired. As a result, it often had to replace women soon after they began work, and officers ended up competing against other units and departments for scarce staff. Although military administrators sought to control their civilian staff and to deploy them according to the army's needs, they found that their employees' ability to quit and easily find new jobs meant that the army did not always possess the upper hand in negotiations or while making job offers. Louise Bouland's career illustrated this phenomenon. Born in in Fontainebleau in 1883, Bouland took a position in an Intendance office in Meaux in January 1917. Despite hiring guidelines that instructed officers not to hire women already employed by the French state, she soon moved to a higher-paying position with a different military office. After gaining experience at Meaux, which is northeast of Paris, she found a new position working for another Intendance office in Melun, which was closer to her family in Fontainebleau. She left that position on October 27, 1918, two weeks before the end of the war.[81]

In March 1917 Léon Abrami, an undersecretary of state in the Ministry of War, sent a circular to the directors of the Intendance offices in each of France's military regions clarifying the position of wartime civilian workers. In addition to issuing new instructions on how to calculate pay, the undersecretary advised administrators that his office was preparing specific instructions to ensure that auxiliary employees received pension credit for their work and would be eligible for the full array of benefits. Abrami's instructions dealt with how to integrate employees hired under the 1916 Regime with civilian employees hired under prewar programs. Although focused on technical questions, the instructions revealed Intendance administrators' concern to protect their prewar male employees from suffering economic or prestige losses as a result of the wartime hiring of women. Women were treated differently from men, in part because some benefits were open only to men, even if there were women doing the same jobs. This was because of how two prewar decrees on civilian hiring interacted with the 1916 Regime. The Decree of February 26, 1887, was applicable to both sexes, but the text of the Decree of May 11, 1897, applied only to men, which meant that any of the enhanced benefits in it could only be given to men.[82]

Although the army did eventually clarify the terms of women's employment, it did not take any action to close the gap between what it paid civilian women and men to do the same job. Although the existence of a pay gap was not surprising, its size and the variation among different regions meant that standardizing and reducing it was one easy way the army could have tried to recruit more women. In June 1917, civilian men's starting pay exceeded that of women by 75 percent in the Thirty-Sixth Corps, and men's maximum pay outpaced women's by 66 percent.[83] Although gender-based income inequality was expected in wartime France, and the Thirty-Sixth Corps' case was extreme, the size of the difference in pay was usually significant. Greater attention to women's pay, which varied considerably between regions, could have had a major impact of recruitment.

Even some supporters of hiring women denied that the army's recruitment problems were real. On July 31, 1917, General Marie-Eugène Debeney, then the commander of France's First Army, rebutted claims that the female labor force was nearly exhausted. He admitted that some units under his command reported being unable to find enough female staff, but cited others that had been able to hire large numbers of women. Debeney concluded that, despite the tight labor market, a skillful local campaign would eventually yield enough applications from well-qualified women if officers were persistent.[84]

Other officers believed that the army should take a more proactive approach to solving the problems it encountered in recruiting women. In November 1916 Mardochée Georges Valabrègue, the inspector general of the First Arrondissement in Paris, wrote to the undersecretary for supplies at the Ministry of War, urging him to change the army's approach to recruiting women. He urged the ministry and the army to adopt a plan to continuously rerecruit existing employees. Valabrègue explained that inadequate attention to women's needs was not only making it hard to recruit women but also creating instability within the army's workforce because of how prone women had become to quit the military for more flexible jobs.[85]

Valabrègue's views were not typical of the officer corps, and he stands out as the most radical proponent of improving women's wages and working conditions. His own background left him out of step with most senior officers despite being extremely well connected. Born in 1852 in Carpentras, he was Jewish and had served as chief for Minister of War Louis André's military cabinet during the Affair of the Cards. He had commanded the École de guerre and in 1914 he was a member of the Conseil Supérieur de la Guerre; in August of that year he commanded the reserve divisions of General Charles Lanrezac's Fifth Army. After Joffre relieved Lanrezac of command on September 3, 1914, Valabrègue's position became precarious. When his group was dissolved on September 30, he was refused another combat command and relegated to inspecting rear-area camps until he was removed from the active list due to age in April 1917. Valabrègue's fall from being one of the most important generals in the army before the war to performing what was essentially a make-work job after September 1914 left him with few opportunities to contribute to the war effort and may have encouraged him to mentally and emotionally invest in advocating expanding women's roles within the army. Although his wartime experience was similar to General Ruffey's, Valabrègue's response to the push to recruit women was to become one of the movement's strongest supporters.

Valabrègue argued that the army needed to do more to recruit and retain women workers, and he developed a plan to provide an array of services to the women and their families. He argued that the army had already made some concessions to women's requests and that his plan was an extension and elaboration of existing policies. Despite initial reticence, the army had given women the right to eat breakfast in military canteens. The canteens were convenient, because they were located at women's worksites, but women also prized the right to use them because their food cost less than the market price. Valabrègue praised that decision but argued that it was a half measure, and that women should be given the right to eat dinner at the same canteens. He gave an example of a post commander who had overcome his inability to hire enough staff by liberally interpreting the guidelines that allowed women to eat breakfast in military canteens to allow them to have dinner there as well—an example that emphasized the power of nonmonetary benefits in attracting women to military employment. According to Valabrègue, it was not just a case of needing to pay a higher wage but of using the power of the government to

privilege its employees, thus producing "important advantages" when recruiting women in particular because they prized convenience more than
male employees did—especially if they had children.[86]

General Valabrègue warned that the army was not taking women's roles
as mothers sufficiently into account when setting working hours, pay, and
benefits. Citing reports from office and depot commanders, he explained
that many women who applied for jobs were mothers of young children,
and they had to return home in order to prepare their children's meals.
Even if the children were in school, mothers still had to leave work to make
their children's afternoon and evening meals before leaving them in the
care of other adults. The time it took to do that prevented them from being
able to take advantage of the subsidized, and otherwise convenient, canteens and made military employment less desirable to them. Valabrègue
citied anecdotal evidence that many women who applied for jobs asked
if their children could eat with them in the canteens and when they were
told that it was not allowed canceled their applications. Allowing women
to bring their children with them to meals would, the general argued, allow more employees to take advantage of the benefits theoretically available to them and provide a further boost to recruitment efforts.[87]

Valabrègue argued that in order to recruit more women, the army had
to listen to women, and that women were the most effective people to
recruit other women. He recommended reaching out to local women to
help improve recruitment, and envisioned the formation of local committees dominated by women who would try to recruit women to work for
the army. The committees would advertise positions and find solutions to
practical problems, including child care, which kept women from taking
army jobs. These committees would rely on local knowledge to actively
search out employees by creating lists of women to target as potential
workers. They would research applicant's backgrounds to make sure they
were suitable employees and would experiment with new methods of
recruitment.[88]

In particular, General Valabrègue thought that base commanders
should be given authority to organize crèches in towns with bases in conjunction with local committees. These crèches would be located close to
the bases to make them convenient for women, would be staffed at government expense, and would provide food for the children. This would

free women from their need to care for their children during the work day, but it would require ongoing arrangements between military and civilian authorities to provide for the maintenance, staffing, and cost of such facilities.[89]

In addition to the civilian committees, Valebrègue suggested that every area with a military presence should have a military commission chaired by the senior local commander and consisting of the heads of services and depots in the area, who would be specifically charged with finding ways to better use women's labor. The commissions would collaborate with the local committees to identify sources of labor to meet the military's needs. He hoped that the combination of the civilian committees dominated by women and military commissions could defeat the entrenched prejudices against women that he felt was slowing recruitment.[90] Valabrègue's suggestions implied that he believed that women's labor was absolutely essential to winning the war. He was calling for the army to accept a significant expense by agreeing to feed women's children at subsidized prices and maintaining crèches. His local committees and military commission implied the creation of a quasi-permanent infrastructure aimed specifically at recruiting women, which would require the investment of a lot of government money and officers' time. An investment that large would only be worth it if he believed that women's labor was crucial to winning the war.

Even Valabrègue's relatively progressive program still maintained a clear hierarchy that privileged military men and maintained a separation between women and the military. By dividing the job of recruiting more women between the women on the local committee and the officers on the military commission, he segregated women and military men even in the bureaucratic structures he wanted to use to integrate more women into the military community.

Valabrègue suggested that the Ministry of War promise the army's civilian employees, men and women alike, that at the end of the war they would receive the same commemorative medal that would be awarded to soldiers. That suggestion was guaranteed to be controversial because it implied that civilian employees of the army were in some way part of the army, and because it bestowed upon women the same honor as combat soldiers. Valabrègue defended his proposal against the anticipated criticisms by explaining that the medal was set to be awarded to soldiers regardless of whether they served in combat or behind the lines; he thus drew an equivalency between women civilian employees and at least a part of the army. The Ministry of War ignored Valabrègue's suggestions, but his proposals made clear that as least some officers were beginning to see women as part of the army and its future.[91]

Throughout the war, battlefield events profoundly influenced the importance military leaders attached to recruiting women civilian employees. The collapse of the Russian Army and widely anticipated German offensives of 1918 forced French leaders to turn their attention to the battlefront and away from pushing subordinates to hire more women. Instead, French generals spent late 1917 and early 1918 marshalling their forces and focusing on the Germans.[92] Almost immediately after defeating the last German offensive at the Second Battle of the Marne in early August 1918, Entente forces began a series of counterattacks that coalesced into the Hundred Days Offensive, which forced German leaders to surrender in November 1918. The fluid battlefield situation and the arrival of American troops kept French leaders' attention focused on strategic debates instead of on maximizing rear-area efficiency by substituting women for men in noncombat tasks. The fact that the number of women the army hired was so sensitive to the degree of pressure that senior leaders exerted to hire women demonstrates that many officers remained skeptical of women working inside the army. Many officers still excluded women from their conception of military identity and membership in the army as an institution. Despite periods when senior military and political leaders were not focused on hiring women, efforts to increase the proportion of female labor continued and the number of women working for the army rose throughout the war.

Regardless of the resistance to the further expansion of women's roles in the army, and some pressure to reduce women's roles, the top of the military hierarchy and the Ministry of War remained committed to moving more men to the front by continuing to hire women to replace soldiers working in the rear areas. In April 1918, the Ministry of War issued orders to replace male servers still working in noncommissioned officers' messes with women. Although there had been some progress with the replacement, the process was far from complete by the fall, and the orders had to be reissued on September 22, 1918, which suggested that there were still managers trying to avoid hiring women.[93]

Although in 1917 the army did not sustain the rate of hiring women it had reached in 1916, significant new hiring continued. On the eve of the ill-fated Chemin-des-Dames offensive, General Pétain, then commanding Army Group Center, reported replacing men of military age with women and older men in staff offices at army group headquarters.[94] On March 4, 1917, Pétain began a new and more intense effort to substitute women and men too old for military service for soldiers and able-bodied men in his headquarters. His order led to thirty-six men being reassigned to combat duty; they were replaced by eight women and fifteen older men. The results were modest, but representative of the ability of officers to squeeze extra manpower out of rear-area unit, even as late as 1917.[95] Pétain's example suggested that women and older men could be more effective than soldiers in some positions because he replaced thirty-six soldiers with only twenty-three women and older male civilians.

During 1917 and 1918 the army continued to open new positions to women in staff offices and depots of territorial infantry regiments and in rear-area support services throughout France.[96] The 39th Infantry Regiment's depot provides a good example of this process. It already had twelve female employees in December 1916 when the 1916 Regime came into force and over the course of 1917 its numbers rose rapidly despite the beginnings of a backlash against hiring women that became apparent near the end of the war. By December 1917 it employed twenty-six women, but over the course of 1918 it only added a net of four new women, bring it to a total of thirty at the end of the war.[97] Another territorial infantry regiment reported success in its bid to replace soldiers, reporting in March 1917 that it had been able to quickly hire eleven women for rear-area work. The unit reported receiving seventy-one applications, including seventeen from underage men.[98] One of the women hired during this period of reduced hiring was twenty-nine-year-old Marie Binctin, for whom the first months of the war had been filled with tragedy: on August 31, 1914, her husband Alphonse was killed in action serving in the 331st Infantry Regiment near Fossé, and on December 20, 1914, her brother was killed in fighting near

Perthes-lès-Hurlus. In April 1918 Binctin took a position doing clerical work for the Army General Staff, beginning a career with the army that would last until 1932.[99]

Within days of the November 11, 1918, armistice that ended the fighting, French officers began to purge their female civil employees. On November 14 the Ministry of War ordered the army to stop hiring women and to satisfy any new job needs by transferring women from positions that were being eliminated because of demobilization. In the past, historians have wrongly surmised that this order led to the firing of almost all of the army's wartime women employees.[100] By the end of 1918, the army was aggressively eliminating its female employees, but an unexpected military labor shortage soon reversed the process.[101] Despite clear indications that the army's leadership was expecting to shed its female workforce, the situation remained nuanced and, surprisingly, the end of the war did not always reduce the ministry's commitment to hiring women. On November 18, 1918, a week after the armistice came into force, the ministry reiterated its order to replace male servers working in noncommissioned officers' messes with women and affirmed the practice's continued validity despite the apparent end of the war.[102]

WOMEN AND THE FRENCH ARMY:
A CONTESTED IDENTITY

Women's labor was vital to the French Army's ability to fight and win the First World War. Before the war, the Third Republic had nearly completed its masculinization of the armed forces and had clearly marked the military domain as conceptually purely male. The near expulsion of civilian women from the army meant that by 1914 most officers were hostile to allowing women to serve as civilian employees; they resisted opening new categories of employment to women and complained about being forced to work beside them. But the brutal logic of total war ultimately broke down senior officers' reticence. When the army began to run low on men in 1915 and then faced a full-scale personnel crisis during the Battle of Verdun in 1916, most senior leaders accepted that they could not afford to refuse women's service.

The reopening of the French Army to women's service as civilian employees forced military men to deal with the contradiction between the prewar gender ideology that held that women were inherently incapable of self-discipline and corrosive to the army's ability to defend the nation and the wartime reality that the army could only successfully defend the nation against the larger German Army if it made extensive use of women's labor. The resulting synthesis was a complex and contingent reconstruction of women's military identity. The process involved an initial phase in 1914 and 1915 in which military leaders rhetorically accepted women serving in roles with a long tradition of conceptual feminization, such as nursing. This early opening was justified by wartime labor shortages within the army and carried little long-term danger to the masculine army because women usually supplemented rather than replaced men, and officers could be confident that when the war ended the supplemental women would not be needed.

During this early phase of the war, women's service did not lead to the construction of a military identity because military leaders could maintain the plausible belief that women were not really serving in the army. They were, however, praised for their commitment to France and for their appropriately feminine compassion for wounded and sick soldiers. Despite occasional references to their skill as healers, which itself reinforced prewar gender roles, women's initial service did not force officers to integrate them into their vision of the army or to construct a military identity for women.

In 1915 and 1916, women's increasingly integral place inside the French Army forced officers to define a place within the military community for them and explain why they were able to occupy it. At first senior officers, including the generals serving as ministers of war, only gave women's presence inside the army their qualified support. Even after senior military and civilian leaders accepted that the army had to systemically replace soldiers with women in March 1916, General Roques's grouping of women with labor-saving technology reflected the ambiguous place women were allowed within the French Army. Throughout the Great War, French officers debated women's proper roles; these debates centered on women's loyalty to the army, their capacity to be self-disciplined, and whether or not they could equal the skill level of male soldiers and civilian employees. Some officers, like General Ruffey, held that women's status as mothers meant that they could never be truly loyal employees because their familial responsibilities would always outweigh their loyalty to the army. But others, like General Valabrègue, defended women's loyalty and reflected Ruffey's criticisms back on the army by arguing that restrictive and shortsighted policies were needlessly burdening working mothers and that a more compassionate policy would allow more mothers to join the military community and help the French Army to win the war.

Other voices debated whether women had the skill to be useful employees. Advocates of integrating women into the army cited their contribution to the war effort in terms of their own hard work and the men they freed for the front, while opponents claimed that any skills they learned were negated by their natural lack of self-discipline. The inability of senior leaders who supported hiring women to fully impose their views on subordinates was a result of a chaotic wartime situation that kept them from focusing on the subsidiary issue of women's roles in the armed forces. It was also a function of the relatively short four-year period of the war. In peacetime the transition would have happened slowly, over many years, and senior officers would have had a long time to persuade recalcitrant officers, but the war accelerated and compressed the transition. As a result, it ended before the high command and Ministry of War had defeated all of the dissidents.

When the war ended in November 1918, women in the French Army were still in the process of establishing their military identity. By the end of the war they worked in offices and depots all over France and North Africa. They had accumulated an impressive record of wartime service, but their claim to be natural members of the military community remained contested, and many officers believed that the end of the war should mark the natural end of women's employment because with total war over, the weapons of total war would no longer be needed.

The fact that women's identity and membership in the military community was strictly circumscribed during the Great War did not mean that it was unimportant. Since the 1870s French generals and political leaders had squeezed women out of military life. By 1914 the military community had been masculinized to the point that almost all of the roles women used to play had been either eliminated or were now performed by military or civilian men. Only a handful of *cantinières* remained with their units, and most of them were in North Africa, where military regulations and laws were more easily ignored. The outbreak of the war thus revived women's nearly extinct place within the French Army. The war provided the shock necessary to derail the forty-year trend toward excluding women by boosting the need for military manpower above the level that the government could meet through conscription. It created a need for a massive increase in service workers at a time when there were fewer and fewer men available and thus forced military and political leaders to reopen the military community to women. Women's wartime service challenged the prewar narrative that linked masculinizing the armed forces with rationalizing the army's structure and culture by creating uniformity. The ability of the army to function with a huge influx of women demonstrated that a gender-mixed force could fight and win a war, but it was left to postwar leaders to come to grips with what the permanent reintegration of women into the military community would mean. Winning a total war had unexpectedly required the efforts of both sexes, and demobilizing from total war proved almost as unpredictable as the war itself.

NOTES

1. "Lynn, *Women, Armies, and Warfare*, 33–36." See also Barton C. Hacker, "Women and Military Institutions in Early Modern Europe: A Reconnaissance," *Signs: Journal of Women and Culture in Society* 6, no. 4 (1981): 643–71; and Mary Elizabeth Ailes, "Camp Followers, Sutlers, and Soldiers Wives: Women in Early Modern Armies (c 1450–1650)," in *A Companion to Women's Military History*, ed. Barton C. Hacker and Margaret Vining (Leiden, Netherlands: Brill, 2010).

2. Lynn, *Women, Armies, and Warfare*, 33–36; Cardoza, *Intrepid Women*, 14–17.

3. Cardoza, *Intrepid Women*, 14–17.

4. Ibid.

5. Ibid., 18–20.

6. Ibid., 30–33.

7. Ibid., 127–28.

8. Ibid.

9. Ibid., 168–71.

10. "Note au sujet des divisions de Réserve jusqu'en 1914," SHD DT 7 NN 142; Maxime Weygand, *Histoire de l'Armée Française* (Paris: Flammarion, 1961), 292–93; *Journal Officiel de la République Française, Lois et Decrets*, July 27, 1872, 893.

11. René Rémond, *La République Souveraine: La vie politique en France 1879–1939* (Paris: Fayard, 2002), 36–48; Steven C. Hause and Anne R. Kenney, *Women's Suffrage and Social Politics in the French Third Republic* (Princeton, NJ: Princeton University Press, 1984), 10–12.

12. Eugène Pierre, *Traité de Droit Politique Électoral et Parlementaire Supplément*, 5th ed. (Paris: Libraires-Imprimeries Réunies, 1924), 343. A soldier or sailor who had a sufficiently long leave, usually interpreted as between one and six months, could regain his right to vote for the duration of his leave. Pierre's interpretations strongly supported parliamentary supremacy over the executive, the armed forces, and even popular sovereignty. His legal philosophy assumed the republic to be an absolute that neither a parliamentary majority nor a plebiscite had the power to abolish.

13. Ibid., 373.

14. Judith Stone, "The Republican Brotherhood," in *Gender and the Politics of Social Reform: France, 1870–1914*, ed. Elinor A. Accampo, Rachel G. Fuchs, and Mary Lynn Stewart (Baltimore: Johns Hopkins University Press, 1995), 28–58.

15. Cardoza, *Intrepid Women*, 208–14.

16. Weygand, *Histoire de l'Armée Française*, 302–4.

17. Cardoza, *Intrepid Women*, 208–14.

18. Ibid.

19. Weygand, *Histoire de l'Armée Française*, 309–10.

20. Cardoza, *Intrepid Women*, 111–13.

21. Darrow, *French Women and the First World War*, 30, 41.

22. Ibid., 235–36.

23. Darrow, *French Women and the First World War*; Antier, *Les Femmes dans la Grande Guerre*.

24. Darrow, *French Women and the First World War*, 260–61. Antier, *Les Femmes dans la Grande Guerre*.

25. "La Novice," *L'Illustration* 3840 (1916): 33–34.

26. Antier, *Les Femmes dans la Grande Guerre*, 82–84.

27. Rachel Chrastil, *Organizing for War: France 1870–1914* (Baton Rouge: Louisiana State University Press, 2010), 128–30, 133–35.

28. Millerand served as minister of war from August 26, 1914 to October 29, 1915.

29. Letter No. 4721 1/5, June 22, 1915, Dossier 2, SHD DT 7 N 159.

30. Ibid.

31. Letter No. 5592-CM, November 16, 1915, Dossier 2, SHD DAT 7 N 159; Order, December 13, 1915, Dossier 2, SHD DAT 7 N 159; "Gallieni," November 10, 1915, Dossier 2, SHD DAT 7 N 159.

32. Ibid.

33. "Buat," SHD DAT 6 YG 260. After remarrying, Georgine Blanchet became Georgine Buat.

34. "Bareil," SHD DAT 6 YG 160.

35. Darrow, *French Women and the First World War*, 137–42.

36. "Replacement des infirmiers par la main-d'oeuvre féminine," No. 10593 4, August 1, 1916, Dossier 2, SHD DAT 7 N 159.

37. "Main d'oeuvre féminine," No. 4919 1/5, May 25, 1916, Dossier 2, SHD DAT 7 N 159.

38. "Exécution des prescriptions de la D.M. No 12738—I/5 du 2 December 1916," February 18, 1917, Dossier Femmes, SHD DAT 7 N 495.

39. "Replacement du personnel du service armé, employé dans l'intérieur," No. 10278 1/11, June 22, 1916, Dossier 2, SHD DAT 7 N 159.

40. Letter, No. IO 582 2/7, June 17, 1916, Dossier 2, SHD DT 7 N 159. Roques served as minister of war from March 16, 1916 to December 12, 1916.

41. For more of the role of family images and metaphors in politics and public discourse in French history, see Lynn Hunt, *The Family Romance of the French Revolution* (Berkeley: University of California Press, 1983).

42. For a discussion of Higonnet and Higonnet's double helix theory, see the introduction to the present volume; see also Higonnet and Higonnet, "The Double Helix."

43. "Auclair," SHD DAT 6 YG 159.

44. "Main d'oeuvre féminine," December 1, 1916, Dossier 2, SHD DT 7 N 159.

45. "Utilisation de la main-d'oeuvre féminine dans les Corps des Troupes, Dépôts et Services," December 2, 1916, SHD DT 16 N 82.

46. Ibid.

47. A military region was a territorial division within France which in peacetime corresponded to an army corps. In peacetime, commanders of military regions were responsible for many training and support activities; although command of a military region was a senior assignment, in wartime it was not a desirable assignment because it did not involve a combat command and many senior officers who had fallen afoul of France's commanding general, General Joseph Joffre, were relegated to the command of military regions.

48. Letter from General Drude to Minister of War, EMA, 1ᵉ Bureau, January 14, 1917, SHD DT 7 N 495; Darrow, *French Women and the First World War*, 251; "Extraits—Procès-verbal No. 497 du 2 Septembre 1916 de l'Inspection effectuée en exécution de l'article 9 de la li du 17 Août 1915 par le Contrôleur Général Weil," SHD DT 7 N 495.

49. "Extraits—Procès-verbal."

50. Ibid.; Robert Doughty, *Pyrrhic Victory: French Strategy and Operations in the Great War* (Cambridge MA: Harvard University Press, 2005), 67–68, 85. Ruffey's explicit attack on working women's sexuality was exceptional in military documents and may have been influenced by his feud with Joffre over his humiliating exile.

51. For more on concerns about the ability of French soldiers to meet the test of their manliness that war implied, see Rachel Chrastil, *Organizing for War: France 1870–1914* (Baton Rouge: Louisiana State University Press, 2010).

52. Gail Bederman, *Manliness and Civilization: A Cultural History of Gender and Race in the United States, 1880–1917* (Chicago: University of Chicago Press, 1995).

53. "Rapport d'ensemble sur l'utilisation de la main-d'oeuvre féminine dans les dépôts et services de la 4e région et observations sur les résultats obtenus," No. 2172 / II-I D, April 24, 1917, Dossier Femmes, SHD DT 7 N 495.

54. "Utilisation de la main-d'oeuvre féminine." SHD DT 16 N 82.

55. "Letter," No. 910 Y/C2, January 17, 1917, Dossier Femmes, SHD DT 7 N 495; "French Generals Shelved," *New York Times*, November 28, 1915.

56. "Execution de la Circulaire No. 12738 1/5 du 2 Décembre 1916," Dossier Femmes, SHD DT 7 N 495; No. 910 Y/C2, January 17, 1917, Dossier Femmes, SHD DT 7 N 495

57. "Utilisation de la Main-d'oeuvre Féminine dans les services de l'Intendance," No. 209 B 7, December 1917, SHD DAT 7 N 495.

58. "Utilisation des Femmes," SHD DT 7 N 495 2/10.

59. "Note pour monsieur le Ministre," November 17, 1916, SHD DT 7 N 495; "Femmes," SHD DAT 7 N 495.

60. Doughty, *Pyrrhic Victory*, 309.

61. Darrow, *French Women and the First World War*, 255.

62. Ibid., 260–61.

63. Controller General Piquet, "Rapport relative à la main d'oeuvre féminine (Régime de 1916)," No. 464, August 29, 1919, Dossier 1, SHD DT 8 NN 36.

64. Darrow, *French Women and the First World War*, 256–57.

65. Ibid, 261.

66. "Nombre total aux femmes embauchées," SHD DT 7 N 2449.

67. Letter to general commanding direction de l'Arrière, No. 2202/E, March 19, 1917 SHD DT 16 N 2449,; Letter from the mayor of Le Bourget, March 2, 1917 SHD DT 16 N 2449; Letter from the mayor of Dugny, February 26, 1917, SHD DT 16 N 2449; Letter from the mayor of Aubervilliers, February 26, 1917, SHD DT 16 N 2449.

68. "Posters Service de l'Intendance de la Gare Régulatrice du Bourget and L'Hôpital d'Evacuation de la gare d'Aubervilliers la Courneuve," SHD DT 16 N 2449.

69. Ibid.

70. Smith, *Confessions of a Concierge*, 34.

71. Ibid., 137.

72. Ibid.

73. Ibid., 39.

74. *Rapport du 2 Juin*, SHD DT 16 N 1521.

75. Denis Rolland, *La Grève des Tranchées: Les mutineries de 1917* (Paris: Imago, 2005), 184–85, 379, 408.

76. Ibid., 399.

77. Guy Pedroncini, *Les mutineries de 1917* (Paris: Julliard, 1968).

78. "NOTE pour la presse," September 4, 1917, SHD DAT 7 N 159; "Arrêt" No. 10611— Q-0 December 13, 1918, Dossier 2, SHD DAT 7 N 159.

79. "Ecole de dactylographie et de sténographie," January 8, 1918, Dossier 2, SHD DAT 7 N 159 No 249-1.

80. "Arrêt" No. 24100 K 1, November 1916, SHD DAT 7 N 159; "Voyages des Dames employées dans le S.A.," No. 28233 I-SA, August 2, 1917, Dossier 2, SHD DAT 7 N 159.

81. "Bouland," SHD DAT 6 YG 353.

82. Au sujet de l'extension du régime des décrets des 26 février 1898 et 11 Mai 1907 à tout le personnel civil et Établissements militaires," No. 5036 1/5, March 28, 1918, Dossier 2, SHD DAT 7 N 159.

83. "Salaires travailleurs civils et main d'oeuvre féminine," No. 782 AC 1619, June 7, 1917, SHD DT 16 N 2449.

84. "Sur l'emploi de la main d'oeuvre féminine," July 31, 1917, SHD DT 16 N 2449.

85. "Emploi des femmes," No. 6159, November 16, 1916, Dossier Femmes, SHD DAT 7 N 495.

86. Ibid.

87. Ibid.

88. Ibid.

89. Ibid.

90. Ibid.

91. Ibid.

92. Doughty, *Pyrrhic Victory*, 425–29.

93. "Arrêt," No. 027 1/5, April, 27 1918, Dossier 1, SHD DAT 7 N 159.

94. Letter from Pétain to Neville No. 70/1 2/C 5232, March 4, 1917, SHD DAT 16 N 2449.

95. Ibid.

96. "Rapport sur l'emploi d'hommes dégagés de toute obligation militaire, de mutilés, de jeunes gens ou d'étrangers", No. 5767, March 16, 1917, SHD DAT 16 N 2449; "Personnel Féminin employé dans les Armées. Services & Formations diverse dépendant du Général en Chef—Année 1917–," SHD DAT 16 N 2449.

97. Piquet, *Rapport à la main d'oeuvre féminine.*

98. *Rapport sur l'emploi d'hommes dégagés.*

99. "Binctin," SHD DAT 6 YG 151.

100. Darrow, *French Women and the First World War,* 8, 230.

101. Note, No. 6517/DA November 20, 1918, SHD DT 16 N 2449.

102. "Militaires mis a la disposition des mess de sous-officiers," No 25.129-I/II, November 18, 1918, Dossier 1, SHD DAT 7 N 159.

2

⸎

The Failure of the Demobilization
Purge, 1919–1923

During the First World War, French officers had reluctantly hired women as civilian employees in order to free soldiers for the front lines. Although women were not allowed to enlist as soldiers, more than 200,000 French women worked inside the French Army and often did the same jobs as soldiers. Given France's shortage of soldiers and the 1,400,000 combat deaths the French Army suffered between 1914 and 1918, women's service was vital to France's victory. Despite women's contribution to the victory, most officers assumed that the end of the war would see a return to the prewar exclusion of women from the military workplace. Like their civilian political counterparts, military commanders believed that with the end of the war, and the return of husbands and fathers from the front, women would have less need to work outside the home to support themselves and their children and that many would immediately and voluntarily leave the army's workforce. Contrary to most officers' expectations, the end of the war did not see the reversal of all of women's wartime gains and after a crisis in early and mid-1919, women consolidated their position in the military community and continued their service with the French Army.

Contrary to Margaret Higonnet and Patrice Higonnet's double helix theory's claim that the First World War did not lead to enduring gains for women, it did reverse the trend toward an ever more rigorous exclusion of women from the military community and began an expansion of women's roles inside the French Army that continued after the November 1918 armistice.[1] The predicted postwar backlash against women's wartime gains occurred, and in some parts of the army was successful, but overall it failed because women not only retained some of their wartime gains but reversed the prewar trend toward exclusion and even witnessed more gains during the interwar era.

The experience of women employees of the French Army also challenges the double helix theory in another way. Because most officers did not see the army's workforce as being divided between men and women but instead saw women as one group among several others, including officers, career enlisted men, and conscripts, women were able to experience prestige gains in relation to the vast majority of military men and to be increasingly included within the pale of military identity while conscripted men increasingly lost prestige because officers lost trust in their self-discipline during and after the war.

While military leaders grappled with women's place in the military community, they also had to deal with politicians who had their own ideas about what the postwar army should look like and were determined that it would not simply return to its prewar status quo. As befitted the ideological diversity of post–World War I France, political leaders supported a broad array of reforms, but every major political group wanted to reduce the size and cost of the military. This began a running debate about how the French Army should be organized that ultimately led to the 1927 and 1928 Army Laws. At the same time, military leaders found that the end of the war did not mean the end of discontent in their institutions. Both the army and navy struggled to conduct operations abroad while they were demobilizing and in April 1919 the French Navy was rocked by the Black Sea Mutiny, which reinforced officers' fears that conscripted men were not trustworthy members of the military community.

THE PURGE

Although women ultimately survived the demobilization purge, the end of the war did bring an extensive contraction of the military's civilian workforce. This contraction fell especially hard on women, whom commanders often viewed as employees of last resort. The exact time and rate of firings varied, but the purge could be rapid and hit civilian employees—

both men and women—all over France. The firings came in two distinct waves and illustrated the diversity of women's functions in the military. In the early months of 1919, roughly January to March, orders from the Ministry of War led the army to begin the large-scale firing of women doing clerical work. The first wave of firings was massive and fell particularly hard on women in combat or other units that could now reassign soldiers from field service to staff and support work. In June and July units began a new wave of firings. This time, instead of targeting office staff, they focused on two different groups: units with kitchens began to purge their female cooks and replace them with soldiers, and logistics units fired women working as laborers in munitions and other depots.

The initial wave of firings began as soon as the fighting stopped. Some offices and units were able to reduce their complement of civilian workers because the end of the war allowed soldiers to be transferred to take over more rear-area duties, while others, like recruitment offices, could cut staff because they had less work to do after the war ended. Le Havre's recruitment office eliminated ten of the twenty-five women who had worked there at the end of the war, and the office in northern Rouen fired seven of its twenty-four women in the same period. The military governor's office in Le Havre reduced its complement of women from seven to two in early 1919. The 74th Infantry Regiment had 120 female employees at the time of the armistice, but by January 1, 1919, it was down to ninety-three and by April that number had been further cut to forty-four. Over the same period, the 11th Artillery Regiment fired thirty-four of the sixty women who worked for it at the armistice.[2]

Some offices accomplished their cuts much more quickly, leading to a massive wave of firings. The 1st Artillery Regiment at Le Havre shrank its female work force from 130 to eighty between November 11, 1918, and January 1, 1919. The magazine at Vernon, a town north of Paris, employed 125 women in November 1918, but by May 1919 it only employed six. The staff of the Third Corps, headquartered at Rouen, fired forty-two of its forty-five women in early 1919. The corps' automobile group reduced its contingent of women drivers from seventy in November 1918 to two by July 1919. The group's annex base at Gaillon reported an even more dramatic contraction: between November 1918 and July 1919 it fired all thirty of its female drivers.[3]

The initial contraction was often brutally effective at quickly reducing the number of women working for the French Army, but it was unevenly applied. Some offices and units found it inconvenient to replace women workers, and others kept them on because soldiers did not want to take over their jobs. This was especially the case in situations where women had replaced soldiers doing menial work. Before the war, many conscripts were happy to be assigned to be assigned to work as servers, cooks, and cleaners in military canteens, but in 1919 it was more difficult to transfer combat veterans to perform what was seen as menial labor.

Following new instructions from the Ministry of War, during the summer of 1919, units began to fire women food workers and to accelerate the purge of women working in munitions depots. In June and July 1919, the 103rd Heavy Artillery Regiment got rid of all three of its female cooks and the five women who worked as handlers in its depot. The 74th Infantry Regiment earned praise for firing all of its women employees, and the 189th Infantry Regiment reduced its female workforce to a single woman working as a handler in a depot.[4] Based on how quickly they were firing women in the wake of the armistice, army leaders expected that they would soon return to a version of the prewar masculinized military workplace. Yet even as officers appeared poised to complete the demobilization purge and expel women from the military community, the process of demobilization began reversing the purge. This reassertion of women's wartime gains undermines the double helix theory because women were able to "step forward" by regaining wartime advances while men actually "stepped back" into their prewar roles.[5]

The demobilization purge was real and had the support of many officers. Despite the army's need for women's labor to help with demobilization, many administrators remained opposed to women's presence inside the army, and complaints from these officers flowed up the chain of command in the spring of 1919. The complaints formed part of a general concern that the army was wasting its resources and taxpayers' money by adapting too slowly to the end of the Great War. In July 1919, Georges Clemenceau, who was both premier and minister of war, ordered the army's controller general to begin an immediate and detailed investigation into the numbers and usage of women, cars, and typewriters in military offices and on bases. Clemenceau's language paralleled Minister of War

Joseph Gallieni's language from a 1915 letter in which he not only urged that women be hired but, in the same circular, called for the adoption of labor-saving devices like telephones and typewriters.[6]

Clemenceau was explicit that he wanted the Office of the Controller General to investigate women's roles in the demobilizing army. He asked it to probe the "conditions of employment of auxiliary civilian personnel, other than those covered by the decree of February 26, 1897, and more particularly of female personnel." Given that the 1897 decree only covered men, Clemenceau's intentions were clear. He went on to demand details of how many cars and typewriters were in service and where, whether offices were still ordering new machines, and whether there were machines going unused. He did not specifically ask for those details for women, but the controller general's officers read between the lines, and the final report on women categorized them in the same way other reports categorized cars and typewriters.[7]

The language in Clemenceau's instruction, whether dictated by him or by one of his military aides, revealed the widespread belief that women were a special category of employee. By combining an instruction to investigate the use of machines and women, the order implied that women were expendable and artificial members of the army. In theory, the instructions requested a report for Clemenceau on the army's employment of civilian employees, but most men were explicitly exempted, and the demand for special attention to women meant that the report would constitute a verdict on the value of continuing to employ women. That verdict was derived from a process designed to be used to study inanimate objects. If men had been subject to the same process, it would have indicated military leaders' concern about the presence of civilians within the army, but the fact that it focused on women highlights military leaders continuing discomfort with women having a role inside of the army.

FAILURE OF EXPECTATIONS

At the same time that the army was purging its women workers, it was also facing growing—and unexpected—demands on parts of its labor force that encouraged some commanders to begin rehiring them. The 39th

Infantry Regiment at Rouen illustrates this point. On June 20, 1919, its commander complied with his orders and fired all four of the women working in one of the depots as laborers, but exercised his authority, granted through the 1916 Regime, to immediately hire back all four women as secretaries; their duties and workplace changed, but they remained employed by the same unit they had previously worked for. The women of the 39th Infantry Regiment were part of a larger trend in which the unexpected pressures of demobilization created new opportunities for women, but in a more restricted domain than had been the case during the war.[8]

Despite a general belief that hiring female civilian employees was a wartime expedient, after armistice the Ministry of War soon recognized that some women's labor remained useful. On May 3, 1919, the ministry issued a decree creating a permanent cadre of stenographic-typists in its Central Administration and a crèche for their children.[9] Administrators created the crèche in response to women's demands for child care because many of the remaining women were war widows with young children. Although the initial cadre included only three hundred women, it marked official acceptance that some wartime changes could not, and perhaps should not, be completely undone. The order specified that postwar employment would be based on a combination of wartime job performance and a continuation of wartime hiring preferences that favored female relatives of dead or badly wounded soldiers.[10] The decree was just one part of a larger, but less self-conscious, process in which officers were hiring or rehiring thousands of women in the late spring and summer of 1919.

The hiring wave raised the ire of officers and civilian officials who wanted to remasculinize the army as well as officials concerned about the cost of maintaining a large civilian workforce. These concerns led to Clemenceau's decision to order the controller general to investigate the army's continued use of women's labor. The Office of the Controller General responded in August 1919 with Controller General Second Class Piquet's *Report on Female Labor: The Abuse of Female Civil Employees*. In the report Piquet urged rapid action to eliminate women employees. He cited a series of inspections by controllers and concluded that although the army still needed women's labor, it was using it on too large a scale. He urged officers and civilian administrators to begin firing women immediately to reduce waste and to prepare for the final elimination of all female civilian employees as soon as that became possible.[11]

Piquet surveyed the situation of women in the Third Military Region surrounding Rouen, which had been General A. M. B. Drude's wartime command. He found that, despite local variations, women's employment had followed a predictable pattern: immediately after the war, the demobilization order led commanders to begin mass firings, but labor shortages soon ended the purge. By the spring of 1919, the demobilization of troops forced local post commanders to return to hiring women under the 1916 Regime. Piquet attributed the reversal to short-term factors, mainly the unexpected increase in the army administration's workload created by demobilization and the contraction of the conscript workforce.[12]

Just as the First World War's unprecedented scale led combatant powers to do things their leaders had not previously expected or contemplated, the demobilization also proved unpredictable, because no society had ever fielded armies on the scale of those in the Great War in an age of bureaucratization. As a result, European governments and armies had no experience disbanding such large armies and underestimated the problems it created. Military leaders had assumed that they would not need women's labor after the war ended, but demobilization created so much paperwork that it threatened to overwhelm the army's administrative capacity. Military units and offices had to prepare and process numerous forms detailing collective information on every soldier demobilized each week and each month from every regiment, division, and corps in the French Army. Headquarters and administrative staffs also had to calculate partial pay and bonuses for soldiers returning to civilian life, arrange for them to be demobilized in appropriate places, and provide them with travel documents to get home. The Clemenceau cabinet demobilized older classes before younger ones, which had the unanticipated result of demobilizing many soldiers assigned to administrative tasks because of their age and civilian managerial experience. Not surprisingly, this combination of a rising workload and a shrinking workforce created a backlog of work and led the Army General Staff, the Intendance, and the Office of the Controller General to spend the spring and summer of 1919 complaining about administrative failures.[13]

Army administrators and post commanders responded by using the wartime 1916 Regime to draw on women's labor; these new employees often worked in the secretarial and accounting fields.[14] Military offices with responsibilities for transportation and demobilization tended to experience the most dramatic growth in workloads, and thus often sought new staff. The Intendance office in Le Havre reported that although its workforce was unstable, its female workforce increased by about one-third from January to August 1919, despite receiving orders to fire as many women as possible. A similar trend held in military units at all levels because of the unexpected volume of paperwork. Units needed more staff to produce the paperwork recording soldiers' military records, while regional administrations needed new staff to deal with the paperwork that certified that soldiers had been legally discharged from the army.

By July 1919 the army was overwhelmed by the effort involved in demobilization. Piquet's investigation of the 39th, 74th, and 129th Infantry Regiments revealed that they were failing to keep up with the paperwork necessary to complete the demobilization process. The 74th Regiment had fired forty-three of its ninety-three female employees, and the remaining administrative staff had become overwhelmed. As a result, only one in three of the unit's monthly bonuses for demobilizing soldiers was finished and the unit commander was asking permission to hire thirty more women to do office work. The 39th Regiment had maintained a constant staff of forty to fifty women since the armistice, but it had only succeeded in finishing 2,000 of its 13,000 monthly bonuses and 2,200 of the 4,300 files it had to complete for dead soldiers. The 129th Regiment had finished 18,000 of its 21,880 monthly bonuses, but its work contained serious and recurring errors that raised questions about the validity of its statistics.[15]

Piquet reported that despite the Ministry of War's instructions stating the units should be reducing the number of women they employed, in many units that number was actually growing. He noted with alarm that many units that had been steadily eliminating positions for women during the spring of 1919 had started rehiring them during the summer. Commanders justified the new wave of hiring by citing their units' need for emergency clerical staff to deal with the unexpectedly difficult demobilization process. Not all units rehired women at the same rate; some commanders preferred to transfer soldiers, others insisted on hiring more expensive men, and a few hired women more slowly because they had fired women more slowly than most units and thus did not have as much of a need to rehire. Even the Army General Staff itself was hiring women in the summer of 1919 despite sending out a steady stream of orders to other agencies to stop doing so. On May 19, 1919, Jeanne Bachet began work as a stenographic secretary in the Administrative Section of the Army General Staff. The never-married Bachet had not been a wartime civilian employee, and at forty was too old to benefit from any preference for orphans, but was hired to help deal with the glut of demobilization paperwork.[16]

Several offices and bases that had eliminated all of their female employees in early 1919 began to rehire women in the summer of 1919. The headquarters in Le Havre hired three women in August 1919, its accounting office added three female secretaries, and the engineering headquarters hired eight women to replace demobilized men. The liquidation of military stocks added another increased workload, and the military region's chief military engineer warned Piquet to expect another wave of hiring to help his office dispose of surplus wartime material.[17]

Even units that had seen less dramatic staff reductions were hiring women again by August 1919. During early 1919, recruitment offices had been able to cut staff because the end of the war had reduced their workloads, but as demobilization began they started to lose soldiers to civilian life, and by summer the loss of soldiers outweighed the reduced workload and the offices began hiring women to make up the difference. The Third Intendance office in Rouen began rehiring women in mid-1919 because of the growing number of requests for military pensions, which swamped its workforce. The 129th Infantry Regiment's depot had originally planned on slashing its workforce, but the rising workload derailed the commander's plans. On March 11, 1919, its commander ordered a one-third reduction in the number of women it employed, but as the demobilization process began, he found that he had to expand his workforce instead of allowing it to shrink. The only reduction he was able to make came when an artillery unit that was temporarily sharing the depot departed, which allowed for a downsizing of staff. The depot of the 74th Infantry Regiment had employed 120 women in November 1918, and by August 1919 it had reduced that number to forty-four. But the demobilization of military secretaries and bookkeepers who were not replaced by new conscripts meant that the commander was planning on hiring thirty new women, including twenty-four clerical workers and six accountants.[18]

The 39th Regiment's depot had a more complex story, but one that illustrated the variability of women's employment. By the end of 1916 it had twelve female employees, but over the course of 1917 the depot's officers expanded their workforce to include thirty-six women despite that being a year in which the overall number of women working for the army leveled off. In the immediate wake of the armistice, the 39th Regiment's workforce fell to thirty women, but demobilization soon led to a new round of expansion. The return of some men from the front led to an increased workload and instead of reassigning soldiers, the commander drew on women's labor. By April 1919 the depot was employing sixty-six women, more than it had during the war. Pressure to shed workers in the spring led to a phased reduction to forty-four women by July 1, 1919, but the inability of the remaining staff to manage the demobilization forced the resumption of hiring that brought the female workforce back up to fifty by August 1.[19]

One of the reasons that officers returned to hiring women was pressure to save money. Because it was legally and socially acceptable to discriminate against women by paying them less than men to do the same job, women became attractive employees when officers needed more labor but had to minimize their payrolls. In Rouen, the army paid newly hired women an average of 7.5 percent less than it did men. In La Havre, the disparity was more significant: there newly hired women could expect to make between 8 percent and 33 percent less than their male coworkers.[20] These figures reflect the official wage, and thus do not take account of discrimination in promotions and pay raises, which often meant that men's salaries would grow more quickly than women's pay.

FAILING IN THEIR DUTY

Piquet repeated criticized civilian women for their inattentiveness to detail and blamed them for making too many mistakes in their work, implying that they were undisciplined employees. He complained about the rising error rate in districts with a large percentage of female civilian employees and singled out the region around Le Havre as a major offender. The report identified the 129th Infantry Regiment's headquarters, which had the largest proportion of female employees of any unit in the military region, as the worst offender. Piquet acknowledged that the unit commander's decision to hire a large number of women had allowed it to process more forms, but warned that it was "necessary to consider the quality of the work." He noted that Le Havre's Intendance office signaled that "its audits . . . revealed many errors, and that it had to return a lot of the dossiers to the local corps." Generalizing based on the 129th Regiment, he castigated the army's female employees for indiscipline, calling them "a personnel insufficiently trained or insufficiently attentive, too numerous to be controlled, and working too quickly." He explained that the women's errors had forced the regional corps command to install a special team of male auditors on-site. The team regularly rejected files and returned them to the staff "covered in red ink." Piquet ignored the role of untrained soldiers reassigned from dissolved combat units and new male civilian employees, who were just as unskilled as their female coworkers, in causing errors. These omissions revealed his assumption that women's gender rather than their inexperience or civilian status explained their alleged lack of self-discipline.[21]

Like General Pierre Ruffey, Piquet feared that women's presence in the army endangered military professionalism by undermining male self-discipline. He argued that officers were saddling the army with needless expenses because they lacked enough self-discipline to properly supervise women. According to Piquet, officers were allowing women to perform make-work tasks and treating lazy or incompetent women too leniently by transferring rather than firing them.[22] He cited a report from the commanding general of the Third Corps that claimed that his staff officers had investigated the possible overemployment of women and found numerous examples of waste. In one example, a staff officer had visited a military office that employed four women to do specialized secretarial work; the day the investigators visited the office they found that the woman charged with processing transfers did not deal with a single transfer. The secretary who dealt with requests for leave processed only four forms, and the secretary who took dictation only typed four short letters and twenty notes.

Meanwhile, the fourth only processed two documents during the workday and spent a considerable amount of time doing her hair and makeup.[23] The officer in charge was content to retain all of his staff, but after receiving the report, the commanding general fired all the women.

In another example, the Third Corps claimed to have found an office that employed two hundred women but had not properly supervised them. When the corps-level staff asked for disciplinary records, it found that between the end of the war and August 1919, the officers in charge had not recorded a single negative note on any of the employees; none had been fired for poor work product, absenteeism, or for personal conduct, nor had any been demoted or even sanctioned for their work. The corps staff refused to believe that "all the secretaries were perfect" and instead concluded that it was a result of "laziness and inattention" by the officers in charge.[24]

Piquet identified officers' failure to supervise women as a major problem facing the demobilization process. He argued that officers were essentially ignoring the deficiencies of women under their command and were failing to demand value for money or maintain accurate records that would allow senior commanders and administrators to evaluate individual women's performances. The report admitted that it was not always the fault of the officers in charge of the offices; sometimes there were too many women for the officers to effectively oversee, and other times the facilities were so hastily organized or overcrowded that it was not practical to observe the work as it was taking place. This was the case with 142 women in one of the 129th Infantry Regiment's posts who worked in a confusing and overcrowded room. But Piquet's report emphasized that too often officers were not even trying to discipline women;[25] his insistence that women had to be constantly monitored by men to make their work productive implied both that they lacked the self-discipline to be independently productive and that when they were effective, the credit for their accomplishments should go to the men whose strong oversight had facilitated such productivity.

Piquet criticized officers' refusal to formally sanction underperforming women. He implied that many of the army's women employees were failing to meet acceptable standards, but that they were not having their poor performance noted in their records. As a result, many were holding on to jobs they should have lost and others were successfully getting new jobs because their commanding officers were either giving them positive recommendations to get rid of them or allowing them to resign from previous positions without noting their failure to adequately perform their duties. Piquet suggested that the army should create a centralized system of tracking women's service records so that their past employment could be more easily verified and so that only those who had been fired as a result of the planned reduction of the civilian workforce would be able to get new jobs with the army.[26]

In his report, Piquet urged Clemenceau to take immediate action to make sure women left the army's workplace as quickly as possible. He suggested the army concentrate women into a few specialized tasks while masculinizing the rest of the civilian workforce. He reasoned that if women were forced to specialize in just demobilization work, once the demobilization ended the army would be in a position to naturally eliminate their jobs without having to make a formal decision to do so. He also argued that forcing women to specialize would make it easier for male functionaries and officers to oversee their work during the brief period they continued to serve in the army.[27]

DEFENDING MILITARY MANHOOD

Piquet's report revealed a gendered conception of military identity that excluded women from membership in the military community and questioned their fitness for any role within the army. In his report, Piquet implied that self-discipline was a purely male trait and essential to the army's functioning. He argued that women's allegedly poor work performance was evidence of an inherent lack of discipline and that they required strong male oversight to make their work useful. According to Piquet, women made more mistakes than their male counterparts, which ultimately created more work for men, because they had to fix women's errors in addition to doing their own work.[28] He also alleged that male officers regularly failed to hold women accountable for their mistakes because they were women. He thus claimed that women's lack of self-control created problems for the army, but the larger problem was that male officers' self-discipline was too weak to allow them to regularly impose the outside discipline that women needed. As a result, women's mere presence in the military workplace was introducing indiscipline into the army and threatening the officer corps' professionalism by undermining male officers' self-discipline, which was the cornerstone of military professionalism and a fragile achievement that could only survive in a gender-segregated environment. For Piquet, a soldier needed to possess manly self-discipline, and a man could only truly be manly in the absence of women. He thus defined women as inherently and irrevocably alien and dangerous to the French Army.

Piquet's construction of manliness and professionalism through self-discipline allowed him to pose as an epitome of military manhood by recalling the army's officers to their duty vis-à-vis women employees. By making self-discipline the major component of professionalism and limiting it to men, he created an image of military identity that reflected a skilled and self-disciplined man. By excluding women from professionalism through denying their ability to be self-disciplined, Piquet constructed military identity against women's gender and indirectly validated male civilian employees and noncombat soldiers' claim to a respected place within the army based on their ability, as men, to exhibit self-discipline and thus professionalism. By focusing on self-discipline instead of courage or self-sacrifice, Piquet appealed to prewar staff and command officers who, like himself, had not experienced much combat during the war yet sought to protect their power and privilege against men who became officers or were rapidly promoted during the war because of their battlefield exploits.[29]

Although Piquet raged against it, the rehiring of women during demobilization was on a far smaller scale than wartime hiring. The army's need for additional labor in the summer of 1919 was significant in some key sectors, but it never approached the levels it had in wartime. Overall figures are not available, but the new wave of hiring probably did not lead to a net increase in the number of women working for the army in the first months after the armistice because even as offices with demobilization responsibilities began rehiring women, other parts of the army continued to fire civilian employees. The result was a slowing of the rate at which women were leaving the army's employment and then a modest rise rather than a dramatic boom. Yet even in its limited form, the rehiring of women changed the dynamic within the army and bought time for women to become better integrated into the service. That coupled with the financial crisis in postwar France made women more and more attractive to military leaders as employees. Women were cheaper than conscripts because they did not need to be trained for combat before being assigned to office work, and they were cheaper than male civilian employees because they could be paid less to do the same job.

DECLINING TRUST IN MALE CONSCRIPTS: THE BLACK SEA MUTINY

At the same time that Piquet was advocating purging women in order to prevent the intrusion of the civilian world into the military community, a mutiny among French sailors in the Black Sea raised the prospect that civilian politics and identities were overcoming military identity and discipline. The April 1919 Black Sea Mutiny greatly affected how French officers viewed political activity in the armed forces and contributed to their declining faith in conscripted men. The French Communist Party's retelling of the story and defense of the mutineers eventually influenced both voters' understanding of the event and the ways that military officers remembered the mutiny. In many respects, the cult of memory that the party built around the April 1919 mutiny was more important that the mutiny itself. The military's own repeated rewriting of its memory of the mutiny incorporated major elements of the Communist Party's description of the event, which led both military officers and party members to see the mutiny as a prototype for future communist-inspired revolts.

The mutiny was a result of Clemenceau's efforts to aid the anticommunism forces, led first by General Anton Deniken and then by General Pyotr Wrangel, in southern Russia during the Russian Civil War. In advance of the crisis, officers had warned that the end of the war with Germany in November 1918 had led to rising discontent among sailors who wanted to go home. Some warned that the armistice had undermined officers' authority, and others signaled growing sympathy with the Bolsheviks among the crews of their vessels.[30] A February 1919 report linked sailors' interest in communism to their complaints about inadequate winter clothing, disruptions in the supply chain, and the irregular delivery of mail from home.[31]

Naval officers in the Black Sea first detected signs of an impending mutiny on April 16, 1919, when informants among the crew of the destroyer *Protêt* warned their captain that André Marty, the chief engineer, was conspiring with some of the sailors to take control of the ship. The ship's captain, Lt. Commander Léon Jules Welfelé, responded quickly by arresting Marty and his coconspirators. The arrests put an end of the revolt on the *Protêt*, but it did not stop mutinies on other ships.[32]

Between April 19 and 25, sailors on at least ten ships mutinied, tried to mutiny, or directly defied their officers' authority. The first mutiny took place on April 19 among the crews of the battleships *France* and *Jean Bart*, two of France's seven dreadnoughts, while they were moored in Sebastopol Harbor. The mutinies did not involve direct attacks on the officers of either ship, though crew members threatened several officers and openly discussed killing the squadron's admiral. As the mutineers were consolidating control of the *France* and *Jean-Bart*, the crews of several other vessels mutinied. On April 20, men aboard the battleships *Justice*, *Mirabeau*, and *Vergniaud* joined the mutiny. The sailors refused to obey orders, sang "The Internationale," and attempted to communicate with mutineers on other ships. These mutinies were, however, less severe than the one onboard the *France*, and by the end of April 21 the officers were back in control of most of the ships. The *France*, however, remained largely under the control of mutineers until it completed sailing from Sebastopol to the French naval base at Bizerte, Tunisia.[33] On all of the ships, the mutinies were generally nonviolent. The mutineers raised red banners, sang revolutionary songs, and refused to follow orders, but they did not kill their officers or fire on loyalist ships.[34]

During the summer a second round of uprisings shook the naval high command. Mutinies took place on the *Voltaire* and *Guichen*, but the main uprising was aboard the battleship *Provence* in Toulon Harbor. On June 6, 1919, the day before the Chamber of Deputies was set to debate the Black Sea Mutiny, sailors on the *Provence* raised a red flag to show their solidarity with the accused Black Sea mutineers. On June 10 the crew of the *Provence* revolted against its officers, refusing to obey orders to sail to the Black Sea to inspect French forces there because the mutineers feared that the ship was going to participate in the war against the Bolsheviks. The subsequent trails convicted seventeen sailors and sentenced them to between one and eight years in prison.[35] By August 1919 the courts-martial had sentenced one officer and seventy-five enlisted men to prison terms ranging from twenty years at hard labor to as a little as a two-year suspended sentence. Ironically, the man who received the stiffest sentence never got to join in: Marty, the chief engineer of the destroyer *Protêt*, was convicted of organizing a mutiny, but his plan was uncovered before he could carry it out and he spent the entire period in the brig.[36]

All of the revolts were soon suppressed, but French officers still had to explain them. Initially naval authorities took a balanced view of the origins of the revolts; they recognized that there was a Bolshevik influence, but they also blamed war weariness and several other internal factors. The navy's initial report on the mutiny identified procommunist propaganda as a contributing factor, but emphasized that the men's desire to return home following the end of the Great War was the most powerful motivation for the mutiny. It also repeated claims noted earlier that the poor quality of the food and winter clothing had been important to the revolt.[37]

Naval officers' initial view was challenged by communist propaganda. During the various mutinies themselves and afterward, Russian, and later French, communists claimed credit for causing the mutinies. They argued that the mutineers had acted in class solidarity with Russian workers and in support of broader revolutionary aims. Communist propagandists painted the mutiny as an overtly political act and demanded that the participants be granted amnesty. They also credited Marty, the only officer to be involved in the mutiny, as the leader of the movement. Despite Marty's marginal role in the mutiny he became its face because of a long and focused propaganda campaign that tried to identify the mutineers as ideologically committed communists who chose to support the Bolshevik cause against their own country's imperialism. In 1919 and 1920 the campaign was organized by left-wing elements within the SFIO (Section Francaise de l'Internationale Ouvrière, the Socialist Party), and after the December 1920 Socialist-Communist split, it was aggressively embraced by the SFIC (Section Française de l'Internationale Communiste).[38]

The Bolsheviks also loudly proclaimed their responsibility for the mutiny and presented it as a communist passion play in which Marty was cast in the role of Vladimir Lenin, the vanguard intellectual leading and organizing the proletariat. Marty's father had been a communard, which further positioned Marty to play the role of revolutionary leader and martyr. Whereas Lenin claimed to act in defense of the abused working class, communist propaganda claimed that Marty acted to defend the Russian revolution, which represented the aspirations of all the world's workers. He allegedly broke the officer corps' class solidarity because he opposed the French mission to aid anti-Bolshevik forces in the Russian Civil War. Their propaganda, which was repeated in France, also claimed that Marty and the sailors were inspired by the pronouncements of Bolshevik leaders, including People's Commissar of Foreign Affairs Gregory Chicherin.[39]

The SFIC reinforced its claim to have been responsible for the Black Sea Mutiny by campaigning for the release of all of those convicted. The party produced posters and pamphlets calling for the release of the mutineers, but often gave Marty central billing. Party newspapers published editorials demanding their freedom, and meetings often involved calls for their immediate release. The effect of those demands was to associate the SFIC with the Black Sea Mutiny in the eyes of most observers.

In 1923 the government granted Marty and the rest of the convicted mutineers amnesty in an attempt to undermine their power as communist martyrs, but this did not end the mutineers' role as propaganda symbols, and Marty became a leading politician and speaker for the PCF (Parti communiste française), as the SFIC had become know, and; in 1924 he was elected to the Chamber of Deputies as representing Seine-et-Oise and continued to campaign against the professional military and call on conscripts to defy their officers.[40] The PCF's campaigns continued to invoke the mutiny throughout the 1920s; the mutineers were evoked in election campaigns and in propaganda aimed at the military. During the Rif War in Morocco in 1925 and 1926, military and police intelligence reports regularly noted that the PCF was invoking the mutiny and the popular press reported communist appeals that soldiers in Morocco should emulate the Black Sea mutineers by rebelling against the government's unjust war.[41]

The PCF's campaign changed the way military officers understood the Black Sea Mutiny. The constant repetition of the story of heroic working-class sailors who followed the call of class solidarity and communist propaganda to defend Soviet Russia from the French government struck at the heart of the French Army's mission and officers' view of their institution. Over the course of the 1920s, their memory of the Black Sea Mutiny's causes was eroded by communist propaganda campaigns and reshaped by it into a new memory that conformed to the party's version of events, but which officers interpreted as a grave threat to their institution and country instead of as a source of hope. Military officers came to see the Black Sea Mutiny as proof that the PCF's efforts to establish a support base within the military posed a direct threat to their ability to control their men and defend France. Officers' internalization of the communists' narrative of the mutiny led them to increasingly view conscripts as potentially dangerous men who could not be trusted to obey orders. Officers' fears that the civilian world was creeping into the army were exacerbated by the seemingly unending debate over reorganizing the French Army.

Discussions about the Black Sea Mutiny largely ignored women because women did not actively participate the mutiny. But as officers' trust in draftees—who constituted the majority of military personnel—declined, it indirectly improved the relative status of every other group inside the military community, including women civilian employees. The officers' belief that the mutiny had been influenced by outside propaganda and the work of communists inside the crews also made them more sensitive to future evidence that the PCF was trying to win converts inside the French Army or to influence French soldiers.

FORGING A NEW IDENTITY

Despite Piquet's complaints about the effects of female civil employees and France's involvement in military conflicts in Cilicia, Morocco, and Russia, the army found that it could not just return to the prewar status quo. During the war the French state had borrowed 110 billion francs to pay for the war, and the combination of economic damage from the war and the cost of servicing the debt left the postwar government with a strong incentive to minimize military spending. The end of the war and the destruction of the German Army created a sense that France was less likely to be attacked than it had been in decades, which reduced public support for maintaining a large army. At the end of the war, the French Army returned to its peacetime legal regime and, at least in theory, it was supposed to revert to its prewar organization based on the 1913 Three-Year Service Law. When the war began, the army had only just begun its transition to its new structure. Its peacetime strength was 747,000 men, including 32,000 officers, who were divided into forty-four infantry and ten cavalry divisions. If the postwar army had been reorganized according to the 1913 law, it would have deployed 979,000 men, including 32,350 officers. The government did not apply the 1913 law, but neither did it immediately replace it. Despite the extensive demobilization of 1919 and 1920, by the end of 1920 the French Army still had 837,000 men under arms, including 40,950 officers. Given the government's need to cut expenditures, it was politically impossible to continue to maintain such a large combat force, let alone implement the 1913 law. Alexandre Millerand's cabinet's solution was to reduce the size of the army by sending conscript classes home early while it worked on a permanent plan.[42]

As soon as the war ended, the French cabinet and France's military leaders faced pressure to use the armistice to fundamentally reshape the French military, and especially its army. In August 1919, at the same time Piquet submitted his report, a group of Socialist deputies, led by Pierre Renaudel and Albert Thomas, presented a proposed law "on a first adaptation of the French military to the Covenant of the League of Nations."[43] Renaudel and Thomas dismissed the value of a professional army and advocated a militia army modeled on Jean Jaurès's 1911 book *L'Armée nouvelle*, which had called for the creation of a militia in which all men would serve; these men would be briefly drafted for training, but then would return to civilian life. He argued that the militia would be able to defend France against any invasion but could not be used to invade another country.

The bill's preamble credited the Republic for the victory in the Great War and blamed France's wartime defeats on the military elite's over aggressiveness and mistrust of reservists. The bill's authors argued, "It can be affirmed today, without fear of being contradicted, that if the nation had listened to the voices—for the most part of nontechnicians—that counseled a defensive military organization on the militia model, that is to say if it had prepared the methodical utilization of all its reserves, France would have victoriously resisted the blows of the enemy, instead of suffering the disaster of Charleroi."[44] The authors thus blamed the professional officers for the early defeats and called for the elimination of the military as an institution distinct from civilian life. They summed up their appeal, writing of their "hope that the will of the people will press against the hesitant action of governments. We hope, when all is said and done, that socialism will bring nearer the hour when general disarmament will allow humanity to organize the labor and leisure of men in the fraternity of reconciled peoples."[45] Military leaders regarded Renaudel and Thomas's bill as dangerously naive and a threat to both their institution and France's national defense, though in 1919 they had little cause to fear it would pass in the face of Clemenceau's solid majority in the Chamber of Deputies.

In 1920, parliamentary Socialists returned to the subject of military reform with a proposal from Vincent Auriol, Joseph Paul-Boncour, Albert Thomas, and Alexandre Varenne; Renaudel was not part of this group because he had been defeated in the November 1919 elections.[46] The 1920 plan repeated the 1919 proposal's call for the internationalization of French defense policy and a very short term of conscript service—in this case eight months, more than half of which would be spent in training or on leave. Thomas and his cosponsors argued that France was in a unique position to strengthen the League of Nations by facilitating Franco-German reconciliation. They hoped that disarmament would strengthen the League of Nations and pave the way for a lasting Franco-German rapprochement. Thomas also argued that undermining the standing army would protect the Republic against the poison of the professional officers' antirepublicanism.[47]

Given that the 1919 elections returned a solid majority for the conservative Bloc National, the Socialists had no hope of implementing their proposals, but even right-wing politicians recognized the need to cut the military's size and budget. In 1920 Millerand's cabinet decided to reduce men's mandatory military service requirement from three to two years and then temporarily reduced that figure to eighteen months. Initially many generals opposed the plan. Speaking in the Conseil Supérieur de la Guerre on June 22, 1920, Marshal Philippe Pétain argued that "to further aggravate an already unsatisfactory thing by maintaining only one class or a class and a half under the flag, constitutes an error the consequences of which will be incalculable."[48] Military leaders were reluctant to endorse the cut, but ultimately accepted it because of the postwar financial crisis. In June 1920 the Conseil Supérieur de la Guerre accepted a reduction in the term of conscript service. The council consisted of France's highest ranking generals, the men designated to hold major wartime commands, and had the legal right to be consulted on military policy. It did not have the power to block government policy or changes to the army's structure or mission, but political leaders were reluctant to enact changes without the council's support.

To accommodate the reduction in conscript service the council approved plans to free 4,500 soldiers for combat duty by replacing seventy-five soldiers doing clerical and mobilization work with civilian employees in each of the army's sixty authorized infantry regiments.[49] The council inadvertently, but effectively, blocked further efforts to eliminate women as civilian employees and registered the failure of the postwar backlash against women's gains within the army. It did so without its members admitting that they were making women a permanent part of the army's organization. This decision saved the jobs of thousands of women hired under the 1916 Regime, although many officially remained temporary employees. On December 11, 1920, the Conseil Supérieur de la Guerre ratified its earlier advice provided the reduction in conscript service was accompanied by a broader plan that increased the numbers and roles of civilian employees within the army.[50]

The 1920 law set the term of service at two years, and the government almost immediately began working on a new law that would further reduce that. The end of the war had made conscript service increasingly unpopular because most French voters believed that the threat from Germany had been greatly reduced or eliminated. In response to continued pressure from the Ministry of War to endorse a permanent reduction to eighteen months, the Conseil Supérieur de la Guerre agreed to support the cut if it was allowed to increase the number of career soldiers, colonial soldiers, and civilian employees.[51] The effect of these pronouncements was to slowly reopen positions to women throughout the early 1920s. By 1925 the number of women working under the 1916 Regime had stabilized at 7,500 out of 10,000 employees in addition to thousands of other temporary and permanent employees.[52] At the same time the French Army had shrunk to 643,400 enlisted men and 32,600 officers.[53]

The shift toward civilian employees was complicated by the lack of a clear central plan. Because most of the decisions were being made at the local level, officers were often left to improvise their budgets in order to pay for the workers they needed. On January 12, 1921, the Ministry of War sent a sent a circular to corps commanders warning them that it still did not know how much money would be available to pay civilian employees that year. It suggested that commanders retain anybody they needed and keep paying them while the central administration worked out a budget.[54] The army's manpower shortage and the cabinet's budget cuts pushed unit commanders to continue to rely on civilian employees, including women, despite the lack of central leadership. During the early 1920s, army leaders tried to reduce the number of soldiers doing nonessential tasks, and some commanders experienced significant successes. On March 20, 1922, one colonial command reported that it had recently repatriated approximately seven thousand soldiers without compromising its forces' effectiveness. The manpower savings were a result of rationalizing services and hiring 2,596 civilian employees to replace them.[55]

During the early 1920s, the General Staff, the Conseil Supérieur de la Guerre, and civilian political leaders virtually ignored the presence of women in the army, but French officers slowly integrated them, and this facilitated the emergence of a military identity for women. This system of administration limited women's job mobility; they could not freely transfer between posts or offices and had to apply to the Ministry of War for permission to move to a new unit instead of just applying for a vacant position or having their commanding officer deal with it bilaterally with another commander. As a result, women stayed with the units that hired them and assimilated into the army's collective identity on the unit level.[56]

Marie-Louise Mercier's experience shows how hard it could be for a woman to get a simple transfer. Mercier, who had been working for the army since 1916, was a war widow and the mother of a child born during the war. After remarrying, she took her new husband's name, Auclair, but when she wanted to transfer to a post closer to her family's home it proved challenging. In May 1922 she asked for, and got, permission to transfer out of the Health Service to an office closer to her home, but she had to wait for the new office to find an employee with the same skills and rank who was willing to transfer to the Health Service, which did not happen until April 1923. In 1925 she unsuccessfully sought another transfer. In December 1928 Auclair appealed to her immediate supervising officer and wrote to officers up the chain of command asking for help to transfer again. In the letters detailing her case she signed her own name "veuve [widow] Mercier" despite having remarried, and her supervisor, Captain Nauches, also referred to her that way. Both Nauches and his immediate superior officer supported her request (which was a renewal of the request she had made in 1925) and the central administration finally approved it, but the move did not happen until September 1929.[57]

The compartmentalized system of overseeing women employees in the 1920s was strikingly similar to the system of overseeing nineteenth-century *cantinières*. *Cantinières* were hired and overseen by unit commanders and remained with their units, often for years at a time. Just as many of the women working in the army in the early 1920s had blood ties to their units, all *cantinières* had been married to a soldier, usually a non-commissioned officer. This suggests that senior officers used their memories of how previous generations of officers had managed the *cantinières* to guide their handling of women civilian employees.[58]

In the early 1920s, midlevel officers and female employees constructed the basis for a military identity for women by emphasizing unit loyalty and blood ties to fallen soldiers. As a result of wartime and demobilization hiring and retention preferences, many women were the widows, mothers, or daughters of soldiers who had died in the war. Indeed, many were working for their deceased relative's unit. For example, Marie Binctin signed on in April 1918 after her husband and brother were both killed in action, leaving her to support herself and her mother. She served until 1934, during which time she was only transferred twice. Her 1929 transfer from the Army General Staff office to an artillery post closer to her home required a personal letter to the minister of war, in which she pleaded for a transfer based on her need to care for her war-widowed mother. Binctin identified herself as a war widow in the first sentence of her letter; she explained that although she valued her job, she was managing to combine her "family obligations with the exigency of daily life" only with "great difficulty" because of the time it took her to commute and her position's demands. After writing two letters to the ministry in the space of a year, she ultimately managed to arrange her transfer.[59]

Women's blood ties to their units were magnified by remaining with the same unit for years, even if it deployed to the armies of occupation in the Rhineland or the Saar Valley in Germany. Women's long-term connections to individual units helped them even when they did not have a blood tie to a unit. Throughout the early 1920s, they developed personal friendships and professional ties with their units' officers and enlisted men, and this encouraged their supervisors to view them as being a part of their units. It also allowed them to develop job-specific skills, which built a case for their competence. Their stable employment meant that they often had a longer institutional memory than their officers.[60]

Over time this led commanding officers to view their units' women employees as regular members of their commands and extend concepts of unit loyalty to them. Female employees could usually rely on their officers' support when questions emerged about their grade, pay, or employment status. Commanders fought attempts to transfer women to other units by citing the bonds of loyalty that had developed between the women and the soldiers in their command—especially if the woman's husband, son, or father had served in the unit.[61]

The case of Madame Hélias illustrates the process by which women slowly integrated into the French Army's culture. In April 1923 Hélias was a civilian employee assigned to the headquarters of the 9th Battalion of *Chasseurs alpins* in the French-occupied Saar Valley. Because of a dispute over her right to be a principal employee, Hélias faced the threat of demotion and a major pay cut unless she agreed to transfer to a unit stationed in France. During a prior period of uncertain promotion standards, she had been promoted to principle employee, which was supposed to be restricted to civilian employees who were in charge of a major office or service, despite not acting as a supervisor of a large office. As long as she remained in France she retained her status, but when her unit redeployed to the Saar she experienced problems because French forces there functioned under a different set of regulations and administrators refused to process her paperwork as a principle employee. The differences between the pay rate that administrators believed she should have received and her pay as a principle employee was dramatic. If her pay had been reduced to a level commensurate with the Saar administration's view of her duties, she would have suffered a 25 percent pay cut.[62]

She had been with her battalion—which appears to be the same unit her husband had served in before his death—since 1918, and refused to transfer to a unit in France despite the threat of financial hardship for herself and her young son.[63] Throughout the dispute, Major Jean-Baptiste Lesieur, her battalion commander, repeatedly intervened with the commander of the Saar garrison, General Georges-Henri Brissaud-Desmaillet, and the Ministry of War in Paris, to press her claim to retain her title and pay as a principle employee without having to return to France.[64] Even after the Ministry of War ordered Hélias repatriated, Lesieur continued to fight to keep her by citing the bonds of trust she had established with his men and the debt the army owed to her husband for his sacrifice.[65] He claimed that Hélias and her son had a "close relationship with the officers and noncommissioned officers" and a "strong bond" with the men in the unit. He also praised her for showing "great loyalty to the battalion" during its deployment.[66]

In the army's records, Lesieur spoke for Hélias, whose own voice never appears in the official correspondence on her case. The surviving records do not reveal what she thought about the controversy or how she viewed her place within the army, but they provide important insights about how officers viewed women. Lesieur's defense of Hélias provides a limited but useful view of the changing construction of women's position within the French Army and reveals the early stages of officers' creation of a professional identity for women. Lesieur, who had worked with Hélias since 1920, highlighted her familial relationship to the army and its obligations to her; in the process he defined her in relation to her deceased husband instead of as an independent person. The letters detailing her case did not even mention her first name; instead Lesieur always referred to her as the *veuve* Hélias. By denying her a given name, he emphasized the moral debt the army owned her husband and cast the dispute in terms of family, making her seem less threatening or presumptuous for challenging her superiors' decisions. This formulation also emphasized that it was her husband's service and sacrifice that entitled her to her job so that the army could minimize his family's suffering.

Hélias's case showed that the hiring preference for war widows, and the army's decentralized personnel management, combined to help women integrate into the officer corps' sense of unit identity. Although Lesieur did not claim Hélias was a soldier, he nevertheless used a modified form of the army's internal language of professionalism to present her as an integral member of his unit by establishing her as a skilled and loyal employee. In pleading Hélias's case, Lesieur mixed appeals to professionalism with a language of dependency focused on familial obligations and avoiding suffering. This combination of languages reflected the slow emergence of a new identity for female civilian employees. Lesieur's appeals exemplified officers' increasing acceptance of women as skilled and loyal employees, though women's claim to a place within the army remained incomplete because they were not yet accepted as fully self-disciplined and independent workers. Military leaders had passively accepted their presence within the army and were creating a subordinate identity for female civilian employees. In December 1923 General Brissaud-Desmaillet and the Ministry of War agreed to let Hélias keep her job and pay until a position equal to her grade became available in the Saar.[67]

When such a position opened in Saarbrücken in March 1924 it sparked a new round of arguments. Hélias was assigned to Saarbrücken on March 19, but on April 26 she still had not left her old post. After an exchange of notes between Lesieur, the Saarbrücken office, and the corps-level staff about whether she had other options, Lesieur wrote to the corps headquarters on May 20 to assure his superiors that Hélias had left for Saarbrücken, but explained that she would only be serving as an accounting secretary and not as a true principal employee. His observation was an implicit complaint that because her new posting still left her in a lower-level position than her official rank, she should have been allowed to stay with the battalion until it returned to France and as a result regained her old position as principal employee.[68]

Lesieur defended Hélias's interests by referencing her skill and loyalty, but this construction of her military identity was limited. By relying on her pseudofamilial relationship to the unit he made her claim to membership in the military community dependent on her dead husband. For women like Hélias this represented a significant redefinition of their relationship to the army since the period of Ruffey and Piquet's attacks on women as military employees, but it was limiting because it conceptually restricted acceptance to women with a preexisting relationship to the army. In practice many women were accepted by officers despite lacking a personal blood tie to the army, and over time the importance of a blood tie inevitably declined. As many of the war widows and daughters of fallen veterans married, remarried, died, or moved on and new hires took their places, the number of women who could fully embody Lesieur's construction of women's military identity inevitably shrank. As a result, even as Lesieur was invoking Hélias's husband's wartime service to protect her job, the link between women's military identity and their male relatives' wartime sacrifices was eroding. By the mid-1920s, most newly hired women were neither war widows nor war orphans.

Most war widows' experiences were much less dramatic than Helias's. When the widowed Georgine Blanchet began her army job on December 15, 1915, she could not have anticipated that she would work for the minister of war's cabinet until July 1940. During that time she rose from the status of temporary auxiliary employee to principal employee and a permanent first-class secretary and became an invaluable source of institutional memory for her office. Like many other women, Blanchet remained with the army even after she remarried. This would have surprised wartime military leaders who had assumed that married women did not need jobs as much as their unmarried counterparts. It reflected the officers' failure to understand that it was common for married prewar French women to work outside the home or to acknowledge the financial distress of interwar French families, which often saw prewar sources of income such as investments and property rents dwindle.[69]

Women who were not immediate relatives of dead servicemen had similar work experiences to those who were. Louise Bouland worked as a civilian employee in 1917–18, lost her job at the end of the war, and then returned to government service, working in the Central Administration of the Ministry of War in July 1927. She remained in that position until June 1945, after the end of the Second World War in Europe. Jeanne Brotier had been a teacher during the First World War and was hired by the army in December 1921; she remained with the army until her premature death at age forty in September 1928.[70] Neither Bouland nor Brotier had a father, husband, or son who was killed in the war and so could not claim a blood tie to the army, but otherwise their careers followed the same trajectory as that of the women who worked continuously for the army. Bouland, in particular, represented the experience of many women working in the military: she worked for the army during the war, left her job during the demobilization purge, and in 1927 was rehired as part of a new wave of hiring and remained in her position for the rest of her career. She continued to work for the army during the Second World War, served under the Vichy Regime, and retired after the Liberation. Both Bouland's and Brotier's careers showed tremendous stability and job security, but also the very limited opportunities for promotion to supervisory roles that women civilian employees had.

During the early 1920s officers accepted that their female employees, including many of the same women whom they once saw as corrosive to male self-discipline and inimical to military professionalism, were skilled and loyal to the army. The experience of working side by side with stable and increasingly experienced cadres of women created bonds of personal and professional trust between career officers and their female civilian employees. This process took place simultaneously with officers' loss of faith in their male conscripts. Taken together, the two processes shook up officers' view of the groups that composed the military community. Officers' growing trust in women civilian employees may have contributed to their loss of faith in conscripts even as that loss of faith definitely boosted the status of women employees. The reduction of conscript service from three years to eighteen months in 1920 meant that officers spent less and less time with individual draftees. By the middle of the 1920s, a typical conscript spent only eighteen months in the military and less than eleven months with a regular unit.[71] Women, on the other hand, benefited from long-term relationships with officers and the skills they developed from familiarity with their jobs. The longer women spent working for the army, the more their officers trusted them; conversely, the less time conscripts spent in the army, the less officers trusted them.

INVISIBLE SERVICE

Although thousands of women were serving in the army, political and military leaders largely ignored their contributions to winning the war or sustaining the forces during peacetime. Instead, when civilian employees were discussed in official circles, leaders usually spoke and acted as if civilian employees were men. In some cases this may have been an oversight, but many times it was a willful choice by political or military leaders to focus on male civilian employees at the expense of women's interests.

Since the end of the war, thousands of civilians had continued to work for the army in positions that had become effectively permanent but were still officially temporary. There were a handful of attempts to make these invisible employees visible, but they focused on men to the exclusion of women. For example, in 1924, Socialist deputies presented a bill designed to deal with that problem by making long-term temporary employees into permanent employees. It specified that the converted employees would receive the same salary and vacation benefits as existing permanent employees. The legislation had the potential to help thousands of women serving with the army, but the authors limited their bill to temporary civilian employees of the French Army and Ministry of War who had been classed as temporary employees since August 2, 1914, before the army began hiring women as temporary auxiliary employees.[72]

There were many reasons why the bill's authors chose to restrict their proposal, but its effect was to set the cutoff at the last possible point that would ensure the plan only helped men. Promoting more women from temporary to permanent employment was a potential threat to existing male civilian employees: making women their equals could have provoked opposition from men who feared that their social position within the army and their prospects for future pay raises would be hurt. In addition, the political reality was that there were few votes to be won by helping women because women were not allowed to vote during the Third Republic. Excluding wartime hires, and thus women, also reduced the potential cost of the measure because most long-term temporary employees were wartime hires.

UNEXPECTED MEMBERS OF
THE MILITARY COMMUNITY

Contrary to most officer's expectations, the end of the First World War did not lead to the total reversal of women's wartime gains in the French Army. Officers like Piquet pushed hard for their superiors to demobilize the army's entire female workforce, but a combination of the economic effects of the war and some officers' support for women remaining as civilian employees frustrated the process. When the government began ordering cuts in the military budget and the army's force structure, women became more and more attractive as an alternate labor force. Before the war the army might have chosen to hire more men rather than reverse the progressive exclusion of women from the military community that the Third Republic had been enforcing, but the wartime inclusion of women changed the dynamic, and military leaders chose to accept women into the postwar military community.

Women's survival might have been accidental, but it was still important. Their continued presence in the French Army allowed them to develop a military identity. In 1919 many officers contested women's value to the army, but many other officers believed that they had a moral obligation to the women serving with their units because many of them were the widows and children of men who had died while serving—sometimes even in the same units—during the war. This created an alternate and subordinate construction of military identity: instead of the dominant construction that defined membership in the military community based on professionalism, which was a function of self-discipline and skill, women's membership was based on combining skill and loyalty. Despite the instability of women's military identity, the 1919–24 period saw women unexpectedly survive the demobilization purge and even reclaim some of the wartime gains that had been reversed at the beginning of demobilization. They forged a military identity for themselves and consolidated the wartime reversal of their progressive exclusion from the military community that the Third Republic had begun in the 1870s.

NOTES

1. For a discussion of Higonnet and Higonnet's double helix theory, see the introduction to the present volume; see also Higonnet and Higonnet, "The Double Helix."

2. Piquet, "Rapport relative à la main d'oeuvre féminine (Régime de 1916)," No. 464, August 29, 1919, Dossier 1, SHD DT 8 NN 36.

3. Ibid.

4. Ibid.

5. Higonnet and Higonnet, "Double Helix," 35.

6. "Note de Président du Conseil Ministre de la Guerre à Monsieur le Contrôleur du 2ème classe de l'Administration de l'Armée Piquet," No. 2698 88/9, July 30, 1919, Dossier 1, SHD DT 8 NN 36; "Letter," No. 5592-CM, November 16, 1915, Dossier 2, SHD DAT 7 N 159; Order, December 13, 1915, Dossier 2, SHD DAT 7 N 159; "Galieni," November 10, 1915, Dossier 2, SHD DAT 7 N 159.

7. "Note de Président du Conseil Ministre."

8. Ibid.

9. Note, No. 5999.1, May 15, 1919, Dossier 2, SHD DT 7 N 159; Darrow, *French Women and the First World War*.

10. "Rapport," No. 5999.1, May 1, 1919, Dossier 2, SHD DT 7 N 159.

11. Piquet, "Rapport relative à la main d'oeuvre féminine (Régime de 1916)." Controller General Piquet was an officer in the Intendance, which was subordinate to the Fifth Bureau of the General Staff of the Army.

12. Ibid.

13. Ibid.; Darrow, *French Women and the First World War*, 262. Margaret Darrow has shown that the demobilization process was so rapid that it overwhelmed the military administration; in many cases the army could not keep up with the demobilization paperwork and was late paying the required bonuses.

14. Piquet, "Rapport relative à la main d'oeuvre féminine (Régime de 1916)."

15. Ibid.

16. "Bachet," SHD DT 6 YG 159.

17. Piquet, "Rapport relative à la main d'oeuvre féminine (Régime de 1916)."

18. Ibid., annex 1.

19. Ibid., annex 1.

20. Ibid., annex 2.

21. Piquet, "Rapport relative à la main d'oeuvre féminine (Régime de 1916)."

22. Ibid.

23. Rapport No. 490 Y/I du Général Commandant la 3e Région à Monsieur le Ministre de la Guerre—État-Major de l'Armée—1e Bureau le 11 Août 1919, cited in "Rapport relative à la main d'oeuvre féminine (Régime de 1916)," No. 464, August 29, 1919, Dossier 1, SHD DT 8 NN 36.

24. Piquet, "Rapport relative à la main d'oeuvre féminine (Régime de 1916)," 9–10.

25. Ibid.

26. Ibid., 10.

27. Ibid.

28. Ibid.

29. Piquet's assumption fits into a broader French belief that women were unable to exercise self-control. In "The Republican Brotherhood," Stone has established that the Third Republic's political institutions were built on gendered understandings of citizenship and republicanism that assumed women lacked the mental discipline to use their reason to overcome frivolity and superstition. Most French leaders believed women's ability to exercise intelligent self-control was so much weaker than men's that it was dangerous to risk allowing them to vote or exercise public responsibilities lest they be controlled by their attachment to religion or their emotions.

30. "Crisis of Authority," SHD DM SS ED 30; "Sebastopol Manifestations d'indiscipline," No. 186 D/2, February 12, 1919.

31. "Sebastopol Manifestations d'indiscipline."

32. Ibid.

33. Ibid.

34. Ibid.

35. "Jugement rendu par un conseil de guerre assemblé à bord du cuirassé 'Provence' en rade de Toulon" SHD DM SS ED 30.

36. "Relevé des informations terminées en cours ou a ouvrir," August 1919, SHD DM SS ED 30.

37. "Marine nationale Armée Navale—Ière Escadre, Cuirassé 'Provence' Jugement rendu par un conseil de guerre assemblé à bord du Cuirassé 'Provence' en rade de Toulon," SHD DM SS ED 30; "Sébastopol Manifestations d'indiscipline."

38. "État des sanctions prises contre militaires qui se sont livres à des faits d'excitation à la désobéissance ou de propaganda" February 11, 1928, AN F 7 13099; Jacques Raphael-Leygues and Jean-Luc Barré, *Les mutins de la mer noire: Avril 1919: des marines français se révoltent* (Paris: Plon, 1981), 142–46, 151–62.

39. "Documents Russe l'Offensive Révolutionnaire de Marty et Badina," SHD DM SS ED 30.

40. "État des sanctions prises contre militaires qui se sont livres à des faits d'excitation à la désobéissance ou de propaganda" AN F 7 13099 11 February 1928.

41. Clipped Article from *Depêche de Brest* AN F 7 13176.,"Pac à l'URSS et Amnistie" and "Les crimes de conseils de guerre" AN F 7 13190.

42. "Note sur l'évolution des forces militaires françaises de 1913 à 1932," SHD DT 7 N 2291.

43. "Proposition de Loi relative à une première adaptation militaire de la France au Pacte de la Société des Nations," No. 6745, Dossier 2, SHD DT 5 NN 10, 1. The bill was sponsored by deputies Paul Aubriot, Alexandre-Marie Bracke, Joseph Lauche, Pierre Renaudel, Albert Thomas, and Lucien Voilin.

44. Ibid., 2.

45. Ibid., 11.

46. Ibid., 8.

47. Ibid., 4.

48. "Pétain to the Minister of War," No. 585, June 22, 1920, Dossier 3, SHD DAT 1 NN 10. The Conseil Supérieur de la Guerre was created early in the Third Republic and chaired by the president of the republic, though its composition and duties changed over time. The council included the generals assigned to the most important wartime staff and field commands, and it had the right to be compulsorily consulted by the cabinet on questions of national defense and military policy, but the cabinet was not bound to follow its advice.

49. "Pétain to the Minister of War," June 22, 1920, Dossier 1, CSG, SHD DT 1 N 5.

50. "Procès-Verbal Séance du 11 Decembre 1920," December 11, 1920, Dossier 3, CSG, SHD DT 1 NN 1.

51. Ibid.

52. General de Division Brissaud-Desmaillet, *Rapport Partiel No. 2. Commission institué pour la créations d'emplois civils nouveaux dans l'armée*, July 1925, Dossier 1, SHD DT 9 NN 1169.

53. "Note sur l'évolution des forces militaires françaises" SHD DT 7 N 2291.

54. No. 03- 1/5 January 19, 1923, SHD DT 19 NN 160.

55. "Document 269," No. 5374 A 3/3 March 20, 1922, Dossier 2, SHD DT 9 NN 359.

56. "Auclair," SHD DT 6 YG 159.

57. Ibid.

58. Cardoza, *Intrepid Women*.

59. "Binctin," SHD DT, 6 YG 151.

60. "Brissaud-Desmaillet to Lesieur," No. 927/T, April 9, 1923, SHD DT 19 NN 160.

61. No. 7141/T 28 April 28, 1922 (Brissaud-Desmaillet), SHD DT 19 NN 160; No. 08-1/5, February 26, 1923, SHD DT 19 NN 160," No. 199 8/C, April 7, 1923, SHD DT 19 NN 160.

62. "Lesieur to Brissaud-Desmaillet," No. 983, April 10, 1923, SHD DT 19 NN 160.

63. "Brissaud-Desmaillet to Lesieur" No. 927/T, 9 April 1923 SHD DT 19 NN 160; Letter May 16, 1923, SHD DT 19 NN 160; Letter No. 6727 I/5, July 20, 1925, SHD DT 19 NN 160.

64. "Brissaud-Desmaillet to Lesieur," ; "Lesieur to Brissaud-Desmaillet."; Letter from the Ministry of War, May 14, 1923, SHD DT 19 NN 160.

65. "Lesieur to Brissaud-Desmaillet."

66. Letter from Brissaud-Desmaillet, No. 927/T, April 9, 1923, Dossier 1, SHD DT 19 NN 160; "Lesieur to Brissaud-Desmaillet."; Letter from the Ministry of War, May 14, 1923.

67. Letter from Ministry of War to Commander Sarre Garrison, No. 289 1/1, December 27, 1923, Dossier 1, SHD DT 19 NN 160; Letter from Commander Sarre Garrison to Ministry of War, No. 289/, December 28, 1923, SHD DT 19 NN 160; Letter from the Payeur particulier du secteur 219, No. 1050.d., April 26, 1924, SHD DT 19 NN 160; Letter, No. 6727 I/5, July 20, 1925, SHD DT 19 NN 160.

68. Letter from Ministry of War to Commander Sarre Garrison; "Letter," No. 289/ December 28, 1923, Dossier 1, SHD DT 19 NN 160; Letter from the Payeur particulier du secteur 219; Letter, No. 6727 I/5, SHD DT 19 NN 160.

69. "Buat," SHD DAT 6 YG 260.

70. "Brotier," SHD DT 6 YG 156; "Bouland," SHD DT 6 YG 353.

71. Under the service law, conscripts served eighteen months from induction to liberation, but approximately six months of that time was spent on basic and advanced training and a month was spent on leave. This left only about eleven months of service in a regular combat or support unit. That time could be even shorter if the conscript was entitled to agricultural leave or if he was selected for special training.

72. "Chambre des Députés—Proposition de loi tendant à la titularisation des agents auxiliaries des établissements et services de la guerre, en functions au 2 août 1914," No. 435 (1945), SHD DT 6 N 441.

The 1927 and 1928 Army Laws

Women's service as civilian employees of the French Army during and immediately after the First World War was marked by hostility and mistrust on the part of many male officers and civilian functionaries, but over the course of the early 1920s, military leaders accepted that women were capable of skill and loyalty, which helped them accept that women had become part of the military community. Conflicts between senior generals and civilian leaders over army organization, the length of conscript service, and extending political rights to soldiers accelerated the evolution of women's military identity. As officers came to see voting as synonymous with indiscipline as a result of the overlapping voting rights and fraternization campaigns of the mid-1920s, women's disenfranchisement became a positive asset within the military world: it marked women as, in one important way, more disciplined than civilian men and as safer employees than the conscripted men whose enfranchisement seemed increasingly possible. Notably, despite the active women's suffrage campaign in the 1920s, officers do not seem to have been worried that women could have become voters. As a result, they saw their women employees as more disciplined than they had in the past, especially when compared to male conscripts, and thus more deserving of being members of the military community. These shifts in officers' views of women civilian employees and male conscripts were linked, though the surviving records suggest officers never explicitly discussed the link.

Officers' responses to the military reform debate divided them into two main factions: one group rejected all calls for further reductions in force structure or changes to the army's relationship to the civilian political and legal systems and wanted to confront the cabinet; the other advocated making concessions to the elected government in order to open negotiations and protect their most important priorities. Some generals proposed shifting more of the burden of national defense onto African men, while others argued for bringing more civilian employees into the army, and a few even suggested co-opting the idea of the militia army and combining it with a plan to emulate Weimar Germany's efforts to evade the Treaty of Versailles. In the end, most generals followed Marshal Philippe Pétain's program of cautious negotiation until the Cartel des Gauches, an alliance of the SFIO and the Radicals, collapsed, after which Pétain and his senior commanders agreed to a comprehensive deal with the new conservative cabinet led by Raymond Poincaré. That compromise protected the army's separate legal system, denied soldiers the right to vote, and brought thousands more civilian women into the army to compensate for the term of conscript service falling from eighteen months to one year. Because of the extensive discussions that went on inside the army's leadership about women's future roles, the 1927 and 1928 Army Laws marked officers' acceptance of women as members of the military community and holders of a form of military identity. From an institutional stand point, the 1927 and 1928 laws also represented the end of the First World War for the French Army because it was not until they were passed that the army transitioned to a regular peacetime footing.

PERCEIVED CRISIS: MILITARY REFORMERS AND SUBVERSION

The May 1924 elections resulted in the defeat of the Raymond Poincaré and the conservative Bloc National by the,Cartel des Gauches under the leadership of Radical Party deputy Édouard Herriot. The SFIO pledged to support the Radicals, but refused to join the cabinet. The Radicals buttressed their cabinet by including smaller center-left factions, including

Paul Painlevé's Republican Socialists.[1] The Radicals and the SFIO ran on separate platforms, but they agreed to a common program that included détente with Britain and Germany, recognition of the Soviet Union, and new anticlerical measures. Their alliance commanded a solid majority of deputies, but was riven with internal divisions, both between the parties and within the heterogeneous Radical Party.

As part of the Cartel's policy of détente with Germany the Herriot cabinet sought to reduce the size of the French Army and to negotiate a mutually acceptable political settlement with Germany. In February 1925 German Foreign Minister Gustav Stresemann offered to open negotiations with France and Belgium with the goal of Germany accepting the losses of Alsace and Lorraine to France. British support for the initiative further encouraged the Cartel to accept Stresseman's invitation to open talks, and over the summer of 1925, Belgium, Britain, France, Germany, and Italy all agreed to recognize and enforce the Franco-German and Belgian-German borders. Britain and Italy guaranteed the agreement by promising to intervene against any party that crossed over the borders. The final agreement, known as the Locarno Agreement, was signed on December 1, 1925, and immediately won broad public support because it appeared to mark French acceptance of Germany as an equal power and German acceptance of the result of the Great War. The "spirit of Locarno" reflected the hope that a new, less militarized European order was at hand. The agreement further reinforced the Cartel's belief that the cabinet could safely cut the military budget because the likelihood of war was increasingly remote.

As soon as it came to power, the Herriot cabinet and its Socialist Party allies began debating plans to reform the French Army. Civilian reformers, including some politicians from the Radical, Socialist, and Communist Parties, wanted to make the army function more like the civilian world. These reformers were not, however, all supporters of the Cartel, and they never formed a cohesive entity. Most reformers shared a desire to reduce the military's ability to wage aggressive wars and limit the authority of professional officers by changing the army's force structure or its legal relationship to the civilian world. Large parts of all of the major left-of-center parties supported some kind of significant change in the army's organization, recruitment, and relationship to civil society. The reform movement never developed an overarching structure that could initially insulate it from the conflicts among its members. The movement was extremely fractious; even the Cartel members could not agree to a joint program of military reform. Instead the reformers presented a collage of often clashing ideas that ranged from slightly reducing the term of service for conscripts to completely abolishing the standing army.

Military leaders worried about even moderate reform plans, but the Radical Party's dependence on the SFIO for parliamentary support made officers most concerned about the Socialists' calls for a fundamental change in the nature of the French Army. After the 1924 elections, Socialist deputies Joseph Paul-Boncour, Pierre Renaudel, and Albert Thomas tried to extend suffrage rights in the face of conservative and centrist opposition; they proposed new army laws and sought to amend other deputies' bills to give soldiers the right to vote. Renaudel, who had returned to the Chamber of Deputies in the 1924 elections, immediately reestablished his place as the Socialists' leading defense theorist, though unfortunately he was often at odds with Léon Blum's more ideological defense policy. The Socialists' 1925 bill repeated the party's call that soldiers should be allowed to vote and advocated a militia army based on eight months of service. The militia would continue to be drawn from universal male military service and encompassed a state run premilitary physical training program. Despite the changed political environment, the lack of movement by the Socialists showed that Blum and the party leadership valued ideological purity and political positioning more than the implementation of immediate reforms.[2]

Not every reformist wanted to implement such fundamental changes; many were content to reduce the term of conscript service. These moderate reformists, including most of the Radicals, supported cutting the term of service from eighteen months to approximately one year, citing budgetary reasons for a reduction in the number of conscripts serving at any one. Others believed that the threat of war was low enough that the country could safely survive with far fewer conscripts, and many supported cuts for both reasons.

Given its handicaps, it is not surprising that the military reform movement did not produced any immediate legislative results. At the beginning of the Rif War in early 1925, the movement began to break apart when its members took different positions on the conflict. The PCF's ardent resistance to the war damaged its political standing and made it even harder for other parties to cooperate with it. But the combination of legislative debates on reform plans and party members' attempts to propagandize soldiers and infiltrate the army while calling for soldiers' enfranchisement kept military leaders focused on trying to defend against legislation and campaigns they viewed as threats to their institution and its ability to defend France.

THE RIF WAR AND SUBVERSION

The Rif Valley in northern Morocco had been a center of Moroccan resistance to colonialism since the signing of the Treaty of Fez in 1912, which divided Morocco into two protectorates. The Spanish had a small protectorate in the north and France had a protectorate over the rest of the country. Under the treaties, Morocco officially remained an independent country, but its internal and external affairs were managed by France and Spain. This effectively made most of Morocco a de facto French colony, though neither France nor Spain was in control of most of its official zone.

In 1921 an army under Muhammad ibn 'Abd al-Karim al-Khattabi, known in Europe as Abd el-Krim, defeated a small Spanish army under General Manuel Fernández Silvestre at the Battle of Annual. General Silvestre's defeat led to the near collapse of Spanish Morocco.[3] During 1924, Abd el-Krim's expansion south into the Moroccan interior began to clash with Marshal Hubert-Louis Lyautey's attempts to consolidate France's hold on its part of Morocco. Skirmishes between French patrols and fighters loyal to Abd el-Krim led to rising tensions as the French attempted to isolate his self-proclaimed Rif Republic. In the fall of 1924, Marshal Lyautey, the military and political head of French Morocco, warned the Army General Staff and the Herriot cabinet that he expected an attack in the spring and urgently requested reinforcements.[4]

In March 1925, Abd el-Krim launched a major offensive against French Morocco. Initially the Riffians made impressive gains, but following victories by Generals Henri Giraud and Gaston Billotte in June and July 1925 that blunted Abd el-Krim's attacks, the French allied with the Spanish and went onto the offensive.[5] In August, political pressure from Paris forced Marshal Lyautey to resign, and Marshal Pétain became the military commander.[6] With the new command structure and reinforcements in place, the French and Spanish opened a combined offensive in September 1925. By the end of the year, the rebellion was collapsing and Franco-Spanish forces were advancing on all fronts. In June 1926, French forces captured and then exiled Abd el-Krim, which effectively ended the revolt, but the military victory did not end the political battle over the war back in France, which proved more traumatic for the French Army.[7]

The tactics used by opponents of the Rif War exacerbated army leaders' fear of expanding the franchise and cutting the term of conscript service. The war triggered an active, though unsuccessful, Communist Party campaign to undermine the war effort from within the armed forces,[8] featuring active-duty soldiers and sailors as speakers at antiwar and party rallies. Party members urged soldiers to strike against their officers and fraternize with strikers, protesters, or the Riffian forces. Speakers also called for conscripts and workers to unite and turn the war into a revolutionary civil war.[9] In 1925, party leaders, particularly the future fascist turncoat Jacques Doriot, called for action against the war. Doriot urged troops to fraternize with the Riffians and predicted that unless it was stopped quickly, the war would lead to another world war.[10] At the Communist Party's October 1925 conference, Secretary General Albert Trient explained party policy as an attempt to use opposition to colonial wars to turn a military defeat into a class revolution and called for troops to fraternize to break the power of "officers bought by French capitalism."[11] Trient hoped to tap into postwar France's deep vein of antimilitarism and encourage more people to join the party.[12]

The Communist Party targeted conscripts with three specialist journals. The first, Le Conscrit (The Conscript) was aimed at men as they were entering into military life. The mainstay of the effort, though, was Le Caserne (named after the French word for a military barracks), which regularly condemned the allegedly brutal and uncaring officers and criticized the poor conditions soldiers were made to endure. At the end of a conscript's term, when he became a libéré (the French word for a soldier released from military service), he could read Le Libéré, which emphasized the poor treatment of reservists.[13] This troika of party papers, which often carried the same content, claimed that living conditions for conscripts were bad, food was substandard, and fatiguing exercises weakened conscripts' health. The attacks were modeled on criticisms of the living and working conditions capitalism created for French workers. The papers trumpeted examples of courageous conscripts who spoke out against their officers and the conditions of military life as examples for others to follow.[14] The September 5, 1925, issue of *La Caserne* reported that sailors stationed in Paris had protested against the poor quality of their food and were facing a court-martial. Shortly after the Rif War began, the May 20, 1925, issue of *La Caserne* accused Foreign Legion officers of abusing their men and using the military justice system to suppress opposition to their brutality. The paper claimed dozens of legionnaires were in jail for complaining about poor food or harsh and unfair treatment by their officers. All three papers' editorials regularly condemned the prosecution of soldiers for protesting against their alleged oppression in ways that would have been legally protected in civilian life, and urged other conscripts to stand up for themselves during the war.[15]

Communist leaders highlighted active-duty soldiers and sailors in their propaganda. In August 1925, the Communist Party had three sailors appear in full uniform at a local party congress to denounce the military justice system and military prisons during the Rif War; their presence signaled the party's rejection of the separation of the military from the political system. Political activity on the part of active members of the armed forces was strictly illegal, and the party's use of uniformed personnel was a challenge to the legitimacy of both the armed forces and France's laws.[16] It alarmed military leaders because they saw it as proof that at least some conscripts would obey orders from the Communist Party to sabotage military operations.

Communist propaganda aimed to puncture the military's mystique by showing that military life was just civilian life with a different set of taskmasters. In May 1925, early in the Rif War, the PCF's posters proclaimed that it was a war "wanted and caused by French imperialism in order to steal the Rif's mineral riches" to "permit the Banque de Paris et des Pay-Bas to realize new and scandalous profits."[17] Communist speakers blamed the war on "high finance" and urged conscripted workers in France to join a general strike because the reinforcements sent to Morocco meant that the weakened army might not be able to break a strike in France if enough conscripts joined with the strikers.[18]

During the Rif War, communist propaganda relied heavily on direct and indirect invocations of the Black Sea Mutiny. Although the mutiny had involved no actual fraternization, it was frequently used by propagandists, including mutineer André Marty himself, as an example for French troops in Morocco to emulate. The military elite and civilian political leaders feared communist propaganda, in part, because they believed the party was successfully infiltrating the French Army.

Military and civilian police forces tried to stop the propaganda aimed at soldiers. Civilian law banned the distribution of material that advocated soldiers disobeying orders, which it termed "provocation to disobedience," and military law prohibited the possession or distribution of any form of propaganda deemed antimilitary or which military leaders believed advocated disobedience. Both the military and civilian authorities repeatedly prosecuted men for possessing and distributing the three Communist Party military newspapers.[19] In October 1925, members of the Communist Party's Action Committee were arrested and charged with inciting soldiers to disobedience by calling on them to fraternize with Riffian forces.[20] Throughout 1925 and 1926, the police maintained steady pressure on antiwar groups trying to propagandize the armed forces. Despite that effort, by November 1925 the police had only arrested 351 people for inciting military personnel to disobey orders; this small number of arrests suggests that although the Communist Party's campaign was real and greatly worried military leaders, the militant antiwar movement was relatively small in numbers.[21]

Counterintelligence officers believed the Communist Party's claims that it had cells operating throughout the army. Intelligence reports warned that there were hundreds of cells in combat units and bases all over France as well as in the colonies and the occupied Rhineland. Military and police investigators claimed there were fifty-two active cells inside units in the Paris Military Region, twenty-seven in Metz, thirty-six in Nancy and Strasbourg, and thirty-two in units outside France.[22] Military and police officials cooperated to identity potential communists among the new draftees. Counterintelligence officers maintained lists identifying the number and names of suspected party members in each draft contingent for each department in France. Over the course of 1925, military observers noted an overall increase in conscripts affiliated with the Communist Party. Although the trend alarmed officers, the numbers were actually modest. For example, in the spring of 1925 counterintelligence officers identified a new communist group in the department of Aisne, but it had only fourteen members. Even though many units were stationed in Alsace and the liberated parts of Lorraine, there were only 121 identified communists in that region.[23] Given French counterintelligence officers' tendency to exaggerate the overall threat of communism, even these figures probably overestimate the number of cells and active party members in the army.

In 1926, security officials worried that the Rif War was causing an increase in the number of soldiers speaking out against the military in public meetings. Investigators determined that many of the active-duty soldiers speaking at Communist Party meetings did not have prewar records as communists or pacifists. They interpreted that as proof that communist propaganda and recruiters were winning converts inside the military.[24] This was enough to convince many senior officers that such propaganda was succeeding in establishing a surreptitious organization that could compromise the army's effectiveness against internal or external enemies.[25]

Communist propaganda convinced some left-wing activists and many military officers that the party was infiltrating the armed forces, but in the processes it exposed the infiltration effort, which relied on secrecy to work, and thus triggered a crippling response from the security services. Soldiers and sailors accused of receiving or spreading communist propaganda were tried before courts-martial. Sentences ranged from eight days for a soldier of the 109th Heavy Artillery Regiment who was convicted of the minor offense of reading *Le Caserne* to as much as ten years for some soldiers implicated in the 1924 Landau affair, which involved several soldiers (including two noncommissioned officers) stationed in the occupied Rhineland being convicted of distributing communist propaganda to other soldiers during the Ruhr Crisis. The propaganda urged French troops to fraternize with German civilians, refuse to obey their officers, and side with German workers against French financial interests. Other common offenses included singing "The Internationale," attending or working at Communist Party meetings, and distributing party pamphlets; one soldier in the 25th Infantry Regiment received a sixty-day sentence for writing an article for the Communist Party daily *L'Humanité*.[26]

In May 1927 Minister of War Paul Painlevé summarized army reports in a letter to Minister of the Interior Albert Sarraut. Painlevé reported that between January 1925 and June 1926, roughly the period of the Rif War, there were 1,371 soldiers and sailors convicted of politically motivated disobedience of orders and concluded, "Doubtless the menacing Communist campaigns of that period had an influence on the grave breaches of military discipline."[27] Painlevé's claims appeared impressive, but they rested on a distortion of military records. While he claimed that all of the arrests were made in the period from just before the beginning of the Rif War to the end of major combat operations, a penciled marginal note on the original list made clear that he was actually citing statistics from January 1924 to December 1926.[28] Painlevé distorted his information in an attempt to convince Sarraut that communists were a mortal danger that needed to be fought. Painlevé's subterfuge underlined the fact that although the Communist Party's infiltration and propaganda campaign was generally unsuccessful at undermining the army, it was very successful at convincing many officers and political leaders that the party could influence or control a substantial number of soldiers if it could reach them with its propaganda.

OPPOSITION TO CARTEL'S REFORMS

Faced with a government committed to a maximum of one year of conscript service, and flirting with even more radical reforms, army leaders initially resisted any more cuts in the term of service. Motivated by its members' concern about the army's eroding combat power and fear of indiscipline in the ranks, the Conseil Supérieur de la Guerre unanimously rejected any further reduction.

On March 30, 1925, Marshal Pétain took the lead in criticizing plans to reduce the army's size. He complained that the government had not fulfilled the promises it made in the 1923 Army Law to increase the numbers of career soldiers and insisted that the generals would not agree to new cuts until the old promises were kept. Pétain argued that the Cartel cabinet's proposals were poorly thought out and focused more on the problem of conscription being unpopular than on a workable solution. He explained that "everybody is in agreement on this point: the existing organization must be modified. But, in what sense? There the problem becomes more complicated and the solution less certain." Later in the meeting he criticized the postwar cabinets for continually changing the term of military service and the army's organization, complaining that, since 1923, the army's legal status had been "essentially provisional; it could be said that it no longer has a legal status." General Maxime Weygand added that rather than the 75,000 career soldiers suggested by the Radical Party–dominated Herriot cabinet, the army required 150,000 and a further increase in civilian employees.[29]

On April 1 1925, the council again resisted the cabinet's proposals. The generals vehemently objected to the cabinet's use of the term *armée nationale* to describe the mobilized force and instead demanded the bill be amended to use the phrase *armée de guerre*. This semantic debate revealed the generals' fear that their power and prestige was being threatened by a move to short-service conscription. The word *nationale* was loaded with symbolic meaning, and its use implied that the wartime army of recalled reservists was the true and authentic military manifestation of the French people, while the peacetime army, which was dominated by career officers and noncommissioned officers was just a placeholder. The phrase *armée de guerre* stripped away the symbolic meaning of the word *nationale* and replaced it with a mere reference to the wartime incarnation of the French Army.[30]

During the meeting a seemingly technical debate about whether the proposed law should specify the organization of units or if it should be left to the discretion of the minister of war sparked a disagreement between the military and civilian members. Marshals Ferdinand Foch and Philippe Pétain and Generals Marie-Eugène Debeney, Adolphe Guillaumat, and Maxime Weygand argued that the bill should specify the internal organization of military units and that the cabinet should accept the council's advice on that point. After the council supported Pétain and the senior generals, the minister of war, General Charles Nollet, rejected Pétain's position and insisted that as minister he had the right to overrule the council. He argued that the organization should be kept flexible and that giving the minister the power to change it by decree would preserve that flexibility better than enshrining military organization in law.[31]

Political and military leaders clashed again at the Conseil Supérieur de la Guerre's next meeting two days later. Nollet opened the meeting by complaining that results of the previous meeting had been leaked to the press in violation of members' oaths of secrecy and customary practice. Although he did not accuse any specific members, his criticism implied that it was a military member of the council, rather than a politician or civilian functionary, who leaked the information in order to destabilize the Cartel's military policy. Minister of the Marine Jacques-Louis Dumesnil interjected to deny that any of his aides had caused the leak. In an attempt to prevent the dispute from escalating, Gaston Doumergue, who was exercising his prerogative as president of the republic to chair the meeting, intervened to declare that he was certain the leak came from outside the council.[32]

On April 10, 1925, a meeting of the Conseil Supérieur de la Guerre again boiled over into open conflict. Pétain opened the meeting with an attack on the cabinet's defense policy, claiming that "the army is in a lamentable state because it has not been accorded the civilian agents and career soldiers asked for by the council." He complained that the cabinet was moving toward a new reduction in the term of service, and thus the size of the army, without having fulfilled the promises previously made. He argued that a further reduction in the term of service from eighteen months to one year would only be possible if the cabinet adopted and implemented major changes beforehand, and explained that he was not inherently hostile to a one-year service law, "but if one -year service is realized in the current state, it would be a debacle. The government promises credits, but is parliament able to accord them?"[33] Pétain's question exposed his concern that the Cartel would try to win the generals' endorsement of its policies by trading promises of long-term funding increases that would never come for immediate concessions from the generals.

When the council moved to vote on its first motion of the day, the minister of the marine attempted to vote in order to strengthen the cabinet's voting bloc. As vice president of the Conseil Supérieur de la Guerre, Marshal Pétain objected and told Dumesnil that although he could vote in the Conseil Supérieur de la Marine, he did not have the right to vote in the Conseil Supérieur de la Guerre because he was merely there in a consultative role. Pétain's intervention provoked an angry reaction from Dumesnil, who asserted that political supremacy over the military required his vote to be counted; this won Nollet's support. But President Doumergue, who was again acting as the council's president, backed Pétain. With the politicians split, and Pétain resolute, Doumergue ruled that the dispute would have to be adjudicated by the Conseil d'État which alone could issue a binding interpretation of the decree creating the Superior War Council.[34]

The meeting witnessed constant open conflict between the senior commanders and Nollet over the size and organization of the army. Nollet tried and failed to convince the generals to agree to separate the issue of the length of service from increases in the number of career soldiers and civilian employees the army was authorized to have.[35] During the debate it became clear that Doumergue, who was a relatively conservative Radical, did not support the cabinet's military policy. In the face of Doumergue's muted opposition and Pétain's explicit hostility, Nollet failed to persuade his fellow generals to support the cabinet's proposals, and the council passed a motion declaring that it was "currently inopportune and dangerous to envision a new reduction of the term of service."[36] Instead the generals advised the government to improve conscript life to alleviate voters' complaints about the burdens of military service. The Conseil Supérieur de la Guerre also presented the government with a letter declaring its military members unanimously believed that if it implemented a one-year service law without first dramatically increasing the number of civilian employees and career soldiers in the army, the "very existence of the army would be gravely compromised and the security of the country could not be assured."[37]

Although initially hostile to the Cartel's reform plans, Marshal Pétain eventually steered France's senior generals toward compromise. He began by rejecting all the proposed reforms, but then got his fellow generals to adopt a series of positions that presupposed the establishment of a one-year service law before actually agreeing to it; these piecemeal proposals were part of an elaborate negotiation with the elected government. Pétain and the rest of the council thus signaled both their own flexibility and the concessions they hoped to get in return. Following this gradualist approach, Pétain secured a series of individual pledges from the government that built toward the council's official acceptance of a one-year service law. This process encouraged the government to focus on the term of conscript service as the central plank in any reform plan instead of enfranchising soldiers or creating a militia. Pétain's approach also prolonged the negotiations, increasing the likelihood that the Cartel would collapse before any changes were made. The process included talks on fortifying the Franco-German border; these talks accelerated after December 1925 and evolved into the Maginot Line.[38]

The advent of serious negotiations did not mean that Pétain muzzled his generals' criticisms of the Cartel's policies. As the financial crisis worsened over the course of 1925 and 1926, the cabinets progressively scaled back their promises to compensate the army for the loss of conscripts. In May 1926 General Weygand attacked the cabinet for reneging on its earlier promises. He complained that in 1924 the Herriot cabinet had promised to allow the army to boost the number of career soldiers to 160,000, but had later reduced that first to 130,000 men and then to 106,000. He explained that he "could not take the responsibility of saying that this number was sufficient" and that the resulting situation was "very grave."[39]

THE FALL OF THE CARTEL

The generals' initial attack against Édouard Herriot's defense policies in April 1925 may not have been part of a larger political plan, but it coincided with a conservative political offensive against Herriot's cabinet. By April 1925 the French budget deficit was growing, and rising inflation was undermining the value of the franc at home and in international exchanges. Herriot's situation worsened when Abd el-Krim attacked French forces in Morocco on April 12, 1925, and began winning victories over French forces. On April 17, 1925, Herriot resigned when one of his finance measures was defeated. His fall did not end the Cartel, but it forced the formation of a new cabinet under Paul Painlevé. Painlevé, a Republican Socialist who had been serving as president of the Chamber of Deputies, had played a key role in creating the Cartel and pledged to continue the alliance. He removed General Nollet from the Ministry of War because of Nollet's obvious inability to secure his fellow officers' support for his policies, and Painlevé took over the ministry himself.

Painlevé was a staunchly nationalistic, moderate leftist who supported military leaders' efforts to defeat Abd el-Krim. He saw France through the crisis of the Riffians' spring offensive, but his inability to solve the financial crisis led to his cabinet's fall in November 1925. Painlevé remained war minister in the following two cabinets, both led by Aristide Briand, and left the Ministry of War for less than a month during Briand's third cabinet before returning on July 20, 1926, as part of Herriot's three-day ministry, which— like Briand's cabinets—collapsed in the face of the financial crisis. He then continued in office as part of Poincaré's more conservative cabinet.

The generals' delaying tactics succeeded in buying them the time they needed to outlast the Cartel. Pétain shifted between criticizing the cabinet's defense policies and negotiating with Painlevé. Ultimately he and his generals succeeded in slowing down the Cartel's reform plans and watering them down. Prolonging the debate ultimately worked to the generals' advantage, because the Cartel was inherently unstable as a result of the SFIO's refusal to fully embrace a coalition with the Radicals. By July 1926 internal conflicts among the Cartel's members brought down the Briand and Herriot cabinets in short succession and led to the creation of a new coalition under former-President Raymond Poincaré that united the Radical with centrist and conservative parties. The new cabinet was much friendlier to the officer corps' vision of how the French Army should work. Regardless of who made up the cabinet, the structural budget deficit was severe enough that any cabinet would have been looking to cut the military budget as part of an overall effort to stabilize the government's finances, which gave military leaders an incentive to find ways to get the same level of productivity from their workforce while spending less money. Replacing conscripts with women civilian employees was one obvious and proven way to do that.

FINANCIAL AUSTERITY AND THE FEMALE CIVIL EMPLOYEES

Substituting women for conscripts played into the government's fiscal austerity plan because one woman could replace more than one conscript.

The regular turnover of conscripts under the eighteen-month service law, and the need to train new soldiers while their predecessors were still serving so that all positions were continuously filled, forced the army to pay an average of 1.5 conscripts for every position it needed a conscript to fill. Because it took almost six months to train a conscript, a new draftee had to be selected to train for a position six months before the end of his predecessor's service. Under the eighteen-month service law the army had to pay two conscripts for a single position six months out of every year, and under the projected one-year law the army would have to pay two soldiers for every position constantly because a soldier would only spend about six months with his unit yet still required six months of training. Moving from the eighteen-month to the one-year service law effectively increased the cost of staffing a position with a conscript by 33 percent even as it reduced the number of conscripts at any given moment by one-third and cut the number of fully trained conscripts in half. Hiring women to replace conscripts allowed the military to save money and manpower while maintaining a higher level of skill and stability, because in addition to the civilian workforce being more efficient than conscripts, hiring civilians also prevented the need to pay two people to do one job.

For some positions the argument appeared to be even stronger. The ad hoc compromise that emerged during demobilization meant that women's opportunities were often unequal in different parts of France. In the mid-1920s, most surplus weapons stockpiles were maintained by soldiers, but in a few regions officers had hired some women to help maintain stockpiled weapons during the demobilization. Officers took advantage of civilianization being back on the table to do a comparative study of women's labor versus that of conscripts. They found that two civilian women could do the work of three male conscripts even before factoring in the background savings of not having to constantly train new conscripts. As a result, under a one-year service law, even if women had been paid twice as much as conscripts, they would have been able to do 50 percent more work than conscripts while still saving the army money after the cost of training was factored in. This appeared to be a result of women spending much longer in a position that a conscript did and thus becoming better at the job, though motivation may also have been an important factor.[40]

Although initially hostile to all of the Cartel's reform plans, Marshal Pétain steered the Conseil Supérieur de la Guerre toward a compromise with the government that further expanded women's opportunities inside the army. Pétain and the council concentrated their efforts on maintaining the separation between the military and the political systems instead of preserving force structure. In 1925–26, Pétain made a series of small compromises with the cabinet that built toward the council's official acceptance of a one-year service law in late 1926.[41]

BRISSAUD-DESMAILLET AND THE COMMISSION ON CIVIL EMPLOYEES

Marshal Pétain's conciliatory approach was not the only avenue open to military leaders in which women and the manipulation of gender roles played an important part. At the same time that Pétain and the Conseil Supérieur de la Guerre were negotiating with the government, other elements of the military elite were expecting the worst and preparing to undermine the cabinet's policies by actively deceiving the civilian government. This faction, which included General Georges-Henri Brissaud-Desmaillet, feared that the Cartel government's reforms would destroy the army; rather than negotiating with the politicians to reduce the reforms' impact, the faction wanted to evade the reforms. Brissaud-Desmaillet envisioned creating a shadow army that would be invisible to the international community and to the French government. Like Pétain and the moderates, this more radical faction also believed women would be vital to preserving the army's institutional future and combat power, which gave them common ground on civilianization.

Despite their differences, Pétain ultimately drew heavily on Brissaud-Desmaillet's ideas as he sought a way to compromise with the cabinet without undermining either the culture or operational capability of the French Army. General Brissaud-Desmaillet, the former commander of the Saar garrison, had seen his career eclipsed as a result of a corruption scandal. While commanding the French occupation of the Saar Valley, one of his staff officers had abused his position to enrich himself through illegal business deals. Although the investigation concluded that Brissaud-Desmaillet had neither enriched himself nor participated in the scheme in any way, it faulted him for failing to supervise his subordinate and covering up the illegal activities after he learned of them. As a result he was reprimanded, but not charged or cashiered. Despite avoiding criminal charges, Brissaud-Desmaillet returned from the Saar with his career in ruins. Before the scandal he was a rising star whose keen intellect and creative thinking had marked him for a senior command or staff position; afterward, he knew he would never receive a senior command nor sit on the Conseil Supérieur de la Guerre.

Brissaud-Desmaillet's first major post-Saar appointment was as president of the Commission on Civil Employees, which was charged with studying the future role of civilians in a reformed army structure, and he became a leading advocate of expanding women's roles in the French Army. He was also a hard-liner in confrontation with the government. His position on women was linked to his belief that the army would have to circumvent the government to preserve itself as a viable professional institution.

Brissaud-Desmaillet used his chairmanship to create a plan to protect the army's political identity and combat capacity. In addition to creating de facto paramilitaries within the army, he advocated manipulating gender roles and the civilian-versus-military distinction to evade government policy by creating a shadow army around the official French Army. He called on his fellow generals to emulate the army of Weimar Germany, which he believed was "trained for war" and "the best professional army in Europe" despite the armaments clauses of the Treaty of Versailles. Using Weimar Germany as a model, the 1925 report of the Commission on Civil Employees articulated a plan to use civilian employees, both male and female, and civilian cover groups as auxiliaries to give the army a larger effective strength than the number allowed by the government.[42]

In its report the commission called for a dramatic increase in the number of women working in the French Army in order to use the civilian world's gender stereotypes to preserve and obscure the strength of the French Army. It argued that increasing the army's reliance on women would preserve its combat power while allowing the government and the world to believe it had embraced disarmament. The report implied that women were more useful than male civilian employees in hiding the true size of the army because French politicians and international observers assumed women could only be noncombatants, while male civilian employees could be seen as part of a paramilitary force.[43]

In both his final report and in the earlier partial reports, Brissaud-Desmaillet argued for a significant increase in the number of civilian employees of both sexes and the creation of *agents militaires* to civilianize much of the administration of the army—including posts down to the battalion and company levels.[44] The male *agents militaires* would all be trained and experienced veterans who could function as soldiers while hiding behind a civilian cover, allowing the army to clandestinely maintain a larger force than the government had authorized.

The commission's report called for major changes, but was within the bounds of loyalty to the civilian government. But Brissaud-Desmaillet developed proposals that he did not publish in the official report; he produced an alternate introduction to the report that included the commission's proposals for better integrating civilian employees into the army's structure but also described the French Army as risking terminal decline in the face of a powerful and vibrant German Army that could strike at any moment.[45] His experiences as a senior French commander inside of Germany and his reputation as one of the more intelligent and energetic commanders of his generation added credibility to his dire warnings.

General Brissaud-Desmaillet accused the French government of systematically destroying France's defenses and preparing the way for the coming German invasion. He urged other officers to use his report as a starting point for emulating the Germans to create a force capable of defending France regardless of the wishes of the French government or international opinion at the League of Nations. Officers on the General Staff saw both versions and forwarded the alternate introduction to at least some commands in France and the empire. One copy survived in a report forwarded to a unit in Tunisia.[46]

The secret report severely criticized the internationalist tone of French foreign policy and mocked the Cartel government for believing that "in order to better assure world peace and facilitate the recovery of trade, France must sacrifice yet again and add to the naval effacement, which was so 'cordially' imposed, the sacrifice of its army, with a security guarantee, under the control of the League of Nations."[47] The general complained that the politicians were surrendering to hostile international opinion that demanded that "having already considerably reduced its armaments, cut its troop strength and defense budget, eliminated divisions, suspended reserve call-ups for training since the peace treaty, reduced the length of military service to eighteen months, studied and prepared for one-year service, France must prove still further its peaceful intentions to the very point of compromising its own security."[48]

Reacting to his own caricature of the reformists' platform, Brissaud-Desmaillet called for major efforts to evade the intent of the reforms should they pass. He called on the military elite to strip their conception of the army down to its foundations and rebuild a new army based on a semiclandestine system of organization. He suggested abandoning the idea of standard military units by emphasizing staff training for professional officers and training in basic soldiering skills for conscripts. The conscripts would spend their entire term of service in training, and command functions would be centralized at the highest possible level to compensate for the conscripts' lack of experience. He also wanted to civilianize as much of the military as possible by training civilians with specialist skills in their skills' military applications and through a massive increase in civilian employees.[49]

Brissaud-Desmaillet was proposing that the officer corps co-opt Jean Jaurès's defense plan, which he originally introduced as a bill and then published as a book titled *L'Armée nouvelle*. He grudgingly accepted the concept of a militia army but wanted to put the militia firmly under the control of a powerful professional officer corps. While Jaurès had faith in his republican militiamen, Brissaud-Desmaillet saw them as dangerously unreliable and barely trained but hoped that giving professionals enough authority over them would allow the small professional component to hold the army together long enough for it to be trained during the war, presumably while suffering atrocious losses as undertrained men were sacrificed to buy time for the rest of the army to learn how to fight effectively. By retaining and strengthening the officer corps, Brissaud-Desmaillet accepted Jaurès's militia concept while mutating it into a vehicle to defend the very group Jaurès intended to destroy.

Brissaud-Desmaillet's reports embraced a gendered division of civilian employees into the all-male *agents militaires* and—in both concept and statistics—the increasingly female civilian employees. *Agents militaires* were retired soldiers, mostly noncommissioned officers, who worked for the army in positions normally requiring active-duty soldiers but who retained their status as civilians. By drawing the *agents militaires* exclusively from retired soldiers, Brissaud-Desmaillet hoped he could prevent communists from joining and thus disrupting vital military functions.[50]

To maintain the hierarchy of rank, *agents militaires* would not command officers or noncommissioned officers but would be allowed to have common soldiers subordinated to them.[51] In effect, the *agents militaires* became de facto noncommissioned officers who together with a new influx of women would cushion the impact of the cut in the term of service. Brissaud-Desmaillet's basic assumptions spoke to a deep crisis of confidence in the political regime among army officers in the 1920s. The official report's support for women civilian employees and *agents militaires* became the basis of Pétain and the Conseil Supérieur de la Guerre's conciliatory response to the Cartel's reform plans, entrenching a gendered system of army organization in the heart of the 1927 and 1928 Army Laws.

Ideally, this ultraprofessional hierarchy would be full of self-disciplined and highly motivated men and women willing to obey and support their military superiors in their effort to defend the army and its hierarchies against the corrupted government. The passage from Piquet's report to Brissaud-Desmaillet's report showed that during the 1920s, the French military elite's gendered construction of military identity shifted in ways that expanded women's acceptance and opportunities within the military community as officers became increasingly worried about the intrusion of civilian politics into the army's internal workings. As the generals began to trust their male conscripts less because of the shrinking term of service and a fear of communist subversion, they saw them as increasingly less professional, more civilian, and more political. The more officers mistrusted the skill and professional loyalty of their conscripts, the more relatively professional and worthy of a place in the military community women employees seemed in contrast.

RACE, GENDER, AND PRESTIGE

French officers also considered increasing the army's use of men from France's colonies to offset the anticipated decline in the number of white conscripts. During the Great War, the same manpower shortages that led to the 1916 Regime also led to the mass recruitment of African men to fight in the French Army. Although African forces showed some limitations in European warfare, they contributed greatly to the Entente's victory.[52] At the end of the war, some political and military elites believed that the war had shown that Africans could take over more of the burden of defending France and its empire. These leaders, such as General Charles Mangin, advocated putting African soldiers into regular French divisions to strengthen the army and reduce the number of white Frenchmen who would die in the next war.[53]

Concerns about the reliability and effectiveness of the colonial force combined with the serial military crises in the empire to hamper any plan to move colonial forces to the metropole. Many politicians feared that fusion would encourage militarism and undermine the alleged pacific tendencies of the nation in arms and that an army of professional or semi-professional colonial troops commanded by professional officers was a recipe for a praetorian military whose reactionary ideology would be a danger to the republic.[54] Ultimately, political concerns and opposition from within the Colonial Army defeated Mangin's plans for fusion in the early and mid-1920s.

The French generals' periodic interest in relying more heavily on African men to defend France did not, however, extend to African women. The combination of gender and race in the colonial context complicated the extension of the General Staff's plans to use women and colonized men to maintain conservative hierarchies; French military leaders could separately rationalize French women and colonized men as collaborators whose subordinate presence would not endanger white prestige and masculine hierarchies, but combining the two groups caused too many problems. Despite the initial attractiveness of using colonial men in the metropolitan army, the military elite's fear of interracial unions at home and upsetting racial hierarchies in the colonies eventually destroyed support for bringing large numbers of African men to France; this narrowed officers' options for adapting to the progressive reduction in conscript service.

In July 1926 the Conseil Supérieur de la Guerre discussed the role of women from the colonies in supporting the armed forces. The council's study committee considered using civilian colonial labor in the French Army and dealt specifically with nonwhite women. Speaking for the Colonial Army, General Peltier stressed "the necessity of not foreseeing, in any manner, the eventual use of *indigène* women in the colonial contingents" and insisted that "this use would be, in effect, contrary to the customs of the population, where women, notably, do not possess any civil personality."[55] Peltier's claim was inaccurate because in many parts of the French colonial empire, women did have important public roles in communal life, but his claim spoke to his fear that if the French called on African women to serve inside the French Army, even as civilians, it would degrade white male soldiers by associating them with black women who they saw as doubly inferior to them.

The military elite's inability to trust foreign and, especially, *indigène* women, was part of a larger conflict over race that was even more acute when generals and politicians discussed interactions between white women and African men. Because of the large number of women working in the army during the 1920s, any attempt to replace French conscripts with African men would have brought the African soldiers into regular daily contact with the women working in the army, many of whom were unmarried.

French military and political leaders feared the social conflicts that surrounded mixing black men and white women; at the same time that it rejected allowing *indigène* women to work in the army, the Conseil Supérieur de la Défense Nationale advised the government to keep French women away from colonial units. Henri Pansot, the Foreign Ministry's representative, argued that "it is of the greatest importance that *indigènes* not have contact with French women. It is a capital question of prestige."[56] General Peltier agreed that it was necessary to keep *indigènes* away from French women, but argued that it could best be done by adopting measures "to satisfy the sexual needs of the *indigènes*" in order to end their "frequenting French women." He further explained that the French women whom colonial troops interacted with both socially and sexually were usually the "least healthy" groups in society.[57] Notably, Pansot and Peltier were concerned about the same thing (interracial relationships), but for different reasons. While Pansot warned that colonized men would threaten social order by having relationships with superior French women, Peltier worried that already degraded French women would contaminate colonial troops morally and physically. The mixture of race and gender proved too explosive for French generals, officials, and political leaders to comfortably handle; the interplay of gender and racial prestige frustrated attempts to bring nonwhite women into army employment or to put colonized men into closer contact with French women.

A combination of military weaknesses in colonial units, demeaning racist stereotypes about nonwhite men, and misogynist fears of exposing French women to African men undermined support for shifting the burden of defending France from white Frenchmen to colonized men and women. The failure of the *force noire* plan in part reflected military leaders' choice to prioritize expanding women's opportunities over relying more on colonized men.

Concerns about integrating non-French elements into the army were not limited to *indigène* soldiers; they also extended to the wives of French soldiers. Although by the mid-1920s the military elite generally trusted its women civilian employees, military leaders continued to distrust non-French women. By 1928 that concern began affecting senior commanders' view of soldiers married to foreign women. A 1928 General Staff directive banned officers married to foreign women from serving in the intelligence units of Morocco and Syria, and in 1929 the order was expanded to cover Algeria and Tunisia.[58] Military leaders trusted certain French women, but were wary of trusting their own officers if they were married to nonwhite or non-French European women. The military elite found the interplay of race or nationality and gender to be far more dangerous and potentially corrosive to military discipline and patriotism than were either gender or race alone.

Senior officers' concern about wives revealed a continuing focus on tightly constructing military identity. The order excluding officers with foreign-born wives did not distinguish between the woman's national origin and citizenship, nor did it distinguish among women based on which country they were from. Being married to an American, Belgian, or Portuguese woman led to an officer facing the same restrictions as if he had married a German or a Russian; merely marrying a foreigner cast a cloud over an officer's loyalty in the eyes of his military superiors. The order was not necessarily unreasonable, but it emphasized that senior officers were becoming more sensitive to fears that outside influences would corrupt soldiers. The fact that the order was issued in 1928, during a period of relative international calm and not during a major domestic or international military conflict, emphasizes that the military identity was continually being redefined within the French Army in both wartime and peacetime.

THE GREAT COMPROMISE: THE 1927 AND 1928 MILITARY LAWS

Under Pétain's guidance the Conseil Supérieur de la Guerre took advantage of the divisions within the military reform movement and Poincaré's return to the premiership by agreeing to a compromise with Paul Painlevé, who remained minister of war in the new cabinet.[59] On October 28, 1926, the council advised the Poincaré cabinet that safely implementing a one-year service law would require special standing units to defend the frontier during mobilization and an increase in the number of junior officers in the peacetime army. At the same meeting, the council signaled it was serious about its offer of support by advising the government to reorganize some units, especially *chasseurs*, to allow them to fulfill new roles under the one-year service law.[60] Under Pétain's guidance, the army chiefs agreed to a compromise with Painlevé: on November 8, 1926, the Conseil Supérieur de la Guerre for the first time pronounced itself in favor of a one-year term of service provided that there was no change in the army's legal relationship to the civilian legal and political systems and the army was allowed to compensate for loss of conscripts by increasing the number of career soldiers to 100,000 and hiring 20,000 more permanent civilian employees.[61] Many if not most of these civilian employees would be women, and despite this anticipated influx, the military elite expressed none of the concern about the effect on military cohesion or efficiency that the Piquet's 1919 report had asserted.

The army's compromise with Poincaré bound most of his coalition, but members of the Socialist and Communist Parties opposed the cabinet and tried to use military suffrage to attack the premier, his military bills, and the Army General Staff. But the generals proved willing to fight to preserve the compromise and maintain their vision of a separation between the French Army and French society. They resolutely opposed granting political rights to soldiers and prioritized protecting the army from the republican political system because they believed it was a greater threat to military cohesion than were further cuts in force structure. The General Staff prepared extensive critiques of every proposed law or amendment granting soldiers the right to vote and aggressively advised the cabinet against any extension of suffrage. During parliamentary debates, the General Staff provided Minister of War Painlevé with detailed responses to speeches or amendments that proposed any change to the total ban on active-duty soldiers voting, holding elected office, or campaigning. One typical example was a July 1, 1927, note from the General Staff advising Painlevé that granting soldiers suffrage was "inadmissible because of the consequences which would result for [military] discipline."[62]

Marshal Pétain and his commanders feared that a politically enfranchised conscript army would become a breeding ground for antimilitarism and antipatriotism; with the ban in place, officers could prohibit political propaganda on military bases and punish soldiers for expressing suspect sentiments. Commanders feared that if soldiers became voters, they would have to allow antimilitary or pacifist political materials and activity inside bases. In response to one of Pierre Renaudel's many amendments to the 1927 Army Bill that would have given soldiers the vote and political rights, the General Staff warned Painlevé that "to accord the right to vote to soldiers would be to recognize their right to express their opinions, to spread propaganda, [and] to criticize the government. The exercise of the right to vote may work with the moral characteristics of other races, for ours, the consequences would certainly be fatal."[63]

A June 1927 amendment of Renaudel's tried to literally redefine military status. Renaudel wanted to rename the old active cadres as career cadres and the reserve cadres as civil cadres, and he described the new career cadres as men who were freely contracted to military employment. The General Staff objected to this semantic change, claiming it would fundamentally redefine what it meant to be a soldier. In a rebuttal that anticipated late twentieth-century linguistic deconstruction, staff officers parsed the nuances of the changed terminology and claimed that it would strip away the army's special status as a unique profession and equate a military career with any other. The term civil cadre implied that the recalled reservists would remain civilians even while under arms. The term itself would not have any legal effect, but redefining the vast majority of the wartime army as civilians while they were serving in the army would blur the conceptual line between the military and civilian worlds. The General Staff responded by claiming that the redefinition would "transform the marriage career soldiers currently make with the army" by reducing it to a contract, which would be "in opposition to the spirit of our institutions."[64]

On July 1, 1927, the PCF group in the Chamber of Deputies presented an amendment to prevent future governments from drafting auxiliary civilian employees or workers doing war-related work. They presented it as an incentive for service and as an effort to protect workers against unfair coercion on the part of the government. The General Staff responded with a note warning that communists were trying to manipulate the conscription laws to facilitate a revolutionary strike and that such an action would take away the government's best weapon against an attempt by a legal or illegal union to hold the country hostage through the disruption of public services or the war economy. The cabinet opposed the amendment, and the chamber voted it down. There was never any real likelihood that it would pass, but the General Staff's reaction to it showed the degree of concern that France's senior generals had over perceived threats to the army or the country's political stability.[65]

On July 4, 1927, a Communist Party amendment would have granted soldiers the right to vote in their home regions: if they were on leave, they could vote in person; if not, they would be entitled to vote by mail. In addition, the amendment would have guaranteed soldiers the right to "receive all advertisements and documents that will permit them to form an opinion" on political matters and went on to declare that "the political liberty of soldier-electors must be respected in the most absolute fashion." The amendment stood little chance of passing and was easily defeated, but its language staked out the PCF's support for military suffrage. It also

THE 1927 AND 1928 ARMY LAWS

reminded officers of the party's previous efforts to establish cells inside the military and to target propaganda at enlisted men.[66]

On July 4, 1927, another PCF-supported amendment tried to enfranchise conscripts in the next war through the back door, specifying that recalled reservists would not be considered active members of the military; such a designation would circumvent the legal prohibition on soldiers voting. The ruse was intellectually clever but politically transparent, and the strong disapproval of the Poincaré cabinet and the General Staff easily doomed the amendment. The chamber also defeated an amendment that would have placed soldiers under civilian instead of military law.[67]

Army leaders opposed any change in suffrage rights related to the army, even when the proposals were designed to deflect changes the generals opposed. On July 7, 1927, Ferdinand Bougère, a conservative deputy from Maine-et-Loire, proposed an amendment to solve one of the problems Socialist deputies frequently pointed out: that it was unfair that conscripts were denied the right to vote during their service, but men who evaded their military service could vote. Rather than enfranchising draftees, Bougère proposed increasing the legal voting age to one at which men would have been discharged from compulsory military service.[68]

The high command opposed the amendment despite its attempt to solve the problem of disenfranchising conscripts without actually giving them the right to vote. The General Staff explained that although Bougère meant well, his proposal was poorly thought out and politically unwise. The generals felt that a conscription law was the wrong vehicle to use to raise the overall voting age. It also advised the minister of war that the proposal would still not solve the entire problem outlined by Socialist deputies because career soldiers and men entering military service at a later age would still be deprived of political rights while civilians of their age could vote.[69]

As the Chamber of Deputies debated the 1927 Army Law, the General Staff kept a close eye on the parliamentary debates. It resolutely opposed any attempt to modify the army's legal relationship to the civilian democratic system. Ultimately, despite pressure from Socialist and Communist Party deputies, Poincaré and the General Staff turned back every attempt to give soldiers and sailors voting rights. But the move came at a cost: to retain the ban on voting rights they had to concede to the shortened term of service and compromise on the organization of the military justice system. The fact that France's most senior commanders, including Marshal Pétain, made keeping soldiers disenfranchised such an important priority shows that they feared the republican political system and saw it as inherently different from—and dangerous to—the army.

The 1920s and 1930s witnessed several failed attempts to enfranchise women, though French officers showed little concern about those efforts. As Steven Hause and Anne Kenney have shown, France had a long-established and active women's suffrage movement throughout the 1920s. The Chamber of Deputies passed bills enfranchising women in 1919, 1925, and 1931, but each time the Radical-dominated Senate blocked them. On July 7, 1927, in the midst of debating the 1927 Army Law, the Chamber of Deputies rejected a new women's suffrage amendment because the deputies were certain that the Senate would defeat any bill that enfranchised women.[70] Official papers do not explicitly indicate whether or not officers expected women might become enfranchised, but neither do they show any concern that they would be. Officers either rightly expected the Senate to continue blocking women's suffrage or, like the right-wing leagues, they believed that enfranchised women would be less likely to be support militant left-wing parties than would men. Such groups as Jeunesses Patriote and the Croix de Feu supported women's right to vote in part because they believed that mothers would favor a more conservative France centered on concepts of family and authority while rejecting Marxist invocations to working-class solidarity.[71]

The final version of the 1927 and 1928 Army Laws followed the compromise laid out by Marshal Pétain and bore the stamp of General Brissaud-Desmaillet's report. The 1927 Law on the General Organization of the Army and the 1928 Law of Cadres and Effectives defined the basic organization and structure of the army until the beginning of the Second World War. The laws' major provisions reduced the term of conscript service from eighteen months to one year, increased the number of permanent civilian employees from 10,000 to 30,000 without removing the army's authority to hire auxiliary employees, created 15,000 *agents militaires*, and boosted the number of authorized career soldiers from 72,000 to 106,000. It also allowed the army to maintain 178,000 *indigène* troops. The increase in the number of professional soldiers, civilian employees, and *agents militaires* replaced some of the manpower lost when the number of conscripts fell because of the cut in the term of service, leaving the army's total force (soldiers and civilian combined) approximately 50,000 people smaller than it had been before the law. The legislators phased the laws' provisions in over a period of several years, so it would not be until 1932 that all of the provisions came into force.[72] In September 1927 the army received permission to spend an addition 15 million francs on hiring new civilian employees to implement the reforms.[73]

Although the political leaders dictated the broad strokes of the 1927 and 1928 Army Laws, they allowed the military elite significant discretion in deciding how to implement the compromises. As part of the compromise orchestrated by Painlevé, Pétain, and Poincaré, the senior generals accepted the idea that the wartime army would have to rely on reservists trained in the short-service conscript force to fight the next war, but officers continued to mistrust such soldiers and filled in the new defense system's details based on their fear of their own troops.

WOMEN, VOTING RIGHTS, AND THE 1927 AND 1928 ARMY LAWS

The 1927 and 1928 laws preserved a modified system of military justice, continued the ban on soldiers voting, and preserved restrictions on political speech for soldiers. In the process thousands of women were legally converted from temporary employees into permanent ones, though many others remained legally temporary despite having positions that were now effectively permanent. Many of the new employees were women, but the generals expressed none of the concerns about women's skills, self-discipline, or professionalism that had appeared in or General Pierre Ruffey's letter or Controller General Second Class Piquet's report. Instead France's generals were planning to use women to help preserve the army's cohesion and professionalism against the dangers of politicized and undisciplined male conscripts.

The bills divided the civilian workforce into two groups: a segregated all-male branch, the *agents militaires*, and a conceptually feminized but still gender-mixed branch. As a result of political leaders' fears that the *agents militaires*, who were drawn exclusively from veterans, could be seen as a paramilitary force, Painlevé limited the number of *agents* authorized in the initial drafts of the Army Laws.[74] Yet as Brissaud-Desmaillet predicted, political leaders raised no objections to increasing the number of women working in the military.[75] The army also kept the right to hire thousands of auxiliary employees who were not counted in its official organizational tables. As a result, these employees, most of whom were women, remained legally invisible employees.

The 1927 and 1928 laws were shaped by the ongoing renegotiation of military identity within the French Army and were strongly influenced by the large-scale reentry of women into the military workplace during the Great War and, later, the declining term of conscript service. During and immediately after the war, officers and civilian administrators accused women of undermining male self-discipline and thus professionalism through their own lack of self-discipline and skills. By defining military professionalism in opposition to women's perceived indiscipline officers constructed women as symbols of a hostile and chaotic civilian world. As the 1920s progressed, officers first credited their female civilian employees with loyalty and skill, and then with self-discipline, which allowed women to be defined as professionals. The integration of women into the French Army as permanent and relatively trusted members of the military community was part of a broader reshuffling of prestige and respect inside the army that was shaped by wartime hiring preferences and triggered by officers' fear of the political and military effects of short-service conscription.

By 1927 the declining status of conscripted soldiers had allowed female civil employees to achieve a position within the pale of military identity. Women remained a subordinate group within the French Army, but their status relative to male civilians and most soldiers had clearly risen over the course of the 1920s as they were written into the officer corps' vision of its institution. In senior officers' eyes, women's lack of voting rights became an asset when they reacted against civilian demands on their institution by trying to strengthen its separation from the republican political system. Within the French Army, at least, the Great War triggered a redefinition of the gendered construction of power and opportunity that helped women gain new opportunities for employment and prestige even as it exposed and reinforced the increasing antirepublicanism of the French officer corps.

The writing of the 1927 and 1928 Army Laws showed the limitations of Margaret Higonnet and Patrice Higonnet's double helix theory's oversimplification of the gendered organization of French society.[76] Although the process of negotiating and passing the laws left women as a whole in an inferior position to men inside the French Army, the interaction of race and class with gender meant that women achieved significant gains. The final transition to a peacetime army reaffirmed officers' dominance over women employees, however women not only kept their jobs but also gained new employment opportunities. In addition, because the majority of men in the army saw their status reduced by the debates surrounding the laws, women employees experienced a relative gain in prestige and respect within their institution, confounding the double helix theory's assertions. The First World War did not end the gendered division of labor, but it did reverse the progressive exclusion of women from the military community, and the long demobilization after the war saw women gain access to new responsibilities and respect.

Studying women's position in the interwar French Army not only reveals that they were far more involved in peacetime national defense than historians have believed but also offers a window into the army's political world in the 1920s. Careful attention to the evolution of women's military identity and the gendered construction of all military identity reveals the importance leaders attached to keeping democratic political culture out of their institution. The willingness of senior generals, including Marshal Pétain, the future head of the Vichy Regime, to prioritize the fight against voting rights over preserving force structure should be considered in light of the same military elite's betrayal and destruction of the Third Republic amid the military disaster of 1940.

NOTES

1. Jean-Nöel Jeanneney, *Leçon d'histoire pour une gauche au pouvoir: La faillite du cartel (1924–1926)* (Paris: Plon, 1997), 1–16.
2. "Proposition de Loi relative à une première adaptation militaire de la France; "Proposition de loi reorganization de l'armée et durée de service militaires," February 5, 1920, Dossier 2, SHD DT 5 NN 10.
3. Paul Preston, *Franco* (London: Fontana, 1993), xvii, 31–47.

4. "Historique des événtements du MAROC en 1925" January 23, 1926, Dossier 2, SHD DT 2 NN 20.

5. Ibid.

6. Ibid.

7. Ibid.

8. David Slavin, "The French Left and the Rif War, 1924–25: Racism and the Limits of Internationalism," *Journal of Contemporary History* 26 (1991): 5–32; Régis Antoine, *La litterature pacifiste et internationaliiste Française 1915–1935* (Paris: Harmattan, 2002).

9. "Séance," October 19, 1925, AN F 7 13091; "Circular," October 10, 1925, AN F 7 13092.

10. M. Marty, "War for Banque des Pays-Bas," May 21, 1925, AN F 7 13171; Report, June 6, 1925, AN F 7 13171; Report, July 3, 1925, AN F 7 13171; Report, May 25, 1925, AN F 7 13171.

11. "Parti Communiste Française," October 20, 1925, AN F 7 13091.

12. *La Caserne*, May 20, 1925, AN F 7 13174; Report on Propaganda from Draguignan, June 6, 1925, AN F 7 13174; Report, October 10, 1925, AN F 7 13175.

13. Report on Communist Propaganda , April 28, 1927 AN F 7 13099. Police records indicate that *La Caserne* published fourteen thousand copies per issue in 1927. Military and police records throughout the 1920s and 1930s indicated that the Communist Party's papers were regularly found inside army bases.

14. *Le Caserne*, May 20, 1925; Report on Communist Propaganda, April 28, 1927, AN F 7 13099.

15. *Le Caserne*, September 5, 1925, AN F 7 13175; *La Caserne*, May–October 1925, AN F 7 13175; *Le Caserne*, May 20, 1925, AN F 7 13174.

16. "7165 Ministre Intérieur (Dir de la Surete Gen) à Min Marine (EMG 2e Bur B) Commandant Chenouard," AN F 7 13090.

17. Poster (Tours), May 31, 1925, AN F 7 13092.

18. Ibid.; Police circular, October 10, 1925, AN F 7 13092.

19. Letter from Military Intelligence (2ᵉ Bureau), May 24, 1927, AN F 7 13099; "Etat des sanctions prises contre des militaires qui sont livres à des faits d'excitation à la désobéissance òu de propagande Communiste," AN F 7 13174; *Rapport Draguignan*.

20. *Le Temps*, October 12, 1925, AN F 7 12919.

21. Police Report October 23, 1925, AN F 7 13171; Police Report November 12, 1925, AN F 7 13171.

22. Report on Communist Propaganda, April 28, 1927, AN F 13099.

23. "Surveillance des Conscrits Communiste 1925," AN F 7 13156.

24. "Congrès des Conscrits région Parisienne," May 2, 1926, AN F 13157.

25. "BE/I Le Ministre de la Guerre À Monsieur le Ministre de l'Intérieur," May 24, 1927, AN F 7 13099.

26. Ibid.

27. Note, April 23, 1927, AN F 13099.

28. Ibid.

29. "Book 15," March 30, 1925, SHD DT 1 N 21.

30. "Book 15," April 1, 1925, SHD DT 1 N 21.

31. Ibid.

32. "Book 15," April 3, 1925, SHD DT 1 N 21.

33. "Book 15," April 10, 1925, SHD DT 1 N 21.

34. Ibid.

35. Ibid.

36. "Procès-verbal," April 10, 1925, SHD DT 1 N 20.

37. "Book 15," 10 April 1925.

38. "Procès-verbal" December 15, 1925, CSG, SHD DT 1 N 20.

39. "Book 15," May 26, 1926, SHD DT 1 N 21.

40. Study No. 10262 1/11, Dossier 3, SHD DT 7 N 2385.

41. "Procès-verbal," December 15, 1925, CSG, SHD DT 1 N 20; "Procès-verbal," October 28, 1926, CSG, SHD DT 1 N 20.

42. "Rapport partiel 1 ," Dossier 1, SHD DT 9 NN 1169; "Rapport partiel 2" July 1925, Dossier 1, SHD DT 9 NN 1169;; "L'Armée Minima," September 25, 1925, SHD DT 7 NN 1169.

43. "L'Armée Minima."

44. Ibid.

45. Ibid.; "Armée Minima," Num 628-1/7, Dossier 1, SHD DT 9 NN 1167.

46. "L'Armée Minima," September 25, 1925, SHD DT 7 N 1169; "Armée Minima," Num 628-1/7, Dossier 1, SHD DT 9 NN 1167. The official report and its supporting material are in Dossier 1, SHD DT 9 NN 1169.

47. "Armée Minima," No. 628-1/8, March 13, 1927, Dossier 2, SHD DT 9 NN 1167.

48. Ibid.

49. Ibid.

50. "L'Armée Minima," September 25, 1925, SHD DT 7 NN 1169; "Gouraud to Brissaud-Desmaillet," No. 28/C5, SHD DT 7 NN29; "Brissaud-Desmaillet to Gouraud" March 10, 1925, Dossier 1, SHD DT 7 NN 29.

51. "Agents militaires," October 24, 1927, Dossier 1, SHD DT 9 NN 1169.

52. Myron Echenberg, Colonial Conscripts: The Tirailleurs Senegalais in French West Africa, 1857–1960 (New York: Heinemann, 1991), 25–46.

53. "Historique du projet de loi des cadres," Dossier 1, SHD DT 7 NN 128.

54. "Historique du projet de loi des cadres."

55. "Projet d'Instruction sur le recrutement et l'emploi de la main d'oeuvre coloniale," No. 627, July 20, 1926, Dossier 1, SHD DT 2 N 10.

56. Ibid.

57. Ibid.

58. EMA—Section études, No. 652 9/11, March 8, 1929, Dossier 1, B20, SHD DT 9 NN 64. The document references an earlier study from June 4, 1928,

59. "Rapport," November 16, 1926, Dossier 1, SHD DT 1 NN 13.

60. Ibid.; "Procès-verbal," October 28, 1926, CSG, Dossier 1, SHD DT 1 N 20.

61. "Procès-verbal," October 28, 1926, CSG, Dossier 1, SHD DT 1 N 20.; "Procès-verbal," November 8, 1926, CSG, Dossier 1, SHD DT 1 N 20.

62. Response to "Amendement No. 70" (BOUGERE) Article 9, July 7, 1927, Dossier 1, SHD DT 5 NN 10.

63. Response to "Amendement No. 14" (Renaudel), July 1, 1927, Dossier 1, SHD DT 5 NN 10.

64. "Amendement 17 Renaudel," Article 11, SHD DT 5 NN 10.

65. Amendement 40, Article 52, July 1, 1927, SHD DT 5 NN 9.

66. "Amendement 32," SHD DT 5 NN 10.

67. Amendement 41, Article 43, July 4, 1927, SHD DT 5 NN 9.

68. Amendement 70, July 7, 1927, SHD DT 5 NN 10.

69. Ibid.

70. Paul Smith, *Feminism and the Third Republic: Women's Political and Civil Rights in France, 1918–1945* (Oxford: Clarendon, 1996); Steven Hause and Anne Kenney, *Women's Suffrage and Social Politics in the French Third Republic* (Princeton, NJ: Princeton University Press, 1984).

71. Daniella Sarnoff, "Interwar Fascism and the Franchise: Women's Suffrage and the *Ligues*," *Historical Reflections* 34, no. 2 (2008): 112–22.

72. "Loi relative à l'organisation générale de l'armée," Dossier 2, SHD DT 1 NN 50.

73. "Note," No. 3464, September 7, 1927, Dossier 2, SHD DT 9 NN 1167.

74. "Armée Minima." Some scholars, following Judith Hughes's lead in *To the Maginot Line: The Politics of French Military Preparation in the 1920's* (Cambridge MA: Harvard University Press, 1971), 174, have misidentified the *agents militaire* as police, perhaps conflating them with the *Garde républicaine*.

75. "Projet de loi des Cadres et Effectifs," October 1926, Dossier 2, SHD DT 1 NN 15.

76. For a discussion of Higonnet and Higonnet's double helix theory, see the introduction to the present volume; see also Higonnet and Higonnet, "The Double Helix."

4

War Clouds, 1929–1938

The 1927 and 1928 Army Laws consolidated women's gains in the post–World War I French Army, but they also marked a slowing of women's progress within the army. The laws had raised hopes that French leaders had finally stabilized the army's organization and were on the verge of adapting the national defense establishment and the structures of the Third Republic to the realities of total war that the Great War had exposed. The text of the 1927 and 1928 laws referred to a comprehensive law that would govern the organization of the home front for total war, and many leaders expected that such a law would resolve the conflict between military service and democratic rights while clarifying women's roles in national defense. Unfortunately, that critical legislation collapsed due to disputes over private property and the role of women during total war. In addition, the beginning of the Great Depression meant that the laws did not end debates over the size, cost, and organization of the army.

The 1927 and 1928 Army Laws gave women more job opportunities and responsibilities within the army, but senior officers' views of women in the army remained one-sided. Despite taking on greater responsibilities, most women were not able to move beyond their temporary status or gain access to senior administrative positions. The implementation of the 1927 and 1928 laws returned the army to a peacetime footing and marked the end of the steady expansion of women's roles that had restarted early in the demobilization process. Political and military leaders' incomplete acceptance of women as members of the military community contributed to the defeat of the Law on the Organization of the Nation in Wartime, which included a serious attempt to delineate the borders of civilian political power and military authority in wartime. The act failed, in part, because political leaders were reluctant to recognize that women had become integral to modern total war and thus, in the eyes of most European military leaders, legitimate military targets. In the 1930s, women's positions in the French Army continued to evolve, but they usually did so farther from senior leaders' attention than had been the case during the Great War or immediately preceding the 1927 and 1928 laws. Although military leaders' mistrust of the civilian world grew after the Popular Front took power in the 1936 election, their mistrust did not extend to purging female civilian employees. In particular, women's status as disenfranchised citizens helped protect them from officers' fear of civilians, even as civilian men were subjected to increasingly robust surveillance programs.

RESIDUAL OPPOSITION TO WOMEN AS CIVILIAN EMPLOYEES

Despite officers' general acceptance of female civilian employees, a handful of officers continued to resist the expansion of women's roles. Whereas officers during the war had derided the very idea of women working in the army as dangerous, by 1929 opponents were reduced to arguing that there were not enough available women to do all of the jobs that were being civilianized. One plea urged the Conseil Supérieur de la Guerre to expand the training and recruitment of noncommissioned officers to work as accountants and bookkeepers in the army on the grounds that it would be impossible to find enough civilian men or women to fill all of the vacancies created by the new system of military organization that shifted conscripts out of accounting functions and into combat units.[1] In November 1929 General Marie-Eugène Debeney, the chief of the General Staff, wrote to Marshal Philippe Pétain explaining that the counterproposal should be rejected because his staff believed it would require new legislation from the Chamber of Deputies to authorize the costs of recruiting, training, and maintaining enough noncommissioned officers to perform clerical and accounting work without taking men out of combat units. He dismissed the proposals by explaining that the women already performing those tasks were meeting all of the army's expectations and there was every reason to think more women could be recruited.[2]

The weakness of the attempts to roll back women's gains in the 1930s reflected the success of previous civilianization efforts and the consolidation of women's military identity. In the early 1930s the biggest obstacles to the further expansion of women's roles in the army were political leaders' unwillingness to let women enlist as soldiers and the previous success of civilian employees. By 1931, civilian workers, including women, were firmly established in many fields that had once been the exclusive preserve of male soldiers, so there were fewer and fewer areas that could be opened to women without recognizing them as soldiers or accepting their presence close to the battlefield. This made it difficult to credibly claim that women could not handle rear-area functions, but is also made it hard to further expand their roles. Actually making women soldiers was a step too far for officers and politicians because it would have clashed with established gender norms that were conditioned by women's lack of full citizenship rights. Opening up many new areas of employment to women would also have run up against political leaders who were refusing to accept that total war required fully integrating women into the war effort.

CIVILIAN EMPLOYEES AND COLONIAL UNITS

The 1927 and 1928 laws shifted many responsibilities from conscripts to civilian employees and forced the army to work harder to recruit enough new civilian workers to meet its needs without sacrificing the quality of candidates. This process was fraught with potential conflicts at a time when political leaders were looking to cut government spending; any part of the budget that was growing was an obvious target for the Ministry of Finance. The transition was especially important at posts that were considered unattractive; conscripts could be sent anywhere, but civilian employees could choose which jobs to take and could quit anytime they wanted. The new law required the army to hire more civilian employees as substitutes for soldiers in North Africa, but the cabinet proposed to keep costs down by reducing the extra benefits civilians received for serving abroad, and military leaders were only willing to hire women if they were European.[3]

Army leaders pushed back against the cabinet and opposed any reductions in civilian employees' benefits. The authors of a July 1929 report on army morale argued that civilian employees in Algeria and Tunisia should retain the right to receive bonus pay. Officers feared that without offering extra benefits they would struggle to recruit and retain enough civilian workers to staff their units. They tried to counter concerns about the cost by reminding the cabinet that increased spending on civilian employees was essential to reducing the term of conscript service. Officers also suggested that if the civilian employees were allowed to continue receiving bonus pay for taking North African postings, they would probably spend that pay while vacationing in France.[4] Their economic arguments were flawed, but ultimately civilian employees were allowed to keep their bonuses because the alternative was recruiting more soldiers, which was even more politically unpalatable than paying the bonuses.

Between 1929 and 1932 the army's implementation of the 1927 and 1928 laws included a renewed drive to civilianize more of the military's labor force. Campaigns to shift work from soldiers to civilians (especially women) that had begun in 1915 had become common by 1929. Unlike many earlier campaigns, the new initiative in 1929 generated almost no opposition to the principle itself and became controversial only when its extension to colonial units brought up sensitive questions about how race, gender, and colonial prestige interacted.

Since many office functions had already been civilianized and feminized in the 1915–28 period, the 1929 initiative extended into new areas and, among other functions, targeted *ordonnance* soldiers. In the French Army a soldier assigned to *ordonnance* duty served as an officer's personal servant. The number of these positions had shrunk since the war, but hundreds of soldiers were still performing these duties in units in metropolitan France and in the colonies.

Initially the focus was on colonial units. While serving in the colonies, officers usually hired local servants or had minimally paid *indigène* soldiers assigned as their servants, but when their units moved to France, these colonial officers sometimes had metropolitan soldiers assigned to them. When the Ministry of War applied pressure to abolish the practice and replace the white soldiers with white civilians, including women, senior officers in the Colonial Army and officers attached to North African units objected vociferously. They claimed that bringing white women into these units would damage morale and internal functioning because it would threaten colonial racial hierarchies. A compromise was finally reached whereby colonial units would stop using soldiers drawn from the metropolitan army as servants and would replace them with men from within the colonial units.[5] This marginally reduced the units' combat strength, but freed conscripts for other duties without creating new expenses. By 1931 renewed pressure from the ministry led the commanders of France's military regions to implement more aggressive measures. They began instructing their subordinate units and offices to replace soldiers performing *ordonnance* duties in the metropolitan army with civilians, both male and female. Colonial units, however, remained exceptions to this rule to avoid the difficult questions that arose from employing white women in nonwhite units. Previous discussions of such had been bogged down with concerns about interracial liaisons and the potential that they would undermine white prestige in the colonies. Exempting colonial units thus made it easier to quickly implement the proposal.[6]

CIVIL CONSCRIPTION OF WOMEN AND THE PAUL-BONCOUR LAW

The Law on the Organization of the Nation in Wartime, which was commonly known as the Paul-Boncour Law (after Joseph Paul-Boncour, the SFIO deputy who oversaw its drafting) was intended to prepare the economic mobilization of the country so that the home front could move from a peacetime to a wartime footing as quickly as the military did. The 1927 and 1928 Army Laws had been written on the assumption the Law on the

Organization of the Nation in Wartime, which focused on military and economic mobilization, would also be passed in short order. Political and military leaders intended the three laws to work together to prepare France for a long war of attrition and worked on them simultaneously, but the process of writing the third law proved to be more controversial than had been anticipated.

Paul-Boncour and the other framers of the law designed it to mobilize all of France's economic resources, including women, for the war effort. The original text spoke of mobilizing "tous les français" (all the French people), which was potentially ambiguous as to whether it referred to men and women or just men, but the Chamber of Deputies' Army Committee added the phrase "without distinction of age or sex," which clearly specified that women would be subject to mobilization. The deputies extensively debated the proper phrasing and interpretation of the proposal's language, but many worried that because the law gave the government the authority to direct—and thus, effectively, to conscript—civilian labor, it would make all civilians, including women, legitimate military targets.[7] Deputies such as Maurice Marchais, a centrist from Vannes, worried that mobilizing civilians could legally justify enemy air attacks against civilian targets and thus added language explaining that people could be conscripted as either combatants or noncombatants. The proposal's opponents used this debate to undermine the legislation by framing it as endangering women and children by making them targets. Military leaders supported the law, but had only a minor role in the pivotal debate over the role of women in wartime, in part because they knew the next war would require the mass mobilization of women and other civilians, and they were already convinced that any enemy would target those civilians, but admitting that view risked alienating some deputies.[8]

The Paul-Boncour Law was essential to Raymond Poincaré's overall reform of French defense policy, and it was approved by the Chamber of Deputies on March 7, 1927. It then moved to the Senate, where the centrist and center-left parties predominated. The Senate accepted the overall principles the chamber had embraced on most issues, though gender and private property proved to be points of conflict; the senators were much more critical of allowing the government to conscript women's labor than the chamber had been. Military leaders made it clear to the cabinet that total war would require mobilizing both women and men, but the senators were not convinced. The Senate Army Committee watered down the chamber's text on civilian conscription considerably and left it unclear how many women could be subject to labor service and under what conditions. During the senate debate, Minister of War Painlevé claimed that women would only be under a moral obligation to help the war effort, but even that promise was not enough to satisfy many critics of mobilizing women. In the end the Senate too adopted a confused compromise in which women's obligations and the government's authority to direct women's wartime labor were both unclear. The Senate did, however, endorse the chamber's decision to allow elected representatives to retain their mandates while serving in the military if they obtained long-term leaves of absence from their political roles.[9]

Ultimately the proposal died as a result of combination of conflicts over the employment of civilian women and civilian property. The Senate and chamber majorities tried to paper over their views of women's mobilization by avoiding taking a clear position on the issue, but they took diametrically opposed positions on the wartime use of civilian property. The Senate and the cabinet preferred to negotiate with property owners to come to prewar arrangements to use their industrial property in the war effort, but the chamber, with its smaller centrist contingent, insisted that the government could limit property owners' wartime profits and wanted the government to be able to expropriate property with relatively little compensation if owners refused to cooperate with the mobilization plan. The result was a running conflict between the two bodies; this, combined with unease about its implications for women, sank the proposal. After more than a year of debate, the bill fell short on February 17, 1928, when the Senate passed a version of it that directly conflicted with the text the Chamber of Deputies had approved in March 1927. Rather than trying to reconcile the texts, the cabinet abandoned its efforts to pass the bill. During the debate, military leaders proved more willing than politicians to accept that women had become integral to national defense and that their labor was absolutely required to allow France to wage total war, but the army's leaders were not willing to put their prestige on the line to insist on the point in the face of political hostility.[10]

THE LIMITS OF INCLUSION: FAILURE TO
REGULARIZE TEMPORARY EMPLOYEES

Despite the consolidation of women's places inside the army, thousands of women remained classed as auxiliary, and thus temporary, employees. They were not alone in that situation, and in 1924 the SFIO had introduced legislation designed to make temporary employees who had been working for the army prior to August 2, 1914, into permanent employees. That proposal had excluded women by setting the cutoff date at the beginning of the mobilization, and thus before the army started hiring women as auxiliary employees.[11] In 1928 Communist deputies sponsored a bill to set a minimum wage for auxiliary employees; as part of the proposal, auxiliary employees, including women, would automatically become permanent employees after five years of service.[12] Both the 1924 and 1928 bills failed to win parliamentary approval because neither the cabinet nor military leaders supported them.

In 1929 Radical Deputies Jean-Robert LaSalle, Maurice Palmade, and Jean Taurines and independent Radical Pierre Deyris presented a bill to convert long-term auxiliary employees into permanent civilian employees, and this would have benefited women as well as men. They argued that it was unfair to treat employees with a decade or more of experience as temporary employees, especially because it kept them from being able to claim the more generous retirement packages available for permanent employees. The bill's authors explained that during the First World War the military had hired temporary employees to replace mobilized civilian workers, and many of these employees had continued working since the end of the war; they argued that it was time to admit that these officially temporary employees were really permanent employees: "today, after eleven years of [peacetime] experience, there can be no doubt that the greater part of those employed as auxiliary agents, though allegedly 'temporary' employees, are really meeting permanent needs." The proposal went on to recognized that some of these employees had performed admirable service under conditions in which their "lives were in peril" during the war. It called on deputies to end the "abnormal situation" of having permanent temporary employees by granting long-term tempo-

rary employees permanent status.[13] Despite the sponsors being moderate
deputies, the plan did not attract much support and languished in the
chamber in part because it would have required paying thousands of employees more money without the government getting anything in return.
The plan's failure set the tone for the decade: in the ensuing years a steady
stream of bills sought to deal with the contradiction of having temporary
employees who had been doing their jobs for five to ten years and, by the
late 1930s, up to twenty years.

Although bills to regularize auxiliary employees sometimes attracted
up to two dozen sponsors, they were usually the work of a small group of
deputies within one party and never had the clear backing of the cabinet.
In 1936, a group of PCF deputies tried and failed to create a binding national salary table for auxiliary employees whose pay was still often being
set by their commanding officers on a region-by-region basis.[14] In June 1939
a frustrated minority wrote a bill inviting Édouard Daladier's cabinet to
present its own plan to solve the anomaly of having permanent temporary
employees. Ultimately, the German Army conquered France before the
problem was dealt with, and when Marshal Pétain took power in June 1940,
his defeated army still had temporary auxiliary employees who had helped
it win the Great War.

The army leadership's disinterest in regularizing its temporary auxiliary
employees revealed its ambiguous attitude toward its civilian employees,
and especially women. Because most of the 1916 Regime employees were
women, they were disproportionately represented among the semiperma-
nent auxiliary employees and thus were more likely than men to be victims
of the high command and government's refusal to admit that they were
permanent employees. Senior officers' disinterest in regularizing women's
positions could have been overcome if the women had been able to call on
reliable support from deputies and senators, but—perhaps because women
could not vote—relatively few politicians were concerned enough about the
situation to settle it, and military leaders did not feel compelled to deal with
the problem. Thus, in the 1930s women retained the employment gains they
had made during the 1920s, and made some new gains, but they found it
difficult to gain additional support from the top of the hierarchy without an
imminent crisis forcing it to pay attention to its civil employees.

Not all women were stuck as temporary auxiliary employees, but many were, and most spent at least part of their careers designated as temporary employees. On January 9, 1928, three days after her twenty-first birthday, Renée Siégin began working for the army as a secretary and was classified as a temporary auxiliary employee. She spent the next twelve and a half years—the entire period before she lost her job during the defeat of 1940—as a temporary employee.[15] It was not just younger women who could be unable to escape the ranks of temporary auxiliary employees. In April 1928, fifty-six-year-old Rose Lépine began an eleven-year stint working for the Infantry Directory in Paris. Upon reaching the mandatory retirement age in 1939 she was still officially a temporary employee and was earning thirty-one francs per day, 75 percent of the minimum pay a woman classed as a permanent employee would have gotten.[16]

THE NEW CARTEL

The Chamber of Deputies elected in April 1928 had contained a clear majority of conservative and centrist deputies who supported Raymond Poincaré, but even as he won the election, he was near the end of his long and distinguished career, a career that saw him serve as president of the republic during the Great War and as *president du conseil* (premier) three times. When he retired from active politics in July 1929 he left his old majority leaderless; for a time his supporters carried on under Aristide Briand, but Briand was a poor fit for the conservative coalition, and by November his cabinet had fallen and was replaced by a procession of short-lived cabinets.

In May 1932 the internally divided center-right majority was put out of its misery by an equally fractious left-wing majority built around the Radical Party and the SFIO. Although the election was close in terms of votes, a return to the two-round first-past-the-post system favored the Left when its members could cooperate and the Radicals and the SFIO created a new Cartel des Gauches that suffered from all of the weaknesses of a sequel. The Socialist deputies again promised to support the cabinet, but Léon Blum's fear that executive responsibility would split the party led him to ban its members from joining the cabinet. That left the Radicals to govern with assistance from smaller parties while trying to retain the Socialists' support.

The Cartel's military policy was vague even to its own members. The socialists continued to demand the implementation of the militia-based defense policy that Jean Jaurès had outlined in *L'Armée nouvelle* despite the fact that by 1932 it was a twenty-year-old document that predated tanks and effective combat aircraft. The Radicals showed their usually tolerance for internal diversity and had several, often contradictory, defense policies: party president Édouard Herriot publically favored the creation of a federal European state to prevent future conflicts; some factions supported building the Maginot Line, while others argued fortifications were obsolete and called for the abolition of the professional component of the army and a move to a "national army" composed of a mass militia. Even Georges-Henri Brissaud-Desmaillet returned to add his perspective. After retiring from the army, Brissaud-Desmaillet had joined the Radical Party and, despite having previously tried to undermine its defense policies, served as the head of the party's defense policy committee in the early 1930s. There he elaborated on his work as head of the Commission of Civil Employees by advocating civilianizing the army and militarizing public education. He called for mandatory physical and military training for young men in schools to prepare them to be better soldiers and reservists. Some of Brissaud-Desmaillet's suggested education reforms were similar to the physical training that boys experienced in Nazi and Fascist youth groups, and they were measures the Vichy Regime later implemented.[17]

In the early 1930s, debates about the military budget took place in the shadow of the deepening depression and the League of Nations–sponsored disarmament talks in Geneva. Although the Great Depression took hold in France more slowly than it did in other countries, beginning in 1930 it put increasing pressure on the budget. The growing budget deficit at a time of increasing unemployment led politicians across the political spectrum to look to cut military spending to defend the franc and maintain social spending. This tendency was reinforced by the Geneva disarmament talks because French leaders feared international isolation and domestic unpopularity if they appeared to sabotage the talks. The disarmament talks also provided a convenient excuse to justify cutting the military budget to free up money to protect social spending while minimizing the deficit.

The year 1933 proved to be a difficult one in French civil-military relations because of the renewed drive to cut the army's budget and the prickly personality of General Maxime Weygand, who replaced Pétain as the designated wartime commander of the French Army in 1932. Weygand spent most of 1933 locked in a battle with Radical Party leaders, and especially Édouard Daladier, over the army's budget and Daladier's plans to cut the number of active-duty officers to save money. These disputes became increasingly bitter until December 1933, when Weygand and Daladier's conflict burst into public view when military sources leaked the results of a Conseil Supérieur de la Guerre meeting in which Weygand had organized Daladier's humiliation by organizing a series of attacks against the minister's position which culminated in Pétain's claims that Daladier's polices could cause French troops to be massacred at the beginning of the next war. Daladier responded by refusing to reappoint Weygand to his position in January 1934, leading to a standoff between the army and the cabinet.[18]

While February 1934 was threatened with being dominated by the growing civil-military crisis, instead a domestic scandal took center stage. While Weygand was defying Daladier, the Radical–dominated cabinet was being undermined by the Stavisky affair, a corruption scandal that implicated several high-ranking members of the party in a fraudulent bond scheme orchestrated by Alexandre Stavisky. When Stavisky was found by the police dying of a self-inflicted gunshot wound, the right-wing press alleged it was a police execution; this led to rioting after Camille Chautemps (who was simultaneously premier and minister of the interior and whose brother-in-law was implicated in the scandal) fired the right-wing prefect of the Parisian police. On February 6, 1934, the right-wing leagues, including both quasi-fascist and clearly fascist groups met in the Place de la Concorde and were only stopped from storming the Chamber of Deputies by police bullets. The next day the second Cartel collapsed and a National Union government replaced it.

The National Union government was led by the conservative Radical Gaston Doumergue, and leaned strongly to the right. Marshal Pétain became the new minister of war and immediately reappointed Weygand to his position of designated commander of the wartime army. The result was a political lurch to the right and an end to major military cuts. For the rest of the 1930s the army became much more autonomous in its operation, which had both positive and negative implications for its civilian employees.

CONTRADICTORY POLICIES TOWARD WOMEN

Because politicians in the 1920s had been focused on cutting the length of conscript service or attacking the existence of the standing army itself, they had largely ignored women when looking to cut the military budget, and had allowed the army to hire more civilian employees to make it easier to reduce the number of conscripts and thus the term of service. In the spring of 1934, however, Doumergue's National Union cabinet acted on Weygand's advice and cut some parts of the army's budget to free up money to fund mechanization and the creation of armored divisions. In response, Minister of War Pétain ordered a number of cuts, including a 10 percent reduction in civilian employees. The cut disproportionally fell on women because they were more likely than men to be classed as temporary employees, and thus were easier to fire.[19]

In conjunction with his cuts, Pétain ordered officials to use a modified version of the 1916 Regime's hiring preferences to decide who should be fired. His list began, intuitively, with any employee who volunteered to quit. Although that was a small group, often composed of those nearing planned retirement or already contemplating quitting for other reasons, it was the least controversial part of the plan. Pétain ordered supervisors to make a list of employees whose professional skills were deemed substandard compared to their colleagues and to fire them first in each group. If necessary, the army would then move on to firing married women who were either childless or whose children had left the home and whose husbands, according to the army, could meet their needs. Only after exhausting these groups would the army proceed to fire other employees.[20] In effect this system gave a preference to mothers and widows that protected them from being fired, just as many of them had benefited from a preference when they were hired.

Pétain ordered that within each group the army would use a point system to determine an employee's relative susceptibility to be fired. The system took account of several factors, including employees' scores on skills tests, the number of months men had served in the military during the Great War, and the number of continuous months of employment as military civil employees that the women and men had completed. This final category was a seniority system, but it treated service as a civilian employee and a solider on an equal basis. For example, when Lucienne Mansuelle turned forty-one in April 1934, she was given credit for 209 months of continuous service as a civilian employee dating back to November 1916. During that time she switched jobs only once, transferring from a position working in the pensions archive to the headquarters of the Army Health Service. She was entitled to the same seniority bonus as a man who entered the army in November 1916 and began working for the army as a civilian the day he demobilized. Pétain's plan administratively equated women's service as civilian employees with men's service in the wartime army.[21] His decisions showed that military leaders still had a sense of obligation to the widows, mothers, and children of men who had died in the Great War; it also reflected one version of the prevailing gender norms of the time. Pétain implicitly assumed that unless a woman's husband had been disabled in the war, a married woman worked in order to earn extra money for luxuries, while her husband worked to provide for their family's needs.

Some women did volunteer to lose their jobs during the purge. In the summer of 1934 Isabelle Jacquet was fifty-four years old and had worked for the army for eighteen years. Isabelle Hallé had been hired on August 14, 1916, and had worked in the minister of war's cabinet since 1921; in 1924 she married Henri Jacquet-Sanches, but the marriage had not produced any children. Pétain's preference system thus worked against her, and rather than risk being fired, she chose to retire from the army on June 20, 1934.[22]

Not surprisingly, the army did not find enough volunteers to meet the staff reductions and thus proceeded with firings in the summer of 1934. Suzanne Maillard, a married twenty-seven-year-old woman originally from Magalas was one of the women the army fired. She had held her job since 1929 and thus had only a moderate level of seniority. In June 1934 she was informed that she was being fired from her job as a temporary auxiliary employee working for the Third Bureau of the Infantry Directory in Paris. When her supervisors put their redundancy list together she was high on the list because she was married but had no children and therefore was presumed to need a job less than other women did. The fact that she had not had a raise in three years suggested that her supervisors were not especially happy with her work, which may also have contributed to their decision to fire her.[23]

Maillard, however, did not accept her firing. In July 1934 she appealed to Albert Sarraut, then the minister of interior in the Doumergue cabinet. Sarraut wrote to the Ministry of War asking that Maillard be rehired, but his appeal failed to get her job back. As Maillard was writing to Sarraut, however, it was becoming clear that fortuitous timing had given her a new avenue of appeal: she was pregnant. In October she wrote to Minister of War Pétain explaining that at the time she was fired she was, unbeknownst to her or her supervisors, already pregnant. She argued that she should be rehired because if her pregnancy had been known she would not have been classified as married without children under the ministry's policies, which counted a pregnant woman as a mother. Her appeal succeeded on the grounds that if her pregnancy had been known she would have had enough points to avoid being fired, and on December 29, 1934, she was informed that she was being rehired with her former seniority.[24]

Maillard's pregnancy allowed her to successfully challenge her firing, but many other women were unable to escape the effects of the budget cuts. The 1934 firings resulted in more women leaving army employment than at any time since the demobilization purge. As usual, the army did not record the overall number of civilians it employed, but based on a sampling of files, it seems likely the army's administration either reached or approached its goal of firing 10 percent of its women employees.

MOBILIZING WOMEN

Even as the Doumergue government approved plans to cut the number of civilian employees, military leaders were further integrating male and female civilian workers into their war plans. Faced with Adolf Hitler's military buildup, senior generals and conservative ministers looked to women to strengthen national defense even as they were calling for a reduction in the number of women employed by the army in peacetime. In August 1934 Minister of War Pétain proposed allowing the Ministry of War to requisition women working for other ministries in the event of war. Although Minister of National Education André Mallermé objected, most generals and several other ministers supported the idea. On November 10, 1934, two days after the formation of the cabinet of Pierre-Étienne Flandin, Minister of Finance Louis Germain-Martin supported an amendment to the text that expanded on Pétain's proposal and proposed the creation of a civilian reserve force that could be mobilized in wartime. Germain-Martin's amendment specified that "functionaries, agents, and employees of the state administration, the departments, and the communes as well as all other public services . . . are, after their retirement and for a period of five years, maintained at the disposition of the administrative service of which they were a party." The provision effectively applied the army's reserve system to civilian public employees of both sexes and made them available for mandatory civilian war work as government employees.[25] Germain-Martin may not have been aware of it, but his proposal echoed Jane Dieulafoy's March 1913 plea for the Ministry of War to begin training civilian women to take over noncombat roles in the military in the event of war. Germain-Martin did not reference Dieulafoy's claims, but he was endorsing the same plan in 1934 that she had advocated in 1913.[26]

The Doumergue and Flandin cabinets' proposals represented an effort to gain more control over how civilian women and men contributed to national defense. During the Great War, civilian employees had freely entered and left government positions. As a result of the 1927 and 1928 laws, the army would have to rely heavily on civilian labor at the beginning of the next major war. The Paul-Boncour Law had sought to create an integrated system to regulate women's wartime labor, but its defeat meant that the wartime system remained ad hoc.

Creating a force of civilian reserve workers made sense because by 1934, civilian women and men were responsible for essential army services and, in the event of mobilization, the army would need to expand those services as quickly as possible. The reserve employee system would emulate the army's existing military reserve and give it access to a pool of trained and trusted workers whose labor could be called upon and deployed as the army's needs increased. By proposing to create a civilian version of a long-established element of the army, Weygand and Pétain were further militarizing civilian employees, including women who would become subject to compulsory service as civilian employees of the army as if they were recalled reserve soldiers. The cabinet's final proposed text made clear that all French men and women were subject to obligatory service in the war effort.[27]

When the bill went to the Senate, many senators objected to the proposal's militarization of women as they had in 1928. Although the generals supported the measure, the senators passed an amendment that specified that only French men over the age of eighteen would be under military obligations or subject to labor conscription. The senators claimed to fear that the more expansive text would give enemy powers an excuse to attack French civilians indiscriminately if they were able to claim that all French citizens, regardless of age or sex, were at least theoretically attached to the army. General Louis Maurin, Flandin's octogenarian minister of war who had replaced Pétain, demanded that the Senate restore the old text, but the senators refused to relent. The bill's eventual failure made the text moot, but the generals' willingness to make civilian employees, including women, subject to a reserve requirement and a form of conscription reflected their acceptance that civilian workers had become indispensable parts of the army and vital to any meaningful plan to wage total war.[28]

MILITARIZED CIVILIANS: SECRETARIES AND POISON GAS

Even though the politicians were reluctant to admit that women's labor was essential to modern war, improved military technology and the spread of strategic bombing theories throughout Europe led French officers to view civilian employees, both men and women, as pseudocombatants, thus furthering women's integration into the military identity at the grassroots level. Female civilian employees were not soldiers, but in the 1930s they began receiving some military training—specifically, training in dealing with poison gas—because senior officers deemed them essential to the daily operation of the French Army in wartime.[29] Many military leaders feared that Germany or Italy would launch poison gas bombing raids against fortifications, depots, mobilization centers, and military offices all over France at the beginning of the next war. If effective, such attacks could cripple the French Army by killing or injuring the women and men who manned its mobilization and support services.[30]

In an attempt to counter these threats and prepare France to withstand the anticipated air raids, Gaston Doumergue's National Union government presented the Law on the Organization of Passive Defense in 1934. The proposal was studiously vague, never specifying how the government would organize France's defenses. The plan signaled French leaders' realization that the ascendancy of total war ideology in the Great War and the subsequent rapid development of the speed and range of combat aircraft had blurred old distinctions between soldiers and noncombatants. It also showed their unwillingness to fully face the implications of that realization by actually preparing the country for such an attack.[31] The General Staff supported the law and provided the cabinet with briefing papers that highlighted the Italian Air Force's attachment to the ideas of air theorist General Giulio Douhet, whose theories of total air warfare emphasized the effectiveness of saturation bombing of cities with a mix of conventional, incendiary, and poison gas bombs.[32]

Fear of gas attacks convinced the military and political elite that civilian employees had to be trained in antigas procedures and the proper use of equipment. In October 1934 the Ministry of War estimated that, in the event of full mobilization, it needed 5,044,000 masks to equip soldiers and another 1,200,000 masks for civilians. This meant that 19 percent of the Ministry of War's wartime defense establishment would be civilians, including hundreds of thousands of women.[33] These preparations extended to civilians working for the army outside of metropolitan France. On November 23, 1934, the Ministry of War wrote to the Ministry of Foreign Affairs, which was administratively responsible for the League of Nations' mandate in Syria and Lebanon, asking for help preparing the region for a possible gas attack. The request specifically noted the need to equip two thousand civilians working inside army units in Syria and Lebanon with gas masks and to train them in their use.[34]

Ironically, the army's antigas training focused more on background and theory than it did on preparing civilians to survive an attack. The training program included a lecture devoted to the history and evolution of the use of chemicals and poisonous gasses in warfare; the lecture took chemical warfare back to the seventh century by describing the Byzantine's use of Greek fire during the first Arab siege of Constantinople (674–75) as an early example of chemical warfare. It simultaneously condemned the Germans for being masters of chemical warfare and claimed that the French had used chemical warfare long before the Germans had even thought of it by classifying the use of smoke to suffocate Vendeans hiding in caves during the French Revolution as chemical warfare. Another section discussed the value of gas shells as an area denial weapon. The program also covered international gas law, with a special emphasis on how Germany had violated prewar conventions by being the first to use gas in the Great War.[35]

After the academic part of the course was over, civil employees moved on to the practical section. Initially this section involved teaching the students how to properly remove their gas masks from their protective coverings without damaging them and how to fit them securely. After 1934 the army revamped its training program and required civilian employees to undergo a more intensive training program that included actually entering gas chambers for thirty minutes;[36] the army maintained these gas chambers throughout France to train its soldiers. The Parisian gas chamber, which was used by both soldiers and civilian employees, was located inside Les Invalides, which contained both Napoleon's tomb and the Army Museum.[37]

When the army began to implement the required program, it faced many obstacles, including the fact that many civilians did not take the program seriously and ignored the presentations. When some civilian workers resisted entering the gas chambers during pilot programs in the spring of 1934, the Directory of Personnel and Material Services pressed officers to compel their employees to attend and demanded that they forward lists of employees who skipped the training or did not pay attention during sessions. The directives emphasized that although some employees were afraid to enter the gas chambers, all employees needed to spend the full thirty minutes in the chamber to complete the training.[38] As part of preparing the antigas training the Ministry of War finally took a complete census of civilian employees in its central administration in August 1934 so that it could organize the sessions. The census, which was limited to just the Central Administration of the Ministry of War, revealed the gains women had consolidated over the previous twenty years. Of the office's 1,303 employees, 759 were women and 544 were men; this ratio of women to men was remarkable given that the original postwar plan called for the Central Administration to be the only office in the ministry to retain a substantial female staff, and the group was limited to just three hundred women.[39] The antigas program was understandably unpopular with civilian employees, but it remained in place until the German invasion of 1940. In April 1936 new guidance offered some concessions to civilian employees by specifying that an employee did not need to go through the program on a yearly basis.[40]

Antigas training acted as a marker of military identity: it proved the self-discipline of those who experienced it and provided a social marker that identified the army's civilian employees as part of the armed forces. Subjecting women working inside the army to gas chambers and other training marked them as capable of self-discipline in the face of danger and as being more valuable to the army than other civilians whose work related to the military but who did not get the training. Sending men and women into gas chambers was designed to reassure them that their equipment worked and to teach them to remain calm and composed during an attack; the experience was, essentially, an exercise in self-discipline, during which soldiers and civilians practiced and proved their ability to control their fear by remaining calm enough to stay in the gas chamber without removing their masks for the allotted time. Undergoing antigas training reinforced women's place in the military community by showing that they were both potential targets of enemy action and, in this particular case, certified to have met some of the same self-discipline standards as the soldiers they worked beside.

The decision to include only some civilians in the training program revealed who the military elite believed was a part of its institution. If military leaders had included all civilians whose jobs were essential to the armed forces' ability to defend the country, armaments workers and civilian contractors would have been included in the program, but they were not. Only civilian employees of the army were part of the training program, which showed that military leaders had accepted that their civilian employees were an integral part of their institutions and not outside support for it, as was the case with civilian contractors.

In June 1939, when the General Staff prepared new plans to protect itself and its officers in the Chateau Vincennes against a surprise attack by the Luftwaffe using gas bombs, it included a precise timetable indicating the order in which bureaus would receive gas masks from central stores. The plan made no distinctions among officers, enlisted personnel, and civilian workers. Instead of rank or military status defining the hierarchy, the importance of the office in which a person worked defined his or her place within the protection plan.[41]

Antigas training served an important practical function, but it also reinforced the idea that the civilians who underwent it were members of a military community that was different from the civilian world. It is unclear to what extent army leaders intended to send that message, but regardless of their intentions, sending their civilian employees into gas chambers clearly established that being part of the military community meant that civilian employees inhabited a different world from their neighbors who worked for private firms.

REVIVING THE LAW ON THE ORGANIZATION
OF THE NATION IN WARTIME

In 1934 the Doumergue cabinet had begun working to revive the Paul-Boncour Law at the same time it was working on the civilian reserve bill. The cabinet of Prime Minister Pierre Laval finally sent the bill to the Chamber of Deputies in June 1935, and the debate reflected political leaders' ambiguous feelings toward women's roles in wartime and the increasing divisions between military and political leaders. Although leaders assumed that the coming war with Germany would require the mass mobilization of women's labor, the chamber included women in the mobilization plan for the civilian economy only as civil defense volunteers. Politicians' refusal to include women in the mobilization plan was an act of willful blindness to the wartime needs of the French economy and armed forces.[42] Because of the effects of the 1933 altercations between Daladier and Weygand, the Conseil Supérieur de la Guerre had ceased to hold substantive meetings and senior generals were not consulted as a group in other forums; instead, ministers of war individually consulted with selected generals in order to claim that the generals supported his plan.

The proposal reflected the civil-military distrust of the 1930s by creating a divided wartime command structure. In wartime, the cabinet as a whole would direct the war, with the aid of the Conseil Supérieur de la Defense Nationale, even though it had not met since 1933 and would never actually meet again. Wartime policy would be directed by the Comité de Guerre, which included the premier, service ministers, and heads of the armed services whose orders would be carried out by army, navy, and air force commanders. Debate on the bill did not finish in time for it to be voted on before the April–May 1936 elections, so the process continued under the Popular Front, which made it even more difficult for military and civilian leaders to agree on a wartime command structure. Despite Marshal Pétain's efforts to obtain a unified command structure in peace and in war, the Popular Front was unwilling to risk giving a single officer— who would almost certainly have been an army general—that level of permanent legal authority.[43]

A watered-down version of the bill finally became law on July 11, 1938. The final text failed to solve the problem of mobilizing political leaders, did not create a national system to mobilize women's labor, and did not create a clear system to control the military war effort. During peacetime the government as a whole would be in charge of preparing for war, with the help of the morbid Conseil Supérieur de la Defense Nationale (it had not met in several years) and a new chief of staff for national defense. The Permanent Committee of National Defense (which included the army, navy, and air force chiefs of staff, but not the rest of the senior military leadership) would assist the government in narrowly defined military matters, though the division of responsibility was not specified. During wartime the government would exercise its authority over the conduct of the war through the Comité de Guerre, though the law never specified how much control it would have over military operations beyond setting broad strategic objectives. Ultimately this confused system for organizing national defense left France without a comprehensive plan for how to organize total war on the home front, its generals lacked a clear guide for how much authority they would have in wartime, and military and political leaders had few opportunities to jointly discuss preparations for war.[44]

POLITICAL POLARIZATION:
THE RISE OF THE POPULAR FRONT

The February 1934 Stavisky Riots did more than bring down the Daladier cabinet; they also shook the confidence of many French citizens in the strength and stability of the Third Republic. Many Communists, Radicals, and Socialists saw the riots as a fascist coup attempt that had come dangerously close to succeeding; fear brought the three groups together. Many Radicals and Socialists mistrusted the PCF but were united with it in their common fear that an Austrian-style, proclerical fascist regime could come to power in France, perhaps backed by Weygand and the army.

The Radical Party had been chased out of power by the riots, and many Radicals saw the paramilitary leagues, such as the Croix de Feu, as a danger to the regime. On July 27, 1934, the SFIO and the PCF agreed to ally against the danger of fascism in France under the banner of the Popular Front. Over the course of 1935 Herriot and Daladier agreed that the Radical Party should cooperate with the SFIO and the PCF in the 1936 elections. Radical leaders expected that as the largest leftist party they would lead any such alliance, which convinced many moderates whose distrust of the PCF was barely concealed to back the Popular Front. The parties ran separate candidates and remained fully independent organizations, but they agreed to endorse a common political program in the elections and to support each other in the second and decisive round of France's complicated two-round electoral system. As the effects of the Depression lingered through 1935 and into 1936, most observers began to expect that the Popular Front would win the April 1936 elections.

Before the Popular Front's election victory, Weygand's successor, General Maurice Gamelin, was able to get the term of service temporarily extended. Gamelin was much more conciliatory and deferential to political leaders than Weygand had been, and he was able to work with the center-right Laval and Sarraut cabinets to secure passage of a law to solve the problem of the so-called lean years (*années creuses*) caused by the Great War. During the war many fewer children had been conceived and born than normal, and by 1936 that would begin to affect the yearly conscript classes. General officers had long hoped the coming of the lean years would force the government to pass a new law to increase the term of conscript service, but politicians strongly resisted even a temporary increase in the term. In the early 1930s Daladier had suggested that the Ministry of War could use its discretionary powers to extend the term of service during the lean years and look for ways to shift conscripts from the years before and after into the lean years to even out the classes, but those plans had not come to fruition.

Although the idea of using administrative fiat had initially been attractive to politicians and many generals, by late 1935 many had concerns about it. With a Popular Front electoral victory looking increasingly likely, neither the generals nor the generally conservative politicians in the Laval and Sarraut cabinets were confident that the Popular Front could or would agree to increase the term of service, and they felt an administrative solution was too dangerous because the Popular Front could undo it with a single declaration. As a result, the Sarruat cabinet brought forward the Army Law of March 16, 1936, which modified the 1928 Army Law by extending the term of service for selected classes in order to cover the lean years. Conscripts who had been inducted in April 1935 were nearing the end of their term of service, but the legislation added another six months to their term. For all later classes—until and including the class that would be inducted in 1939—the term of service was lengthened from twelve months to twenty-four. After that it would revert back to twelve months. In effect, children born during the Great War would be forced to perform their own military service and that of the missing members of their cohort. This ensured that the army would not be shrinking as the threat from Hitler's Germany increased.[45]

The Laval cabinet had opened the debate on the two-year service law in the fall of 1935 and it proved controversial. On December 27, 1935, Minister of War Jean Fabry barely escaped being defeated in a preliminary debate by referring the bill back to the Army Committee.[46] Sarraut's cabinet was more successful, in part because the remilitarization of the Rhineland encouraged many wavering deputies to pass the bill as a symbol of French resolve. This was a major policy achievement by the Sarraut cabinet, which is rarely credited with an excess of foresight or ingenuity. By raising the term of service, even for only four years, Sarraut reversed a trend that had held since the end of the Great War: it was the first time the term of service had been raised since the 1913 law that, on the eve of the Great War, mandated three years of service. The 1936 Army Law's passage represented an early stage in transitioning the French Army to a war footing.

The 1920, 1923, 1927, and 1928 Army Laws had all included plans to boost the number of civilian employees, and thus women, working for the French Army, but the 1936 law did not, for two principle reasons: first, unlike the previous acts, the 1936 law increased the term of service and so there was no need to discuss how to compensate for the lost troops; second, the collapse of the organs of civil-military consultation meant that the law was not submitted to an extensive debate within the military hierarchy and did not have the chance to evolve into a broader reorganization of France's defense policy, as the 1927 and 1928 laws had. In the past, plans to hire more women had come from the generals, so it was not surprising that with the generals sidelined the 1936 Army Law did not mention women. But despite politicians leaving women out of the bill, military leaders soon found that they needed more personnel than conscription alone could provide and began hiring more women in order to further extend the army's labor pool and keep pace with Germany's military buildup.

WOMEN, THE ARMY, AND THE POPULAR FRONT

Despite the high command's deep mistrust of the Popular Front government, Blum's accession to power in June 1936 might have led to useful improvements in the plan to mobilize domestic labor in wartime. Blum had often spoken in public about the need to strengthen the home front, and his rhetorical support for Jaurès's popular militia implied that he recognized the importance of fighting the next war against Germany using all of the nation's resources. Unfortunately, the Popular Front's major home front initiative was the nationalization of several major arms makers. Despite the claims of the conservative press at the time, Blum's government expanded military funding and sought to strengthen France's alliances in the face of rising German power, but the government's domestic reform agenda crowded out significant changes in how national defense was organized on the home front.

Almost as soon as it took power, Blum's new cabinet targeted arms makers for nationalization. The measure was popular with the SFIO's political base because it responded to the widespread, if poorly supported, belief that World War I had been a result of armaments makers promoting a war spirit through politicized arms races. Nationalization thus weakened left-wing resistance to necessary increases in defense spending and made it much easier for the government to fund capital improvements to rapidly expand production, though little such funding was made available.

The nationalization of arms makers could have been the first step in a broader program of reorganizing the home front and preparing for domestic mobilization, but rather than embark on an ambitious program of preparing the war economy, the Popular Front merely continued work on the revived Paul-Boncour Law, which the previous conservative cabinets had been working on since 1935. It eventually passed, but the law did not give the government new powers to mobilize women for government service during the war and did nothing to create a coherent system to centrally organize or expand women's wartime roles within the French Army.

PREPARING CIVILIAN EMPLOYEES FOR WAR

As the diplomatic situation darkened in 1938, the Ministry of National Defense began preparing to deal with its civilian workforce during the expected war. The final Popular Front cabinet collapsed in April 1938, and in November 1938 Daladier's more conservative cabinet faced a call for a large public-sector strike on November 30. On November 28 Daladier, who was then both premier and minister of national defense and war, signed a notice instructing supervisors to warn military civilian employees that they did not have the right to strike and that any attempt to avoid doing their jobs would result in severe sanctions;[47] this sent a strong message toward deterring future strikes that could seek to pressure the government during a moment of international crisis. Daladier's cabinet was in the process of weakening many of the Popular Front's reforms, and he feared a combination of a working-class backlash and active pacifism among both the working and middle classes.

In the summer of 1939 the army tried to get all of its forces, including the women working for the army, ready for war: on June 7 the Ministry of National Defense and War issued orders for all civilian employees to undergo a new round of antigas training, and on June 14 the Infantry Directory ordered its subordinate units to make sure that the training happened regardless of potential civilian opposition, which included verbal objections and refusals to enter the gas chambers. It was to include theoretical instruction and, the report emphasized, actual exposure to gas in a gas chamber. By urging Daladier to approve these orders, Gamelin and his generals showed that they believed their civilian employees were likely targets for German gas attacks and that they were important enough to merit devoting scarce resources and time to training them. Significantly, the army did not pressure civilian businesses to follow suit—not even government-owned armaments firms whose factories and workforces were also obvious targets. The similarity between the General Staff's efforts to improve the training of combat units and civilian employees and its disregard for civilians working for defense contractors was striking; it showed that the senior military leaders viewed civilians who worked for them, including women, as part of their community in a way that other civilians who supported the military were not.[48]

ACCEPTED BUT NOT EQUAL

After the passage of the 1927 and 1928 Army Laws, women's positions within the army continued to evolve, but more slowly than they had in the 1920s. In retrospect, the momentum behind women's further integration into the army abated after the 1927 and 1928 Army Laws ended the drawn-out demobilization process and adapted the French Army to the changes caused by the Great War. The end of demobilization saw a further reexpansion of women's opportunities inside the army, followed by a consolidation of their previous gains, but after the transition to a peacetime organization new gains were harder to come by as senior commanders lost interest in expanding women's roles within the service. Women remained in place, continued to do their jobs, and slowly became so accepted within the structure of the army that their presence became increasingly unremarkable. There was some resistance to their slow progress, and there were occasional attempts to remasculinize the army's work environment, but by the early 1930s women were so firmly established as members of the military community that all but the most misogynist officers had to couch their criticisms in calls to increase the size of the army instead of as criticisms of women's loyalty, self-discipline, or skill.

Senior officers' failure to support legislation that would have allowed temporary auxiliary employees to be recognized as permanent revealed the limits of women's membership in the military community. Women remained lesser members of the military community who had to make special appeals to their leaders in order to win relatively small favors, but their inclusion in antigas training showed that officers recognized that they were on the military side of the civil-military dividing line. During this period women were rarely the center of attention, but issues of gender and women's roles in national defense continued to bubble to the surface in ways that often complicated civil-military decision making.

NOTES

1. "Étude," No. 378, November 29, 1929, Dossier 5, CSG, SHD DT 1 NN 5.
2. "Letter—Debeney to Pétain," No. 11738 1/11, Dossier 5, SHD DT 1 NN 5.
3. Rapports sur l'État d'esprit de l'Armée pour l'année 1928, No. 199, Dossier 6, SHD DT 1 NN 8.
4. Ibid.
5. Order February 5, 1929, Dossier 3, SHD DT 7 NN 153.
6. "12th Region," No. 1356 ER/1, Dossier 3, SHD DT 7 NN 153; "13th Region," No. 2000 CH.P, SHD DT 7 NN 153.
7. "JO, Chambre," March 4, 1927, Dossier 10, SHD DT 1 N 5, 489–93.
8. Eugenia Kiesling, *Arming against Hitler: France and the Limits of Military Planning* (Lawrence: Kansas University Press, 1996), 16.
9. Ibid, 21–23.
10. Ibid., 23–24.

11. "Proposition de loi tendant à la titularisation des agents auxiliaires des établissements et services de la guerre, en functions au 2 août 1914," No. 435, 1924, SHD DT 6 N 438.

12. "Proposition de loi tendant à accorder un minimum de garantie de salaire et de sécurité à tous les auxiliaires (ouvriers ou employés) des services publics et des établissements civils et militaires de l'État," No. 769, 1928, SHD DT 6 N 441.

13. "Proposition de loi relative a la permanisation des employés auxiliaires de l'état," No. 1828, 1929, SHD DT 6 N 441.

14. "Proposition de loi tendant à modifier le régime de salaries des employés auxiliaires, des ouvriers et ouvrières des Ministères de la Guerre, de l'Air, de la Marine, des Écoles nationales d'arts et métiers et des centre d'appareillage, des pensions, par la substitution du salaire national au salaire régional," No. 1027, 1936, SHD DT 6 N 441.

15. "Siégin," SHD DT 6 YG 238.

16. "Lépine," SHD DT 6 YG 238.

17. *Ere Nouvelle*, October 25, 1929, AN F 7 13192; *Le Matin*, October 25, 1929, AN F 7 13192; "1934 Nantes," October 26, 1934, AN F 7 13192.

18. Philip Bankwitz, *Maxime Weygand and Civil-Military Relations in Modern France* (Cambridge MA: Harvard University Press, 1967), 104.

19. "P.C.E.," No. 11.641, June 2, 1934, SHD DAT 6 N 368.

20. Ibid.

21. Ibid.; "Mansuelle," SHD DT 6 YG 266.

22. "Jacquet," SHD DT 6 YG 165.

23. "Maillard," SHD DT 6 YG 239.

24. Ibid.

25. "Note," No. 838, August 6, 1934, Dossier 1, SHD DT 2 N 206; "Note," No. 4319, November 10, 1934, Dossier 1, SHD DT 2 N 206.

26. Darrow, *French Women and the First World War*, 30, 41.

27. "Note relatif à changes du Senat," Dossier 2, B1, SHD DT 2 N 206.

28. Ibid.

29. Ministère de la Guerre, "Direction de Services du personnel et du matériel de l'administration central," No. 2.O/2-2, Dossier 1, SHD DT 9 NN 24; "Instructions 'Z' en 1936." May 18, 1936, Dossier 1, SHD DT 9 NN 24.

30. Instructions 'Z' en 1936"No. 2.O/2-2, Dossier 1, SHD DT 9 NN 22; André Meyer, "L'Organisation de la Protection contre les Attaques Aériennes, spécialement au point de vue chimique et industriel," CSDN/12, SHD DT 2 N 195 Dossier 1 "Instructions 'Z,'" May 2, 1934,, Dossier 1, SHD DT 9 NN 24.

31. "Projet de loi relatif à l'organisation de la défense passive," No. 350, June 14, 1934, Dossier 2, SHD DT 7 NN 90.

32. "La D.A.T. en Italie," December 18, 1934, Dossier 2, SHD DT 7 NN 90.

33. Estimate of France's gas mask needs, October 1, 1934, Dossier 2, SHD DT 7 NN 259.

34. "Ministère de la Guerre à Ministère des Affaires Etrangères," November 23, 1934, Dossier 2, SHD DT 7 NN 259.

35. "Instruction 'Z.'" The document refers to the Hague Convention of November 30, 1912, though it seems more likely that the author meant to refer to the 1907 Hague Convention.

36. "Ministre de Défense National et de la Guerre," No. 3140, June 7, 1936, Dossier 1, SHD DT 9 NN 22; "Direction de l'infanterie," No. 7638, June 17, 1939, Dossier 1, SHD DT

9 NN 24. Ministère de la Guerre, "Direction de Services du personnel et du matériel de l'administration central"; "Instructions 'Z' en 1936."

37. "Instruction," No. 1897-2, April 23, 1934, Dossier 2, SHD DT 9 NN 24; "Instructions 'Z'"; "Instructions 'Z' en 1936."

38. "Note," June 13, 1934, SHD DT 9 NN 192.

39. "Note," September 1, 1934, SHD DT 9 NN 192; Note, No. 5999.1, May 15, 1919, Dossier 2, SHD DT 7 N 159.

40. "Instruction," No. 1576, April 15, 1936, SHD DT 9 NN 192.

41. "Note," No. 6.244, June 5, 1939, Dossier 4, SHD DT 7 NN 263.

42. Kiesling, *Arming against Hitler*, 26–27.

43. Ibid., 27–33.

44. Ibid., 34–35.

45. "Extrait du Journal officiel du 16 Mars 1936," SHD DAT 7 N 2292.

46. Édouard Bonnefous, *Histoire politique de la troisième République*, vol. 5 (Paris: Press Universitaires de France, 1962), 360–61.

47. Note, No. 1080, November 28, 1938, SHD DM 1 BB8 2.

48. "Instruction," No. 3240, June 7, 1939, SHD DT 9 NN 22; "Instruction," No. 7638, June 14, 1939, SHD DT 9 NN 22.

5

"She Remained at Her Post until the Very End"
Women and the Second World War

The collapse of the Popular Front in the spring of 1938 marked a return to a familiar political pattern in interwar France. As was the case after the 1924 and 1932 elections, the left-of-center government that initially ran the country based on the election results gave way to a center-conservative cabinet after the Radical Party abandoned its alliance with the SFIO, and this time Édouard Daladier emerged as the new premier. Daladier had a close relationship with General Maurice Gamelin, that allowed the two men to prevent open conflicts between the cabinet and the armed forces by substituting their personal relationship for a broader process of institutional coordination.

Although the public was largely unaware of it, in the summer of 1939 the largest expansion of the military community since 1914 came about when the General Staff's war plans explicitly anticipated hiring tens of thousands of civilians, women and men alike, to help run the wartime army. This was a major change from 1914 and reflected the generals' recognition that they could not win the war against Germany without the large-scale participation of women. Initially the generals and politicians refused to allow women to join the French Army as soldiers, but in April 1940 President Albert Lebrun signed the decree formally opening the army to women, and for the first time ever women were allowed to serve legally and openly as recognized soldiers.

Ironically, women finally achieved formal membership in the army just weeks before the Third Republic collapsed in defeat and military betrayal.

Before the decree could be properly implemented, the German Army broke the French line near Sedan, beginning the military and political crises that saw the French Army defeated by the Germans and then the Third Republic overthrown in a move led by France's most senior military leaders. Through it all, though, women continued to serve their country by participating in the Resistance, serving in the Free French Forces, and working as civilian employees of the Free French and Vichy armies.

FIGHTING THE GERMANS AND FIGHTING NEED: CIVIL EMPLOYEES AND THE WAR

Despite Daladier's attempt to avoid war during the Munich Crisis of September–October 1938, after Adolf Hitler's annexation of the remainder of Czechoslovakia in March 1939 most French leaders expected another war. As Hitler's attention turned toward Poland in the summer of 1939, he offered Soviet dictator Joseph Stalin a deal to partition Poland between Germany and the Soviet Union. Despite the Soviet defection, the French and British reaffirmed their support for Poland. After Germany invaded Poland on September 1, 1939, France and Britain mobilized and declared war on Germany on September 3.

In accordance with prewar plans, French reservists had been called up in late August. Despite what many officers had feared since the 1920s, the process went smoothly: the German invasion of Poland meant that the army did not have to mobilize while defending the frontier against a German invasion, and there was very little unrest or opposition to mobilization. None of the major unions struck against mobilization, civilian workers loyally facilitated it, and the reservists obeyed mobilization orders and reported for duty. All the while, the cities—including the working-class neighborhoods—remained quiet.

At the beginning of the Second World War, the army's leaders reacted differently from their predecessors in 1914. In 1914, military leaders had tried to limit women's participation in the war effort, but in 1939 they responded to the declaration of war against Germany by hiring thousands of women to help staff the wartime army. When the army had finally accepted the need for women's labor during the First World War it had created a system of hiring preferences that favored groups whom officers viewed as especially trustworthy and worthy of preferment. French officers in 1939 responded in a similar way and created a new system of hiring preferences that favored disadvantaged French citizens with whom officers sympathized.

Even before the declaration of war itself, officers and civilian officials in the Ministry of National Defense, a superministry created by the Popular Front government to oversee the three service ministries, teamed up to study potential wartime hiring preferences. The study expressed skepticism that preferences for disabled veterans and war orphans would matter much because they already benefited from hiring preferences, and disabled veterans were also entitled to a quota of jobs in armaments factories, but plant managers reported that they struggled to find enough applicants to fill the quotas.[1]

The declaration of war brought a series of pleas for special treatment in hiring. The ministry responded by reminding officers that wartime hiring was subject to special conditions. Because the army assumed that most such positions would vanish at the end of the war, newly hired employees were to be classed as temporary employees and were thus ineligible for some of the benefits associated with peacetime employees or were eligible for them only at a reduced level. But the army also established clear rules to channel the benefits associated with an army job to those whom officers considered needy, deserving, and politically safe.[2]

In response to the requests to give veterans a hiring preference, the staff at the Ministry of National Defense discovered that the army already had a complex preference system, and apparently to the surprise of some of its administrators, the 1916 Regime was still being used by base commanders. In 1932 the Ministry of War had issued new guidance in the face of budget cuts; the instructions applied preferences that gave relative protection from being fired, but did not apply to hiring decisions. As a result, the regime remained the army's official hiring policy for temporary civilian employees when France entered the Second World War.[3] In this one way, at least, the French Army really was using the weapons of the First World War to fight the Second World War.

Staff officers at the Ministry of War quickly began to fine-tune their hiring policies. They never abolished the 1916 Regime but they did amend the twenty-three-year-old policy and passed it off as a new departure. The revised policy gave the highest preference to applicants designated as victims of the war and veterans of the Great War. Next came those wounded in the "present war" and the wives of mobilized soldiers who were in financial distress because of the mobilization.[4] The 1939 policy's new elements focused on differentiating among women: it gave the highest preference to "women without support," which included the "wives of mobilized men receiving neither benefits nor salaries, [and] refugees." Next came women acting has heads of families. This preference was weighted on a sliding scale that first favored women with the most children to support; then came evacuated women who did not fall into any of the higher categories. The policy's explicit goal was to help those women who had the fewest resources of their own.[5]

The army, navy, and air force agreed in principle to the hierarchy of preferences but disagreed about whether to impose age limits on jobs. During peacetime many civilian employee positions had age limits for job applicants; often they could not be older than fifty, although some jobs allowed employees to be as old as sixty-five. Enforcing maximum retirement and hiring ages could prove controversial, especially as the threat of war grew. Rose Lépine began working for the Infantry Directory on April 2, 1928, and reached the maximum age limit for her job when she turned sixty-five on April 7, 1937. Her supervisor called her "an auxiliary employee of great merit and robust health who it would be desirable to keep" and asked to retain her. The intervention won her three extra months, but then the ministry insisted that the age limit could not be further breached and she was forced to retire despite her desire to continue working and her supervisor's requests to retain her.[6]

In early 1939 the military was already preparing for the war its leaders considered to be inevitable, and some managers wanted to wave age limits for civilian employees, but there was a split between the different service branches over what to do. The army favored increasing the age limit during the war on the grounds that mobilization was likely to severely reduce the number of younger applicants. Naval officers, however, objected that raising the age limit could transform its support services into "old age homes." The navy eventually agreed that workers between the ages of fifty and fifty-five could be individually screened to determine if they were vigorous enough to be allowed special waivers to take positions, but rejected raising the age limit as a general policy. Daladier, as minister of national defense and war, sided with the army and decided that all services should have the same hiring policies by increasing the maximum hiring age for women to fifty-five.[7]

The paucity of available sources makes it hard to directly access women's views about their positions within the army, but some were willing to protest against the deprivations of the war and to demand the government, often through the army, do something to help them. On October 13, 1939, women calling themselves simply "a group of French mothers" wrote to Daladier asking him to accord them a hiring privilege. The letter explained that the mobilization had disrupted their household economies. Many had seen their husbands called up, and claimed that their husbands' military pay did not cover their families' household expenses; others pointed out that the mobilization had depressed the civilian economy and their husbands, who had not been mobilized, could not find work in their regions. One woman explained that her husband had been wounded in the Great War and was unemployed because his job disappeared when the owners of the firm he worked for were called up and the business was suspended.[8]

Their stories focused on mobilization-related suffering and asked for compassion in a language that was very different from the way officers had spoken about women and their needs during and after the Great War. Major Jean-Baptiste Lesieur had justified the widow Hélias's request for special treatment in 1923 by referencing her husband's wartime sacrifice and her loyal service, but the Group of French Mothers presented their appeal using the language of social justice to demand that Daladier rectify what they saw as the unfair effects of the mobilization. They highlighted the difficulties of feeding and caring for children on the meager salaries their husbands were drawing. One women explained that the 160 francs per month she received was not enough to pay for housing and food for herself and her two children; she told Daladier that she had stopped buying meat and heating her home, but when her son asked for a sweater she could not afford to give him one. She finished by asking Daladier, "What do you want me to do with 160 francs?"[9]

Another woman, whose husband had a civilian job, objected to the hours he was required to work and the pay he received by combining the language of inequality with invocations of her husband's prior military service. She informed the premier that her husband had been wounded in the Great War and that they had one child still living with them. Her husband worked in an airplane factory, but he was only paid eight or nine francs per hour, which was less than his peacetime wage, and would be required to work sixty hours. She claimed that the reduced pay rate meant that he was only being paid for the equivalent of forty-five prewar hours. She went on to say that it was unfair to make veterans of the Great War suffer again during this new war, especially when their sons had now replaced them on the front line.[10]

This language, reminiscent as it was of that of the Popular Front, may have been a calculated attack on Daladier. In addition to highlighting the suffering that he was allowing, the letter personalized the situation, asserting that "we cannot believe that you have abandoned the worker to this point." The statement was a brutal indictment of Daladier, who had championed the Radical Party joining the Popular Front before abandoning it in 1938 to form his own government in alliance with the Right.[11]

Most letters were less confrontational, but in the fall of 1939 military and public officials were bombarded with requests for help finding employment and demands that they create a system of hiring preferences. Many of the letter writers were asking for preferences that already existed, making it unclear if some officers were misapplying or ignoring the official policy, as had often happened during the First World War. It was also possible that applicants were assuming that they did not receive a preference because they did not get the jobs they applied for or that they were writing to politicians to help them find a job despite never having applied for a position with the military. Regardless of the reasons, most women concentrated on demonstrating their acute need for help while deploying their husbands and sons' military service as a secondary factor that added to their moral case. These competing, but not necessarily clashing, justifications reflected different ideas about the origins of the government's obligations to alleviate suffering. Civilian workers appealed to general economic suffering while many officers believed they owed more to families of fallen veterans.

The letters were rarely addressed to officers, but instead were forwarded to the army by the politicians who received them—particularly senators, who were less likely to be of military age than deputies. For those French men and women whose deputy had been mobilized, their senators were their most important remaining elected representatives. Most letter writers complained that the subsidies they received from the government were not enough to meet their expenses; they also asked for help in finding a government position, and several asked for policy changes ranging from hiring preferences to extra pay for the wives of servicemen or veterans and mothers of large families.[12]

Over the winter of 1939–40 military and political leaders made a number of changes to hiring policies aimed at ameliorating some of the discontent and better differentiating among applicants. The result was the creation of different sets of hiring preferences for different classes of employees as well as gender-differentiated preferences. In January 1940 the Ministry of National Defense released its consolidated hiring policies. The hiring policy still bore the mark of the 1916 Regime, but showed the signs of bureaucratization. It divided civilian employees of the military into male workers, female workers, and "employed personnel" who were not segregated by gender.[13]

Men applying to be workers would receive the greatest preference if they were the sons of civilian employees who had been killed or totally disabled. A lesser preference went to war orphans, and then to sons of mobilized fathers who were bereft of financial support because of their fathers' mobilization. Next in line were demobilized men and veterans of previous conflicts, and after them came men supporting families who had lost their jobs because they were evacuated from the frontier. Then came the rest of the male population on France.[14]

The preference list for women was similar, but not identical. It began with the daughters and wives of killed or incapacitated workers, and then added widows and war orphans. Although it was possible that there would be widowers whose wives had been killed while working on a military base, there was no preference category for those men. After widows and orphans, the government added a new category: women who were certified victims of war under the June 1919 law. Then came women facing deprivation because their breadwinner had been mobilized, followed by women who were evacuated from the frontiers. The smallest preference went to women "without support" or resources for other reasons. Then came the remaining female population of France.[15]

Although the ministry had split applicants according to their sex, it did not do so with applicants to the usually lower-paid positions who were grouped together in the new category of employed personnel. It mirrored the previous list by giving the biggest preference to the wives, sons, and daughters of workers or employees killed or permanently disabled in the line of duty. The second preference went to war widows and female and male war orphans. Notably, the policy specifically mentioned both female and male orphans (*orphelines et orphelins de guerre*) instead of relying on the masculine form's ability to cover both men and women. A fourth-level preference went to veterans and mobilized men who had been demobilized, and after them came applicants who had lost their support because of the mobilization. A sixth preference went to needy evacuees, and the lowest preference went to women without a breadwinner who had exhausted their own resources. A note at the end of the list gave women priority over men within each category.[16] All three policies retained the 1916 Regime's focus on family members of fallen veterans, but the 1940 policy expanded the regime to include family members of civilian employees, except for husbands, on equal terms with soldiers. By equating civilian employees killed in the line of duty with fallen soldiers, the 1940 policy acknowledged civilian employees' membership in the military community, and because officers thus accepted civilian employees as being part of the army, they recognized their families as deserving of military solidarity. There was, however, a limit to this: whereas the widows of soldiers and male civilian employees could claim a preference by virtue of their husbands' service, widowers of female civilian employees were not entitled to any such preference. This reflected the military's sense that the preference system existed, at least in part, to protect vulnerable women and children who had lost their male guardian in defense of the country; the preferences were an extension of military men's patriarchal sense of honor, which included a duty to protect vulnerable women and children.

Madeleine Cadet was one woman who benefited from the preference system. Born in February 1916 in wartime Paris, she applied for an army job in April 1940. Cadet demonstrated that even the "phony war" could be fatal because her husband, a mobilized soldier, had been killed in January 1940. Her husband's death made the twenty-four-year-old Cadet eligible for a high level of preference, and she was almost immediately offered a position. Cadet remained in her job during the battle for France and left military employment in July 1942.[17]

The new policy required hiring officers and civilian administrators to maintain lists of applicants for positions (effectively, waiting lists) and to rank applicants according to the preference lists. In some ways it was similar to the hiring reforms General Mardochée Georges Valabrègue had suggest in November 1916. Officers were then required to fill vacancies based on the applicant's order in the hiring list. Unqualified candidates could be ignored, but the new lists were supposed to prove that the government was being fair in the way the army hired employees. The process was bureaucratic and took no account the army's experience in the Great War, when in 1917 the army had found that, far from needing to rank applicants, it was happy to have enough applicants to fill its positions. Presumably, if the French Army had withstood the German assault in May and June 1940, such a situation would have recurred, but France in 1939 was still suffering from the effects of the Great Depression, which had been exacerbated by the financial panic of the Popular Front period. As a result, there was still a lot of unemployment in the French economy at the moment of mobilization, and this could explain the difficulties women and men were still having in finding work in the fall of 1939.

This policy was, however, a fundamentally different system of hiring than that used in World War I. During the Great War, the politicians had almost no role in deciding how the army hired civilians or who they would be; the army had taken the lead in creating a preference system that was refined by the generals who usually headed the Ministry of War—that is, until Georges Clemenceau, who scarcely cared about hiring policy, took over in November 1917. Rather than centralizing and bureaucratizing the process, during the Great War hiring had been left to local commanders who were told to use a preference system but otherwise hired women and men based on their own sense of what they needed and who would do the job best. During the Second World War, however, women civilian employees were no longer seen as a temporary emergency measure but as regular parts of the army's basic structure; as a result, the central administration asserted increased control over how officers hired them.

The gender-segregated hiring system was a compromise. Ministers had been bombarded with complaints from women seeking hiring preferences, and that was reflected in women receiving an expanded hiring preference over men. But the ministers also showed their hostility to the idea of women benefiting from the war by employing gender segregation for the more lucrative positions in order to set aside the best jobs for men. The divided preferences system meant that officers were told to keep separate hiring lists for men and women; that effectively barred women from even applying for many of the best positions because they would be assigned to the male worker list instead of the female worker list. This tactic was imposed by Daladier's civilian staff at the ministry, and it departed from the army's previous practice of benign neglect regarding gender in wartime hiring matters. It was indeed ironic that in early 1940 the generals—who as a group were about to play a crucial role in creating the deeply reactionary Vichy Regime—were the ones being pushed into a regressive gender policy by republican politicians who wanted to ensure that women did not make gains at the expense of male voters.

By April 1940, complaints about insufficient pay had led civilians in the Ministry of National Defense to issue a strident defense of paying women less than men. As the ministry noted, "The nature of their work and their inferior performance justify a lower hourly salary for women than men, [and] that is why all the salary tables for women are lower than the tables for men." The report admitted that in the past some officers and managers had paid women the same salary as men doing the same job and had objected to paying women who replaced mobilized men less than the men had been paid. The Ministry of National Defense accepted that sometimes it was permissible to pay women the same wage as men, but only "in the very rare case where the product of a woman's labor is strictly equivalent to that of a man." In that "very rare case," it was permissible for "the woman's salary to be equivalent to that of the man who she replaced." This strict standard required officers to show that women performed their jobs as well in terms of quantity and quality of product as the men who had done those jobs before the war. Although theoretically it created the possibility of equal pay for equal work, the standard implicitly warned any officers thinking of paying women and men equally that they would be expected to prove that their decision was justified by a strict but amorphous standard that was contained in a report that explicitly justified paying women lower wages.[18] Although such officers were presumably a small minority, the fact that the ministry felt compelled to promulgate a regulation to stop them suggests that the practice was common enough to concern civilian leaders.

On May 10, 1940, as German troops were launching their feint into Belgium and creeping through the Ardennes toward Sedan, the Ministry of National Defense was reporting on consultations with the three service branches on whether or not to raise the wages of women doing what was deemed to be abnormally hard work. The ministry reported that some officers had asked to be allowed to provide extra pay for women who were doing work that was more physically demanding than had been the norm in peacetime. All three services rejected the proposal, with the army's representatives arguing that there was no need to establish special pay bonuses for women and that their salaries were high enough already. Air force officers were openly dismissive, arguing that "the Air Ministry finds it neither opportune nor logical" to boost women's pay, despite the clear gender disparity in compensation. The entire exercise was, of course, about to be rendered pointless by the impending military disaster, but in the meantime the services continued to struggle with the best way to integrate women into the wartime structure.[19]

WOMEN AS SOLDIERS

Between September 1939 and June 1940, 6,600 women volunteered for service as drivers and military nurses, but they were not recognized as soldiers.[20] In addition, the rapid expansion of civilian employees led to thousands of women taking paid positions inside the French Army but, unlike during World War I, the French government eventually decided to allow women to officially serve in the military. The Decree of January 31, 1940, which was clarified by the Order of February 16, 1940, set out rules for quasi-militarized positions for women that would be treated differently from those reserved for civilian employees. The rules applied to women serving in the Infirmières Pilotes et Secouristes de l'Air (IPSA)and Sections Sanitaires Automobiles Féminines (SSAF). Women serving in these two medical services were allowed to wear a khaki uniform but forbidden to have rank or other insignia. They served as volunteers and did not draw military pay, though the Red Cross, the organization for which they were officially working, could pay them. This partial step toward mobilizing women as soldiers echoed the special status that some female military drivers received during the First World War, and thus was not a significant departure from previous precedents, but a more important change was in the works.[21]

In April 1940, after more than twenty-five years of integrating women into the military as civilian employees, French military and political leaders finally agreed to create a women's auxiliary corps within the French Army. The Decree of April 21, 1940 set the stage for women's participation in the Free French Forces and in the French Army after World War II. The decree laid down basic rules for "female auxiliaries of military formations," and under these new rules women could enlist for one year at a time, would be allowed to hold military rank, and would be paid according to their service.[22] Opening the armed forces to women represented a major advance for French women's rights: it demolished the claim that women should not have the right to vote because they were incapable of exercising the responsibility of defending the country. Another decree, on May 21, 1940, further expanded women's roles in the medical services even as the front lines collapsed.[23] Due to the German invasion, however, it proved impossible to fully implement either of these decrees.

THE DEFEAT

On May 10, 1940, German land and air forces began the invasion of Belgium, France, Luxembourg, and the Netherlands. General Gamelin responded by ordering his French and British units to execute the Breda variant of the Dyle Plan in order to meet the German attack outside of France and thus come to the rescue of the Belgians and the Dutch. Unfortunately for the French, their generals' plans played right into the hands of the German strategy.[24] While French troops surged north into Belgium to take up position along the Dyle and reached north to linkup with the Dutch at Breda, German panzer divisions broke the French line at Sedan in the middle of the Western Front. By May 20, German armored forces had reached the English Channel at Abbeville, cutting off the main body of the French Army as well as the British and Belgian forces. In the midst of the collapse Paul Reynaud, who had replaced Daladier as premier in March, fired Gamelin and recalled General Maxime Weygand, who had been serving as supreme commander in the Middle East. By the time Weygand returned to the high command it was already too late to save the military situation, but he arrived just in time to participate in the French Army's final collapse and betrayal of the Third Republic.

When the Germans defeated the French Army in its bloody last stand along the Weygand Line in front of Paris, the government and the army abandoned the capital. In 1914 the fleeing government had left General Joseph Galieni in charge of Paris with orders to hold it to the last man, but in 1940 the cabinet declared Paris an open city. As the army and the government were preparing to leave the capital, the Ministry of War ordered the army to fire any civilian employee whose job would not continue during the retreat. As a result, thousands of people—including a large proportion of women—were fired on June 1, 1940, as part of a defeat purge. There were many reasons for the purge, including cost, transportation logistics, and a desire to protect civilian employees.

The defeat disrupted many military services and meant that the regular administration collapsed. As a result, there was no need to pay people to do the daily work of record keeping in Paris when there would soon be no army left. In addition, if employees were to continue doing their jobs, they would have to be evacuated before Paris fell, which would have further strained France's overburdened transportation system. Finally, given the concern that the Germans would treat civilians working for the army as combatants, officers may have been trying to protect civilians who were about to fall into German hands from reprisals by severing their official connection to the army.

One of the victims of the defeat purge was Raymonde Juliette Siger, who had been born in St. Loup de la Salle on December 24, 1906 and hired by the army in 1929 as part of the implementation of the 1927 and 1928 Army Laws. The defeat of the army created by those laws cost Siger her job in June 1940. She had mainly worked for the Directory of Artillery, but had recently transferred to the Directory of Colonial Troops. Unfortunately for her, the 1940 firings did not follow the guidelines Marshal Philippe Pétain had laid down for the 1934 contraction of forces. As the mother of four children, three of whom were born while she was a civilian employee, she would almost certainly have been deemed worthy or needy enough to keep her job, but in June 1940, firings were often arbitrary and employees had no ability to appeal the decisions.[25]

Not all of the women working for the army lost their jobs during the retreat. Women who were attached to mobile posts and unit staffs often stayed with their units, though this left them separated from their homes and families at the end of campaigns. During the battle of the Weygand Line, Clémence Robin, a single woman and the daughter of a retired civilian military engineer who had worked for forty years at the École Centrale de Pyrotechnie in Bourge, was working for the Directory of Colonial Troops and retreated with her headquarters unit to the south of France. Her unit managed to stay ahead of the Germans and avoided capture, and after the armistice she found herself stranded in the south, far from her home in Paris. After she was laid off she had to lobby the army for a train pass so she could get back to her home in occupied Paris. Robin's experience reflected the physical, political, and administrative chaos created by the military defeat of 1940. Returning home required getting permission from the government to take a train that would pass through German lines as well as procuring the fee for a ticket or a train pass.[26]

Robin was far from the only women who continued serving the French Army during the chaotic retreat. On May 28, 1940, General Weygand transferred Andrée Parreux from her position in Paris to General Julien Dufieux's command staff. The forty-year-old Parreux had worked for the army since March 1917, and she was handpicked by Weygand to copy a set of extremely secret files that he had entrusted to Dufieux's care on May 25, 1940. Soon after Parreux's transfer, however, Weygand was forced to order the evacuation of Paris. Although she was a civilian who lived in Paris and had the right to quit her job at any time, Parreux stayed with Dufieux's headquarters as it retreated west into the Loire Valley and then south toward Vichy in an attempt to keep one step ahead of the advancing Germans. She kept retreating, toward La Courtine military camp, and finally she ended up in Montauban after the armistice. On July 8, 1940, Dufieux commended Parreux for protecting the files he and Weygand had entrusted to her and for completing the process of copying them despite the long retreat and extremely rough conditions under which she had worked.[27]

Parreux's loyalty to the army and dedication to her job was in stark contrast to the army's treatment of her. When she reached Montauban in early July and reestablished contact with the chain of command, she asked what she should do with her cache of secret files. To her great surprise, she found that not only were her superiors unaware that she had the files but they had fired her more than a month before as part of the June 1 purge because they assumed she was still in Paris. General Dufieux intervened on her behalf, praising her in a letter for her "courage and good humor" during the "disagreeable" retreat. He singled her out for having volunteered to retreat with her unit instead of taking the safer option of remaining behind in Paris and described her in military terms, saying she "remained at her post until the very end" and executed every command he gave her while rendering the "most valuable services during the forty days she spent with my headquarters." Dufieux's intervention caused her firing to be redefined as temporary leave, allowing her to continue working for the army in a new capacity and at the same salary and seniority she had had before the fall of Paris. It did, however, mean that officially the army was erasing her brave and self-sacrificing decision to stay at her post throughout the defeat and to risk her life by remaining with her unit even though it could have come under attack by German ground or air forces. Instead of being officially recognized for loyally serving her country in its darkest hour, her experience was legally redefined as a personal decision to flee Paris.[28]

Other women also volunteered to help the war effort and persisted in their efforts to help defend their country even after defeat had become inevitable. Some of these women, such as thirty-one-year-old Andrée Leonard, had to fight against the government's rules in her attempt to volunteer. Leonard, a lifelong resident or Paris, had been a civilian employee of the army since 1931 and was working for the General Staff in May 1940. When her office was ordered to retreat to the Loire Valley, she wrote a letter to her superiors asking for permission to be transferred to an office that was staying behind in Paris because she had been trained as an *infirmière Z*, a nurse who treated victims of poison gas. She explained that she had volunteered for the SSAF, an ambulance service working with Marshal Louis Franchet-d'Esprey's Comité des Amitiés Africaines to help France's African troops; The SSAF was itself part of the Catholic Associations des Dames de France and thus part of the Red Cross. Leonard told her superiors that she expected be called up by the group at any moment, and she wanted to remain in Paris so that when the call came she would be able take her place behind the collapsing front.[29]

Her military superiors initially granted her request, but on June 1, 1940, she was told by the Central Administration of the Ministry of War that she could not have her transfer because as a civilian employee she was already providing an essential contribution to the war effort and that she was thus forbidden by ministry regulations from joining any organization that could interfere with her duties as a civilian employee of the army. She was then instructed to report to her old job immediately. Ironically, that same day she was officially fired by the army as part of the June 1 purge.[30]

In the midst of the defeat, the Ministry of National Defense implemented emergency measures to try and salvage what it could of France's defense capacity. On June 17, 1940, a decree authorized the enlistment of women as auxiliary pilots. They were not supposed to be sent into combat, but they were authorized to fly transport planes and to shuttle planes away from advancing German forces. Women who enrolled as pilots would be commissioned and paid as officers and would be able to volunteer for the duration of the conflict. This emergency measure was soon made obsolete by the impending armistice; when it took effect, only four women had been integrated into the military as servicewomen. Those four—Maryse Bastié, Paulerre Bray-Bouquest, Maryse Hilsz, and Claire Roman—were pilots and IPSA volunteers who joined the French Air Force.[31]

With the Germans taking more territory every day and the French Army collapsing, Reynaud had to impose his will or resign. With the cabinet bitterly divided and the high command united behind Weygand and Pétain's call for an armistice, Reynaud concluded that he could not win and resigned on June 16 in favor of Marshal Pétain, who quickly formed a government and immediately asked the Germans for their terms.

Although Hitler's terms were harsher than Pétain had hoped, he had come to power as a result of a conspiracy to sign an armistice; he thus had little choice but to accept Hitler's demands. The armistice of June 22, 1940, left two-thirds of France under German occupation, capped the size of the French Army in Europe at just under 100,000 troops, and imposed a large reparations bill as well as occupation costs on the French. The armistice allowed the French government to continue and part of its army to survive, and for the moment the army, through Pétain, was in control of that government. But the end of the military crisis would eventually lead to reassertion of civilian power when Pétain tried to govern and needed the cooperation of the legislature. Pétain acted quickly to consolidate his position by summoning the Chamber of Deputies and the Senate to debate a plan to revise France's constitutional laws by granting him powers to rewrite them by decree.

When the legislature met in July 1940 in Vichy to debate revision, it was a distorted version of the body that had been elected in 1936. The Popular Front had long since dissolved, and the PCF deputies had been expelled after the Hitler-Stalin Pact. In addition, many of the antiarmistice leaders in the parliament, including Daladier, Georges Mandel, and twenty-five other deputies and senators, had sailed for North Africa on the *Massilia* and were not present to oppose Pétain. A handful of remaining parliamentary leaders, including Socialist leader Léon Blum, opposed the granting of full powers to Pétain, but the combination of the army's obvious support for Pétain, his overwhelming popularity, and the shock of the German conquest made it a hopeless task: it was likely that even if the legislators had voted against Pétain he would have used his military support to simply impose his new regime by force.

Pétain proceeded to declare himself chief of the *État français*, making it clear that the Third Republic was coming to an end. Initially Pétain had strong popular support, but that waned with time, especially after the November 1942 German occupation of the unoccupied zone in southern France. Pétain's new state made the resort city of Vichy its provisional capital; it began to implement the armistice and tried to reform the French government and society around the motto *"Travail, famille, patrie"* (work, family, country). His patriarchal and racist policies fit into the interwar army's concept of military identity, and like the interwar officers he led,

Pétain defined Frenchness through the lens of workplace skill and hard work, patriarchal family familial relationships, and unquestioning patriotism, which he defined in opposition to Marxism.

The army's military defeat and political victory left it in an ambiguous position: as a combat institution its prestige was shattered and its size and power severely limited, but its conquest of the government meant that its senior officers assumed broad political powers. Counting Pétain himself, five of the sixteen members of the cabinet were serving military officers. Pétain's government sought to impose its unstable mix of traditionalism, conservatism, and fascism on the French state, but the revolution largely left the French Army alone. Not surprisingly, the antisemitic laws drove Jews out of the army, but otherwise it was allowed to largely govern itself. The military retained control over its own justice system, and the civilians in the government steered clear of imposing reforms on the marshal's army.

WOMEN IN PÉTAIN'S ARMY

The Vichy Regime has been rightly condemned for its regressive gender policies, and its leaders abandoned the women's auxiliary forces, but it made no attempt to purge civilian women from the French Army. The armistice limited the army to roughly 100,000 men in the unoccupied zone of metropolitan France, but it also allowed a colonial force of some 120,000 men, most of whom were in North Africa. Given the strict limits on the number of soldiers who could be stationed in France, the elimination of the women's corps seemed to be an obvious step, especially given that it had yet to be formed, but the restricted size of Vichy's army encouraged an increased reliance of civilian employees, which meant that women remained an important part of the Vichy Regime's national defense establishment.

Despite having conducted mass firings in the June purge, the army responded to the limits imposed by the armistice by hiring women as civilian employees beginning in July 1940. Thus, despite Pétain's rhetorical commitment to a patriarchal concept of family that defined women as dependent wives and mothers, his regime's army kept hiring women; this included women who had only recently begun working for the army, like Geneviève Bailley, who took a job with in September 1939 and continued her service under the Vichy Regime, as well as women like Louise Bouland, who had worked for the army on and off since February 1917.[32]

The armistice created the need for the military to open new offices to deal with the consequences of defeat at a time when it was shrinking and many civilian men were missing from the labor force. This led the army to hire additional women. The armistice left 1,800,000 French soldiers in German captivity, and their families were desperate for information about them. To deal with public demand for information about and contact with prisoners, the army created the National Center for Information on Prisoners of War (it's French acronym was CNIPG) in the summer of 1940, and it soon became a sprawling bureaucracy with a large workforce. Because it was a new organization, the CNIPG had to hire a lot of people almost immediately, and although the managers were men, many of the caseworkers and staff were women.

In August 1940 Christiane de Belloy de Saint-Lienard applied for a job and was hired by the CNIPG as a temporary auxiliary employee. According to a background check conducted in 1942, de Belloy de Saint-Lienard, who was sixty-three when she was hired, had never held a paid job before in her life. Since 1927 she had lived in an apartment on Rue de Monceau in Paris; her ability to pay the apartment's monthly rent of 2,500 francs suggested that her prewar income was substantial. Her file does not make it clear if she went to work for the CNIPG because her income had dried up as a result of the war and occupation or if she felt moved to help the families of France's prisoners of war, but both motives commonly drew women to apply for military jobs during the occupation.[33]

In the spring of 1942 the CNIPG informed Christiane de Belloy de Saint-Lienard that she would be fired when she reached the mandatory retirement age of sixty-five on March 25, 1942. She asked for permission to keep working, and mobilized her family connections to help her. Her cousin, a colonel and an army doctor who held an important administrative post in Paris, intervened on her behalf and wrote to her administrator asking him to reconsider. The administrator responded apologetically, but explained that Article 2 of the decree of September 9, 1927, set the maximum retirement age and that he lacked the ability to change it. It is interesting to note that the letter was dated the day after her firing was official, and a background check was completed the following month, but she was not rehired despite passing it.[34] Not every women working for the CNIPG stayed as long as de Belloy de Saint-Lienard, who had a seventeen-month tenure. On August 28, 1940, Jeanne Lotte began working for the organization but quit on December 15, 1940.[35] Simone Levesque, a forty-two-year-old divorcée who had been working as a buyer, took a job as a secretary with the CNIPG on August 9, 1940, because her previous employer had shut down operations, but she quit on October 15, 1940.[36]

Because the Vichy Regime's officers continued to see it as their job to protect veterans' families from suffering, they tried to respond positively to appeals from war widows and the wives or female children of disabled veterans. In August 1940, eighteen-year-old Yvonne Lucie wrote to the director of the Civilian Personnel Office at the Ministry of War and asked that he find her a job because of her family's need. She emphasized that her father was a veteran of the Great War who could no longer work because of an injury and that her mother's employment was restricted by the need to care for Yvonne's baby sister Alice, who was just nineteen months old. Yvonne explained that she had been working in a civilian business but it had closed as a result of the war; she was asking for a job so that she could help support her parents and her sister. Despite a glut of applications, her particular appeal was successful and she was offered a secretarial position.[37]

There were, however, some major changes in how hiring worked. The Vichy Regime's contested legitimacy and its leaders' hatred of communists and Jews was reflected in how it hired civilian employees. For example, when Suzanne Alexeline applied for a position as a secretary in 1941, she underwent an intensive background check. Military and police investigators looked into her political opinions and social connections to make sure that she was not a communist, Gaullist, or Jew.[38] Similarly, in January 1942 Marie Bardou had to certify that she was not a Jew, communist, or Freemason before she could begin her job; specifically, she had to swear that she did not have three or more Jewish grandparents and that she did not have two or more while being married to a Jew.[39]

Government positions were sought after because women viewed them as relatively stable and because they sometimes came with special benefits.

In addition to a hopefully reliable salary, a civilian employee could also get special food and housing privileges. When Andrée Brun took a position with the Automobile Transport Service of the Ministry of War's Central Administration on December 1, 1942, she received a fairly modest salary of 1,500 francs per month, but she also received a rent-free room in the Hôtel des Bains.[40] For Brun, the apartment might have been nearly as valuable as her salary was in economic terms, and unlike her salary the apartment was immune from the effects of wartime inflation.

Like many other women, though, Brun found that her government job was much less stable than it would have been before the war. The Vichy government's chronically bad finances meant that it was forced to repeatedly order mass firings in an effort to control government expenses. Brun was caught up in one such wave of reductions when she was fired on March 1, 1943 as part of a general plan to cut costs by shrinking the government's workforce. She was not alone: in the fall of 1940 there had been a large wave of cuts as the army tried to deal with its new, much smaller military force, and there had been periodic staff cuts throughout the war.[41]

Even after the defeat, women tried and sometimes succeeded in furthering their careers by pressuring administrators to help them get jobs and improve the terms of their employment. Madeleine Benoit had begun working as a civilian employee in 1929, but was fired during the June 1940 purge. She wrote several letters to military administrators asking for her job back and arguing that her firing had been technically flawed due to alleged procedural errors, such as her dismissal having been certified by her bureau head but not the central administration (as was normal in peacetime). She also pleaded her eleven years of faithful service as evidence for her skill and her loyalty to the French Army. After several entreaties, in October 1940 she accepted a position as a lower-paid secretarial worker for the Army General Staff's intelligence division, the Second Bureau, but she continued to lobby for her old job back.[42]

Benoit's experience also shows the limits of women's abilities to negotiate with and pressure the military. After accepting the new job, she kept trying to get promoted back to her previous position. On May 16, 1941, Benoit wrote to the director of the Civilian Personnel Office at the Ministry of War, explaining that she was overqualified for her job but had accepted it because she was desperate for money to support herself and her daughters; now, however, she feared that it was preventing her from being reconsidered for the higher-level secretarial job she used to have. She explained that before taking her first job with the army, she had spent an even longer period working for other parts of the government and that she had been fired just three years before being eligible for her full retirement benefits. She then quoted from one of Marshal Pétain's own speeches about protecting the rights of workers against capricious employers: "As Marshal Pétain has publically said: 'I don't want an employer to be able to tell his employee: I hired you because I needed you, but I do not care what happens to you if I no longer need you.'" But despite her best efforts, Benoit was not able to secure a better position.[43]

During the war, civilian employees experienced the same general political and moral pressures as did the rest of the army and the French population. Like the uniformed men they worked beside, the women's loyalty to Marshal Pétain's regime varied widely from person to person and changed over time. Their political views shaped their experiences, but the single greatest variable was geography. Women who worked for military units and bases in metropolitan France could not easily join the Free French Forces, but they had the option of secretly supporting the resistance. Although the present study has not uncovered archival evidence of women civilian employees who were part of the Resistance, it is likely that some women used their positions to aid it by passing along information or obstructing efforts to hunt down resisters—especially in the later years of the war, when support for Pétain's regime flagged.

AN ALTERNATE PATH:
WOMEN AND THE FREE FRENCH

French women were not immune to the political cleavage the June 1940 armistice caused. Because Pétain's government retained control of most of the military and all administrative offices in France, almost all of the army's prearmistice female employees were, initially, part of the Vichy Regime. Yet women were also among the early recruits to Charles de Gaulle's Free French Forces. When de Gaulle fled to London to carry on the fight against Hitler and Germany, he called for French soldiers and civilians to rally behind him. But as he began amassing troops, de Gaulle soon found that there were some women who wanted to volunteer for military service. The April 1940 decree opening the military to women had not yet been translated into a functioning force when France fell, but it had established women's legal right to serve in the military. While the Vichy Regime had abrogated the decree, de Gaulle embraced the path it laid out.

In the summer and fall of 1940 some women joined the relatively small number of men who responded to de Gaulle's call to join him in Britain. At first this tiny movement had no plans to militarize women, though there were indeed women who were willing to join the Free French Forces. During the defeat Jeanne Bohec reached Britain by boat and was determined to carry on the fight for France's freedom from British soil. Bohec had been a student at the University of Angers, and had taken leave from the school to work at a chemical plant during the war. When she arrived at Carlton Gardens, de Gaulle's headquarters, an engineering officer told her she could work in a factory they were planning on organizing in the future. Bohec eventually succeeded in joining de Gaulle's army in January 1941, though she would later be reassigned and parachuted into occupied France to act as a liaison between the Free French and the Resistance.[44]

On November 4, 1940 de Gaulle created the *Corps des volontaires française* (CVF), the Free French Forces' women's corps, which initially comprised twenty-six women and was under the command of former tennis star Lieutenant Simone Mathieu; by October 1941 the CVF had 126 members, including Hélène Terré and Jeanne Bohec. De Gaulle's decree required potential women soldiers to be between eighteen and forty years old and to be French citizens by birth or marriage; it also forced women to undergo a medical examination to prove they were fit for service. They were required to wear the army's uniform and were subject to military law and discipline. Members of the CVF were recognized as soldiers in the Free French Forces, but their exact branch of service was not always specified because the CVF eventually included army, navy, and air force sections within the overall organization. In January 1942 the CVF underwent an

important change when it was reorganized to include all-female companies that would be commanded by women. Other French women continued to serve de Gaulle's movement as civilian employees.[45]

Hélène Terré was one of the first women to join the Free French Forces
as a soldier. In August 1939 Terré was thirty-six years old and already an
experienced and successful publisher. Days before the war she volunteered
for the SSAF, a military ambulance service organized by the Red Cross,
and was charged with producing recruiting materials. She stayed with her
unit during the defeat and was temporarily retained by the army at the end
of the war. From July to September 1940 she worked with the General
Staff's Second Bureau (Intelligence and Counterintelligence) before
being arrested by the British in London while officially on a Red Cross–
sponsored trip to Bristol. After being released from detention she signed
on as a civilian employee of de Gaulle's fledgling Free French movement.
In October 1941 she accepted a commission as a captain in the Free French
Forces and replaced Simone Mathieu as commander of the CVF.[46]

Terré's career was exceptional not only because of her relatively senior
position but also because she worked in all three of the main capacities
open to women wishing to support the military during this period. She
began as a Red Cross volunteer in the SSAF which allowed her to work
inside the French Army in a uniformed and quasi-military capacity, but
she remained legally a civilian and an employee of the Red Cross, not the
French Army. She then served the Vichy Regime in an ambiguous capacity, but probably as a civilian auxiliary employee before defecting to de
Gaulle's movement. She began her service to the Free French cause as
a civilian secretary in the main recruiting office in Britain. Until October 1941 her career at least superficially resembled that of a woman in the
First World War, but that month she received an officer's commission and
thus joined the uniformed service. Although her records do not explicitly
indicate it, her prewar managerial experience, her service during the Battle
of France, and even her intelligence work for Vichy probably combined to
convince Free French leaders to tap her to replace Mathieu as the leader
of the main women's military formation. To that extent her individual
career could be seen as an allegory for French women's military experiences during the world wars.[47]

By the time of the Anglo-American invasion of French North Africa in November 1942, the Free French Forces' women's corps had grown to roughly four hundred women serving in all three services.[48]Most of these women were French, but some foreign women were also allowed to serve. Despite being a British citizen, Susan Travers was one of the earlier Free French recruits. Having spent most of her life in France, she volunteered for services as an ambulance driver soon after Daladier had declared war on Germany. In her memoirs she explained that she volunteered to be a driver and a nurse for the French Army—rather than the British—because "[i]t had been eighteen years since I'd lived in England; more than half of my life had been spent in France. I suppose I felt more French that anything."[49] In March 1940 Travers left with a small force to aid the Finns against the Russians and ended up trapped in Sweden when Paris fell. She later recalled that "my fellow nurses and I listened on a crackling wireless to the emotional and powerful broadcast by General de Gaulle" and that she had "felt affronted" at the idea that "Nazi troops were marching in the Champs-Elysée." After returning to Britain in July 1940 she went to London, volunteering to join the Free French Forces in mid-August.[50]

After a cursory medical examination, Travers was accepted as a sergeant in the Free French Forces more than two months before the CVF was established. She was desperate to get out of nursing, but did not transfer to office work as some other women did because "I couldn't type—I'd never used a typewriter in my life." While serving in Sudan and Eritrea with the 13th Demi-Brigade of the Foreign Legion she became a military driver. Travers followed her unit through the Ethiopian campaign and then into the Syrian and North African campaigns. In the process she became General Marie-Pierre Konig's driver and then his lover.

When General Konig's brigade held Bir Hakim against Erwin Rommel's German and Italian troops during the battle of Gazala, from May 26 to June 11, 1942, the brigade had women, including Travers, serving in it. Before the battle she sometimes accompanied reconnaissance columns that probed into the desert and behind German and Italian lines. Although women were officially assigned to noncombat roles, the reality was that everybody was in combat, and during the battle Travers was issued a rifle and ammunition. The realities of field service meant that being assigned to a noncombat role did not always keep women out of combat, especially when enemy aircraft attacked their units. "The Stukas were the worst," Travers would later write. "I could hear them several miles away, like a vast swarm of bees droning in the distance, heading directly for us across the endless desert sky. At first sight they looked like a plague of silver locusts hovering above us, with nothing to prevent them from swooping down and picking at out beached bones."[51] Before the Germans finished encircling Bir Hakim, the British ordered the women evacuated, but Travers succeeded in returning to the camp and stayed with the brigade throughout the siege. During General Konig's daring nighttime breakout to rejoin the retreating British Eighth Army, Travers participated by personally driving him through German and Italian lines while their car was raked by machine gun and artillery fire. She was later awarded the Croix de Guerre for her bravery.[52]

BETWEEN VICHY AND DE GAULLE

Women in North Africa had a different experience than either the women who rallied to the Free French in London or worked for the army in France. When Vichy's army stabilized after the armistice, the Armée d'Afrique became its most important component. Because the Germans wanted to keep France's empire out of British hands, the 100,000-man limit the victorious Germans imposed on the French Army only applied to French troops in Europe; as such, the Armée d'Afrique was able to survive in North Africa. When Admiral François Darlan ordered the commander of French land forces in North Africa, General Alphonse Juin, to defect to the Allies after the Anglo-American invasion of Morocco and Algeria in November 1942, Juin and his men joined US General Dwight D. Eisenhower's battle against German and Italian forces in Tunisia. Just as the men who served in North Africa found that they were reentering the war, so too did the women who were working for the army. In addition to the civilian employees who rejoined the war with the Armée d'Afrique, other French women volunteered for military service and were accepted by the non-Gaullist French military administration of North Africa.[53]

On 20 November 1942 Colonel Lucien Merlin created the Corps Féminin des Transmissions (CFT). The corps eventually grew to over two thousand
women, and they soon became known as the Merlinettes. The Merlinettes
served with field headquarters units, but most worked in rear-area offices
managing telephone, telegraph, and radio transmissions. Although some
Merlinettes were able to serve at the front, most performed the same tasks
that army had assigned to civilian women during the First World War. But
the women of the CFT were better integrated into the army. Initially Merlin had to deal with political and legal obstacles while organizing his new
unit; the first volunteers served under the political authority of Admiral
Darlan; after Darlan's assassination on December 24, 1942, they served
under General Henri Giraud, and legally they were part of an institutional
continuity with Vichy's army and not de Gaulle's Free French Forces. As
such, the Vichy Regime's decision to abrogate the decrees opening the
military to women hampered Merlin's efforts. In December 1942, just before his death, Darlan allowed reforms that let women function as if they
were soldiers within his portion of the French Army, but legally they remained civilians in uniform. It was not until June 1943 that the women of
the CFT were recognized as having a "military character." Any lingering
questions about whether they were truly soldiers under French law were
finally eliminated when they merged into the Auxiliaires Féminines
de l'Armée de Terre (AFAT, sometimes known as the Arme Féminine de
l'Armée de Terre) in 1944 and became part of General Charles de Gaulle's
Free French Forces; these forces were created from a variety of different
organizations whose personnel had served under a host of varying
conditions.[54]

The French Army's reunification occurred in phases, culminating
in the liberation of continental France in 1944. Each time another French
territory joined de Gaulle's forces, either through defection or liberation,
new military and civilian personnel had to be melded into the Free French
Forces. That process usually involved the newly rallied forces adopting
Free French organization and training, but it also involved the Free French
accepting some of the Vichy Regime's innovations. Although de Gaulle
claimed that the Vichy Regime was illegal and illegitimate and that its acts
were thus null and void, in practice many Vichy-era regulations and even

laws governing the military and its administration survived the liberation of France, including pension and accounting reforms that regulated civilian employees' retirement system. As a result, in 1948, when Marie Basset—a civilian employee of the army since January 1917—retired, her benefits were set according to rules that Pétain's government had brought in 1943 to regularize how different classes of employees received pension benefits.[55]

As part of the process of uniting the different military groups, de Gaulle moved to combine the various women's military organizations into a single force under his control. By early 1944 he had at least 3,100 uniformed women serving under various organizations under his command. On April 26, 1944, he merged the different women's organizations into the Auxiliaires Féminines de l'Armée de Terre (AFAT), including the 430 women of the old CVF.

By the time of the Normandy landing in June 1944, the AFAT had grown to 4,000 women, and another 1,300 were serving in the Formation Féminine de l'Air which was created on July 3, 1944. In the wake of the liberation of France, the number of women in de Gaulle's forces swelled again as thousands of resisters and others joined. In January 1945 Hélène Terré, who been arrested by the British in 1940 as a potential Vichy spy and then begun her Free French Forces career as a civilian secretary, was promoted to commander of the AFAT; by September of that year the AFAT alone numbered fourteen thousand women. Some of its members continued to serve after the war, and Terré herself briefly served on a mission to Indochina in September–November 1946 before leaving the army in 1947.[56]

Integrating women into the French Army's history provides important insights into the political and military history of France during World War II. Postwar French leaders spent decades claiming that the Vichy Regime was an illegal aberration and that the postwar state had no relationship to Pétain's regime. The military history of the Free French movement was always in conflict with this claim because it was obvious to anybody who cared to look that elements of the Vichy Regime had merged into de Gaulle's movement over the course of the war. The defection of military units in Central and North Africa clearly added to de Gaulle's military strength, and some of his best commanders served in Pétain's army at some point during the conflict. The Gaullist myth survived despite this uncomfortable truth, and de Gaulle himself strongly denied that his post-liberation government was built on Vichy's foundation.

Adding women to the story provides compelling evidence that the Vichy Regime—far from being the legal dead end the Gaullists claimed, strongly influenced the post–World War II French Army. Both Vichy's army and the Free French Forces were firmly rooted in the Third Republic's army and politics; during the war they diverged, but the liberation of France fused them back together instead of representing the destruction of Vichy's military at the hands of the victorious Gaullists.

Just as many of the French Army's soldiers who landed in France were veterans of Vichy forces, so the postliberation army's administration was a fusion of Free French leaders and staff who had served the Vichy Regime. The Gaullists stripped out overtly antisemitic laws and rules, but the army administration continued many of the rules and practices that had begun or been modified during the Vichy period. Military leaders implicitly recognized this reality by giving their employees seniority and retirement credit for the time they spent working for the Vichy military. Women's experience illustrates the reality that, far from being destroyed, the influence, personnel, and some of the laws of the Vichy Regime survived inside the postwar French state.

THE LIBERATION

The success of Allied armies in liberating France put General de Gaulle in a powerful political position: the war and many prewar leaders' collaboration with the Vichy Regime had effectively swept away the power structure of the Third Republic. Although the Vichy Regime was theoretically the continuation of the Third Republic, its antidemocratic structure violated the 1875 Wallon Amendment, arguably making the legislature's granting of full powers to Pétain in July 1940 illegal. The legal situation was murky, and de Gaulle's own claim to democratic legitimacy was tenuous, at best, but during the war he emerged as the recognized ruler of France. One of his most important responsibilities as president of the provisional government was to place the regime on a democratic path by holding elections.

De Gaulle took advantage of his unique position to issue a decree on April 21, 1944, that laid out who would have the right to vote in the upcoming elections. He could not use the Vichy Regime's antisemitic voting laws, but neither could he simply revert to voting laws that had been in force in June 1940. Instead de Gaulle cut through decades of political deadlock and extended voting rights to French women and soldiers at the stroke of a pen. The first article of the ordinance specified that the new assembly would be "elected by a single stage secret ballot by all adult Frenchmen and women [*tous les français et françaises*]." Article 17 further specified that women were "electors and eligible candidates under the same conditions as men."[57] The ordinance did not mention active-duty soldiers, but because there was no clause denying soldiers the right to vote, Article 1 effectively extended the right to vote to servicemen for the first time since 1872. When the electoral rolls were drawn up, the provisional government included men and women serving in the French Army. Women and soldiers thus received the right to vote from the same words in the decree, but did so without the democratic political process that crowned the success of suffrage movements in most of the rest of the Western world. The enfranchisement of women and soldiers removed voting rights as a significant contributor to military identity and paved the way for a true army of citizens to emerge within most of the French Army, excluding the still substantial Foreign Legion and colonial units.

The decision to enfranchise active-duty soldiers and women was conditioned by the experience of the occupation and the need to re-create a democratic government in the middle of the war. Many local elected leaders had been discredited by their actions during the occupation, and new elections were needed to begin rebuilding both the local and national governments. By 1944 France stood out as one of the last Western states to deny women the right to vote. That fact, combined with women's contribution to the Liberation as part of the Resistance and in the Free French Forces, made it necessary for de Gaulle to endorse women's suffrage.

De Gaulle's decision to grant military suffrage was also conditioned by the political realities of newly liberated France. Until the Liberation, the majority of de Gaulle's forces were colonial and foreign troops, but after it the Free French Forces ballooned to some 1.3 million men and women. The vast majority of those troops were neither well trained nor well armed, and most were never intended to be used in combat. De Gaulle and his generals knew that a large proportion of the men and women flocking to the military were enlisting because the economy was in ruins and the military guaranteed food, housing, and a basic salary. De Gaulle had reason to believe that the troops were likely to support candidates favorable to him if he let them vote. Indeed, membership in the army became a benefit doled out as part of Gaullist political patronage; thus, the new army contained a large number of Gaullist supporters. Disenfranchising his strongest supporters would have undermined de Gaulle's ability to retain control of the provisional government.

In particular, adding women and soldiers to the electorate weakened the communist vote. The PCF's strong support for the Resistance—at least after June 22, 1941, when Hitler's invasion of the Soviet Union ended the party's passive acceptance of Pétain's government—meant that its support base grew dramatically during the war. Moderate and conservative leaders believed that women were less likely to support the PCF than were men and that enfranchising women would reduce the Communist share of the electorate. Studies of the postwar electorate bear this out, showing that women gave the largest share of their votes to the Christian democratic Mouvement Républicain Populaire (MRP).[58] By allowing the army to vote as well, de Gaulle further diluted the PCF's share of the electorate.

De Gaulle's decision to expand voting rights to cover soldiers and women meant that he was using groups the Third Republic had disenfranchised for being a threat to democracy to defend the republican political system against the danger of the antidemocratic Communist Party. In some important ways de Gaulle's decision was faithful to the logic of officers in the interwar army, including that of his former mentor, Marshal Pétain, who had used women to help insulate the army against potentially dangerous forces in the civilian world. Whereas in 1927 officers' fear of working-class men had led them to defend military disenfranchisement while expanding women's roles within the army, in 1944 it led de Gaulle, an interwar military intellectual, to call women and soldiers into electoral politics to help insulate the republic—and by extension, the army—from left-wing political groups. The fact that enfranchising the military neither politicized the barracks nor militarized politics emphasizes the fact that decades of civil-military relations had been based on fundamentally flawed assumptions.

The influx of women into the army after the liberation of France consolidated the expansion of women's roles in France's military, but it did not put an end to their service as civilian employees. It did, however, create challenges for de Gaulle's new government; in particular, it was necessary to decide what to do with the people who had worked for the Vichy Regime. High-profile leaders like Philippe Pétain and Pierre Laval faced prosecution for their actions, but the new government had to deal with tens of thousands of everyday French citizens who had worked for Pétain.

De Gaulle's new administration did not attempt a wholesale purge of civilian employees who worked for Pétain, and often Gaullist forces rolled wartime Vichy regulations into their own rules. This meant that a woman like Marie Basset, who had been a civilian employee of the French Army since January 1917 and remained at her post under the Vichy Regime, was able to seamlessly integrate as a civilian employee in de Gaulle's army; in fact, she was even able to count her service to Vichy toward her pension eligibility when she retired in 1948.[59]

After the Allies liberated France many women applied for jobs working for either the Ministry of War or one of the branches of the armed forces, and a significant number of these women had previously worked for the military. Some of the women who had been fired in the June 1, 1940, purge took advantage of the change in regime to request their old jobs back. Although not all applicants were successful, fifty-six-year-old Marie Barre did succeed. She applied soon after Paris was liberated, but had to go through a background check to certify that she had never worked for the Milice. Working for the Vichy government was considered acceptable, but former Milice members were specifically defined as collaborators and banned from military employment.[60] The new government initially accepted most requests from former civilian employees to return to work, but after 1944 it became increasingly hard. When Emilie Bense applied to return to work in 1947, her application was rejected on the grounds that she had waited too long to apply despite the fact that she had served the army continuously from April 1916 to January 1941.[61]

The liberation of France also led to changes in women's work experiences. The first such change was that de Gaulle's government, which was financially supported by the United States, granted its former Vichy employees a substantial raise. Gabrielle Bassier had worked for the French Army since 1928, and after the liberation her pay rose from 2,300 francs per month to 3,300. The pay increases reflected the continuing effects on inflation in France on the eve of the liberation and the greater financial strength of the new provisional government.[62]

Women also experienced changes in how they were managed. Before the war a decentralized system of management and employment meant that women typically stayed with one unit or office for years, and because they were rarely transferred unless they lobbied for a change, they had a lot of control over whether they were reassigned. After the liberation, employee management was centralized and women found they were now more tightly controlled by administrators who routinely moved them between assignments; they sometimes had three or more assignments in the same year. As a result, women lost their close links to individual units. Marguerite Baudion's experience illustrates the change. Baudion began working for the army in 1917, when she was only sixteen years old, and she served continuously until 1948. She had spent the entirety of the 1920s working for the same office, but she was transferred three times in 1945.[63]

Marie Basset's experiences show that although women were moved more frequently after the liberation, their jobs did not necessarily become less secure. Basset began working for the army in January 1917, just two months after her sixteenth birthday, and she continued until after the Second World War. Starting in 1941, her previously positive performance reviews turned increasingly negative. Her 1941, 1942, and 1943 reviews warned that she was making too many mistakes in her work and that her attitude was hostile. In 1943 she received a written reprimand for absenteeism but was not dismissed; she was still there when the Allied armies liberated France, and she transitioned to working for de Gaulle's government. The change of regimes did not improve her performance, and in 1945 her supervisor tried to fire her by claiming that his workload was down and so he did not need her and that her poor performance over a period of years meant that she should be fired instead of transferred. Despite his pleas, she was given a new posting and kept working until 1948, when she qualified for a full pension because of more than thirty years of continuous service.[64]

WOMEN AND THE POSTWAR FRENCH ARMY

The liberation also changed women civilian employees' military identity by bringing thousands of uniformed women into the French Army. These female soldiers were able to more fully embody a female military identity than women civilian employees had been because they were now legally soldiers and thus stood fully on the military side of the civil-military divide. Even so, women remained legally different from men in the world of the French Army: they were, at least officially, forbidden to enter combat and, unlike men, they were all volunteers. Because the Fourth and Fifth Republics maintained conscription, the postwar French Army was mainly composed of conscripted men, but all of the women who served with them were volunteers. It would not be until 2001, when the last all-male conscripts mustered out of the French Army and it became an all-volunteer force, that women and men would joined the army in the same way. However, even after the end of conscription, women and men continued to serve under somewhat different conditions because men could not choose whether or not to serve in combat roles and women were prevented from serving in some roles.

The Second World War precipitated a fundamental legal change in French women's national defense roles, but that change was conditioned by the contributions women had made over the previous twenty-five years. By granting women opportunities to serve in the military so soon after the beginning of the war, French leaders broke with the precedent they had set in World War I when they had refused to enroll women in the military. By 1918, the inability of French women to volunteer for military service was in stark contrast to American, British, and Russian women's legal right to enlist in their countries' militaries. The slow expansion of women's roles within the army in the 1920s meant that women were positioned to take on more responsibilities in World War II. In 1918, French women had had fewer opportunities to contribute to national defense than American or British women, but by May 1940 they had legally caught up to their British counterparts. And they actually surpassed American women's gains, because new US laws in the 1920s had restricted their ability to volunteer for military service.

French women experienced significant advances in their political rights and ability to serve in the armed forces during the Second World War. Because of decisions taken by politicians and officers before June 1940, as well as both Gaullist and non-Gaullist leaders later on, women emerged from the war with the right to vote and the ability to defend that right as soldiers of France. These military gains began under the Third Republic, but really came to fruition later in the war, when military leaders were free to innovate without being restrained by politicians. Faced with a greater freedom to expand women's roles and a critical shortage of soldiers, Gaullist and non-Gaullist officers fighting to liberate France actively recruited women into their forces. Together with the extension of suffrage rights to women and soldiers, these changes were a direct result of the logic of total war before June 1940 and, later, the collapse of the Third Republic, which gave de Gaulle the ability to cut through decades of delays and grant women and soldiers new rights at the stroke of a pen.

NOTES

1. Note, No. 3621, July 21, 1939, Dossier 6, SHD DT 6 N 317.

2. "Note au sujet de l'âge limite d'embauchage des ouvrières dans les Etablissements de l'Etat relevant des Ministères de Défense Nationale," December 18, 1939, Dossier 1, SHD DT 6 N 317.

3. "Note Pour le Secrétariat Général," No. 1661 SA-PR, October 10, 1939, Dossier 1, SHD DAT 6 N 317.

4. "Projet de circulaire relative au recrutement de la main-d'oeuvre pendant le durée de la guerre," No. 1932, November 10, 1939, Dossier 1, SHD DAT 6 N 317.

5. "Note Pour le Secrétariat Général."

6. "Lépine," SHD DAT 6 YG 238.

7. "Note Pour le Secrétariat Général."

8. "Letter from 'Union des victimes de guerre et anciens combattants titulaires et auxiliaires dans les administrations et établissements d'état," No. 2105-CM, October 23, 1929, Dossier 2, SHD DAT 6 N 317.

9. Ibid.

10. Ibid.

11. Ibid.

12. Letter, October 7, 1939, Dossier 2, SHD DAT 6 N 317.

13. "Note sur le recrutement," No. 2431 SA-PR, January 17, 1940, Dossier 1, SHD DAT 6 N 317.

14. Ibid.

15. Ibid.

16. Ibid.

17. "Cadet," SHD DT 6 YG 275.

18. "NOTE au sujet la rémunération du travail féminin," No. 2801 SA-PR, April 2, 1940, Dossier 2, SHD DT 6 N 317.

19. "Rémunération du travail féminine dans les Etablissements de l'Etat relevant des Ministères de Défense Nationale," No. 2942 SA-PR, May 10, 1940, SHD DT 6 N 317.

20. Carol Mann, *Femmes dans la Guerre, 1914–1945* (Paris: Pygmalion, 2010), 207.

21. Luc Capdevila, "La mobilisation des femmes dans la France combattante 1940–1945," *Clio: Femmes, Genre, Histoire* 12 (2000), https://clio.revues.org/187.

22. Ibid.

23. Jean-François Dominé, *Les femmes au combat: L'armé feminine de la France pendant la Seconde Guerre Mondiale* (Paris: Service historique de la Défense, 2008), 26.

24. General Gamelin's strategy sought to take advantage of the Maginot Line to ensure that the French Army would meet the Germans inside of Belgian territory. The Dyle Plan involved rapidly responding to the expected German invasion of Belgium by moving troops to the Dyle River in central Belgium. The Breda variant committed the most mobile units of Gamelin's reserves to extend his line to the north by occupying Breda in the Netherlands in an attempt to save the Dutch if Germany invaded the Netherlands too.

25. "Siger," SHD DT 6 YG 238.

26. "Robin," SHD DT 6 YG 239.

27. "Parreaux," SHD DT 6 YG 266.

28. Ibid.

29. "Leonard," SHD DT 5 YG 238.

30. Ibid.

31. Capdevila, "La mobilisation des femmes," 4; Dominé, *Les femmes au combat*, 25.

32. "Bailley," SHD DT 6 YG 267; "Bouland," SHD DAT 6 YG 353.

33. "de Belloy," SHD DT 6 YG 269.

34. Ibid.

35. "Lotte," SHD DT 6 YG 238.

36. "Levesque," SHD DT 6 YG 238.

37. "Lucie," SHD DT 6 YG 239.

38. "Alexeline," SHD DT 6 YG 251.

39. "Bardou," SHD DT 6 YG 268.

40. "Brun," SHD DT 6 YG 275.

41. Ibid; "Auchon," SHD DT 6 YG 267.

42. "Benoit," SHD DT 6 YG 190.

43. Ibid.

44. Jeanne Bohec, *La plastiqueuse à bicyclette* (Paris: Éditions du Félin, 1999), 31–32.

45. Dominé, *Les femmes au combat*, 31–32.

46. "Terré," SHD DT 16 P 173684; Dominé, *Les femmes au combat*, 56.

47. "Terré," SHD DT 16 P 173684; Dominé, *Les femmes au combat*, 56.

48. Capdevila, "La mobilisation des femmes," 5.

49. Susan Travers and Wendy Holden, *Tomorrow to Be Brave: A Memoir of the Only Woman Ever to Serve in the French Foreign Legion* (New York: Touchstone, 2007), 36–37.

50. Ibid., 44–45.

51. Ibid., 3.

52. Ibid., 128–90.

53. Luc Capdevila, François Rouquet, Fabrice Virgili, and Danièle Voldman, *Hommes et Femmes dans la France en Guerre (1914–1915)* (Paris: Payot, 2003), 89–91.

54. Ibid.; Dominé, *Les femmes au combat*, 45–46.

55. "Basset," SHD DAT 6 YG 347.

56. Capdevila, "La mobilisation des femmes," 5; "Terré," SHD DT 16 P 173684; Dominé, *Les femmes au combat*, 56.

57. "Ordonnance du 21 avril 1944 relative à l'organisation des pouvoirs publics en France après la Libération," http://mjp.univ-perp.fr/france/co1944-2.htm.

58. Maurice Larkin, *France since the Popular Front: Government and People, 1936–1996*, 2nd ed. (New York: Oxford University Press, 1997), 169.

59. "Basset," SHD DT 6 YG 347.

60. Ibid.

61. "Bense," SHD DT 6 YG 160.

62. "Bassier," SHD DT 6 YG 286.

63. "Baudoin," SHD DT 6 YG 347.

64. "Basset."

Conclusion

No form of identity is ever static, and military identity was constantly changing in France between 1914 and 1940. Before the Great War the French military was deep into a long-term process of conceptually, and to a large degree physically, removing women from the military community. That process was linked to the imposition of an increasingly uniform universal male military service that steadily increased the army's available manpower but also reflected the gendered ideology of citizenship in the Third Republic. This exclusion of women can be seen in the phasing out of the *cantinières* (women sutlers): they were not eliminated in a single dramatic purge, but instead political and military leaders slowly choked off the possibility of women entering the profession and made it increasingly hard for existing *cantinières* to make a profit. By 1914 there were only a handful of women still surviving as *cantinières* within the hypermasculinized French Army.

The First World War reversed the progressive elimination of women from the army and changed the path French military identity was taking. Though it did not lead to a resurgence of *cantinières*, the war triggered a flood of women into military service. At peak strength, the number of women working as civilian employees inside the French Army exceeded 200,000 and might have been as high as 300,000. At first officers convinced themselves that these women were just another wartime expedient and that at the end of the war, things would return to prewar norms, but those hopes proved misplaced.

Instead of victory bringing a return to the prewar status quo, as most officers had assumed, demobilization after the war reflected an underappreciated effect of total war: the army had become dependent on civilian women's labor to function on a day-to-day basis. Historians have long recognized that total war militarizes civil society, but the present study shows that it also civilianizes the military. Despite military leaders' efforts to purge them from the postwar French Army, women proved too useful. The war had changed French politics by reducing the threat from Germany and making conscription more politically unpopular. The steady reduction in the term of conscript service, and thus the number of conscripts in the army at any one time, made civilian staff increasingly vital to the army as an institution, and this ensured that women remained part of the military community. It took civilian and military leaders years to come to grips with the political, social, economic, and military changes the war had caused, and it was not until 1927 that they finally came to an agreement on how to adapt the army to the realities of postwar France.

A number of policies and concerns helped women to integrate into the peacetime army. One of the most important was an affirmative action program for war widows and orphans. Because wartime hiring regulations gave a preference to the family members of soldiers who were killed in action, many civilian employees were the widows or children of fallen soldiers. Many officers viewed employing these women as a social duty because it protected the family members of fallen comrades-in-arms from potential suffering. The significance of this blood tie faded over time, but in the early 1920s it was an important part of facilitating officers' acceptance of women's membership in the military community.

External political factors also influenced this transition and the evolution of women's place within the military. The rise of communism in 1920s, combined with efforts by the French Communist Party to infiltrate the French Army, increased officers' doubts about the loyalty and self-discipline of their conscripts and male civilian workers. Because officers' trust in and respect for groups within the army was relative, their increasing doubt made officers see women as more natural members of the military community than had been the case in the past.

Ironically, political leaders' refusal to grant women the right to vote also helped facilitate women's acceptance as civilian professionals inside the army. Because officers viewed the prospect of conscripts gaining the right to vote as a threat to order and discipline, women's disenfranchisement became another factor marking them as acceptable members of the military community. During and immediately after the First World War, military leaders did not worry much about voting rights, but after enfranchising soldiers became a significant political issue during the 1924–26 Cartel cabinets, it became another factor helping officers accept and trust women. Notably, this happened despite the continuing women's suffrage movement.

The experience of women in the French Army during the 1920s defies the predictions of Margaret Higonnet and Patrice Higonnet's double helix model.[1] Instead of the postwar backlash erasing women's gains, the 1920s saw both the consolidation of some of women's wartime gains and the reversal of the prewar trend of excluding women. The 1927 and 1928 Army Laws legally consolidated women's place in the military and showed that the First World War had led to both a permanent expansion of their opportunities and a change in the gendered construction of military identity and privilege in the French Army. There were, of course, clear limits to this redefinition: women remained civilians, and thus inferior in terms of power and prestige to male military leaders; their opportunities to rise to even junior leadership positions were extremely limited, and many women remained trapped in long-term, but officially temporary, positions that paid less than legally permanent positions.

This transition ultimately paid important dividends during the Second World War. When the war began, the army immediately called on tens of thousands of civilian women to fill out its rear-area services. The legal opening of the military to women as servicewomen in April 1940 marked an important milestone in both French military history and women's rights in France. The German conquest of France in 1940 prevented the Third Republic from raising its women's units, but it helped facilitate women's wartime service in Charles de Gaulle's Free French Forces. Obviously de Gaulle's desperate need for soldiers of any gender or race helped explain his decision to recruit women, and some scholars have credited memories of women's contributions during World War I to explain the decisions of both de Gaulle and the Reynaud cabinet. But they have overlooked the critical role played by women and officers in creating a viable military identity for women during the interwar era.

WOMEN, THE ARMY, AND FRENCH POLITICS

Using women's history to study the politics and culture of the French Army yields important insights. By tracing the evolution of women's places within the army, it is possible to trace changes in how the army's senior officers understood their institution and its relationship to the civilian world. During and immediately after the First World War, France's generals were split between those who accepted the need to bring civilian women into the military community in order to defend France and those who saw women as inherently alien to the military community because they represented the undisciplined civilian world; even so, the generals with the greatest overall responsibility for the war effort were most likely to support bringing women into the army as civilian employees. Women's progressive integration into the military community reveals not only how much the construction of military identity was changing in reaction to officers' growing mistrust of conscripts and working-class men but also the degree to which officers continued to fear the civilian political world.

Officers' fear of the civilian world was reflected in Controller General Piquet's 1919 report to Georges Clemenceau; the report excoriated women's indiscipline and implied that women not only corrupted the military community through their own inefficiency but that they actually eroded male officers' military professionalism by making them undisciplined as well. Piquet's condemnation of women was reminiscent of General Pierre Ruffey's claims that women dissolved military men's self-discipline and thus their ability to do their duty by bringing sexuality into the army workplace. Both during and after the war, these objections failed to roll back women's roles within the army because of how valuable women had become to officers and male civilian managers who needed to keep their services functioning despite a shortage of soldiers to do the work.

As more and more officers got used to women's permanent presence within the army, membership in the military community was redefined to allow women to be part of it. That process began with the uses of blood ties to fallen soldiers to justify accepting their surviving family members as worthy members of the military community. Later in the 1920s, officers used women's gender as a defense against the civilian world as they became worried about some politicians' efforts to give soldiers voting rights. The army's excessive fear of communism and voting rights created a space that women could occupy within the military community as accepted, but subordinate, members. It also showed that military leaders' attitudes toward the republican political system were actually hardening in the 1920s, a period most scholars see as relatively quiet in terms of civil-military discord.

Future studies could build on this realization by questioning the claim that the Vichy Regime grew out of civilian fascist politics or that it was a rupture with French politics that was brought on by the German conquest. The fact that anticivilian and antidemocratic attitudes were hardening inside the officer corps in the mid-1920s suggests that civil-military relations and the role of the army in France's governmental and political systems deserve more attention from scholars trying to understand the origins of the Vichy Regime.

WERE WOMEN CIVILIAN EMPLOYEES SOLDIERS?

During the Second World War, 1,047 American women served as Women Air Force Service Pilots (WASPs). Despite wearing a uniform and performing the same job as US Army Air Corps pilots, these women pilots were not recognized as performing military service; instead they, like many French women, served as civilian employees. In 1977 President Jimmy Carter signed legislation that retroactively recognized the WASPs as members of the military, and in 1984 President Ronald Reagan awarded all of the women the World War II Victory Medal. Changes in how Americans constructed military service and identity led to these 1,047 civilian women becoming veterans at the stroke of President Carter's pen, proving that contemporary concepts of who was part of the military need not always bind later generations.

   Although the present study does not advocate legally militarizing civilian employees of the French Army from the 1914–45 era, it does argue
that women civilian employees of the army should be recognized by historians as integral parts of their service. They were not soldiers, but they
were part of the French Army. Women like Marguerite Baudion were
never recognized as soldiers, and there is no reason to suspect that Baudion ever thought of herself as a soldier, but she and hundreds of thousands of other French women dedicated parts of their lives, and in some
cases their entire working lives, to the army. Throughout her career, Baudion worked beside soldiers acting as military secretaries, many of whom
she probably helped train. She was never counted as part of the French
Army's muster strength, but her presence indirectly added manpower to
combat units, and her skill helped to make her office work more efficiently
further strengthening the army. Baudion and hundreds of thousands of
other civilian women were critical to the daily functioning and combat
capacity of the French Army from the time they began working there in
1915, and civilian employees have only become more important to the
army since conscription was abolished in 2001. They have never been recognized as soldiers, but they ought to be recognized as an integral part of
the army and, by extension, important contributors to France's national
defense.

   In the February 2004 issue of *Terre*, the monthly magazine of the
French Army, General Michel Poulet defended France's recent transition
to a professional army. He praised women soldiers, reservists, and civilian
employees for taking on more responsibilities and argued that professional male soldiers should accept them as indispensable comrades in the
new French Army. Responding to concerns that the army's reliance on
women was a weakness, General Poulet praised France's women solders
for displaying "incontestable qualities: pugnacity, efficiency, precision,
energy, [and] determination" on a daily basis. He went on to recognize the
increased importance of reservists and called attention to the vital role of
civilian employees, fully 20 percent of the army's personnel. After reminding his readers that the army would collapse without its women
soldiers, reservists, and civilians, Poulet concluded with a call for military communities to unite "in discipline and in the fraternity of arms" to

complete the transformation and protect France's national interests.[2] Poulet's call for unity and mutual respect was more eloquent than what most
French leaders managed during World War I or the interwar era, but its
underlying logic would have been instantly recognizable to General Pierre
Roques when he was trying to overcome entrenched hostility to women
working inside the army while creating the 1916 Regime. By taking a broad
view of who was part of the French Army it becomes clear that women,
and indeed men, did not need to have been soldiers to play an important
role in France's national defense or to be a functioning part of the force.
The breaking down of barriers that prevent women from playing a full and
equal part in contemporary armies is a welcome process, but it should not
obscure the fact that even in times and places when women were prevented from being soldiers, they still played critical roles within their
country's armies and in national defense more broadly. In other words,
women have long found ways to help protect their countries without having to be Jeanne d'Arc.

NOTES

1. For a discussion of Higonnet and Higonnet's double helix theory, see the introduction
to the present volume; see also Higonnet and Higonnet, "The Double Helix."
2. Général Michel Poulet, "Hommes-femmes, active-réserve, civils-militaires: meme
combat!" *Terre* 151 (2004): 4.

SELECTED BIBLIOGRAPHY

Archival Sources

Archivès nationales (AN), Paris

Series F/7—Police and political surveillance

Archivès de la service historique de la défense (SHD), Vincennes

Département de l'armée de terre (DT)

Series L
Series N 1871–1940
Series NN 1919–40
Series YG

Département de la marine (DM)

Series BB
Series SS ED

Books and Articles

Accampo, Elinor A., Rachel G. Fuchs, and Mary Lynn Stewart, eds., *Gender and the Politics of Social Reform: France 1870–1914*. Baltimore: Johns Hopkins University Press, 1995.

Alexander, Martin. *The Republic in Danger: Maurice Gamelin and the Politics of French Defense, 1933–1940*. Cambridge: Cambridge University Press, 1992.

Antier, Chantal, *Les Femmes dans la Grande Guerre*. Paris: Soteca, 2011.

Bankwitz, Philip. *Maxime Weygand and Civil-Military Relations in Modern France*. Cambridge, MA: Harvard University Press, 1967.

Bederman, Gail. *Manliness and Civilization: A Cultural History of Gender and Race in the United States, 1880–1917*. Chicago: University of Chicago Press, 1995.

Berkin, Carol. *Revolutionary Mothers: Women in the Struggle for America's Independence*. New York: Vintage, 2003.

Blanton, De Ann, and Lauren Cook. *They Fought Like Demons: Women Soldiers in the Civil War.* New York: Vintage, 2003.

Bock, Fabienne. *Un Parlementarisme de Guerre 1914–1919.* Paris: Belin, 2002.

Capdevila, Luc. "La mobilisation des femmes dans la France combattante 1940–1945." *Clio: Femmes, Genre, Histoire* 12 (2000). https://clio.revues.org/187.

Cardoza, Thomas. *Intrepid Women: Cantinières and Vivandières of the French Army.* Bloomington: Indiana University Press, 2010.

Chrastil, Rachel. *Organizing for War: France 1870–1914.* Baton Rouge: Louisiana State University Press, 2010.

Darrow, Margaret. *French Women and the First World War: War Stories of the Home Front.* New York: Berg, 2002.

Davis, Belinda. *Home Fires Burning: Food, Politics, and Everyday Life in World War I Berlin.* Chapel Hill: University of North Carolina Press, 2000.

Dominé, Jean-François. *Les Femmes au Combat: L'arme feminine de la France pendant la Seconde Guerre mondiale.* Paris: Service historique de la Défense, 2008.

Doughty, Robert. *Pyrrhic Victory: French Strategy and Operations in the Great War.* Cambridge, MA: Belknap, 2005.

Downs, Laura Lee. *Manufacturing Inequality: Gender Division in the British and French Metalworking Industries, 1914–1939.* Ithaca, NY: Cornell University Press, 1995.

Echenberg, Myron. *Colonial Conscripts: The Tirailleurs Senegalais in French West Africa, 1857–1960.* New York: Heinemann, 1991.

Elshtain, Jean Bethke. *Women and War.* Chicago: University of Chicago Press, 1987.

Frader, Laura. *Breadwinners and Citizens: Gender in the Making of the French Social Model.* Durham, NC: Duke University Press, 2008.

Grayzel, Susan. *Women's Identities at War: Gender, Motherhood, and Politics in Britain and France during the First World War.* Chapel Hill: University of North Carolina Press, 1999.

Hacker, Barton C. "Women and Military Institutions in Early Modern Europe: A Reconnaissance." *Signs: Journal of Women and Culture in Society* 6, no. 4 (1981): 643–71.

Hacker, Barton C., and Margaret Vinning, eds. *A Companion to Women's Military History.* Leiden, Netherlands: Brill, 2010.

Hanna, Martha. *Your Death Would Be Mine: Paul and Marie Pireaud in the Great War.* Cambridge, MA: Harvard University Press, 2006.

Hause, Steven C., and Anne R. Kenney. *Women's Suffrage and Social Politics in the French Third Republic.* Princeton, NJ: Princeton University Press, 1984.

Higonnet, Margaret, Jene Jackson, Sonya Muchel, and Margaret Weitz, eds. *Behind the Line: Gender and the Two World Wars.* New Haven, CT: Yale University Press, 1987.

Horne, Alistair. *The French Army and Politics 1870–1970.* London: Macmillan, 1984.

Hughes, Judith. *To the Maginot Line: The Politics of French Military Preparation in the 1920's.* Cambridge, MA: Harvard University Press, 1971.

Hunt, Lynn. *The Family Romance of the French Revolution.* Berkeley: University of California Press, 1983.

Jaurès, Jean. *L'Armée Nouvelle.* Edited by Jean-Noel Jeanneney. Paris: Imprimerie Nationale, 1992.

Jeanneney, Jean-Nöel. *Leçon d'histoire pour une gauche au pouvoir: La faillite du cartel (1924–1926).* Paris: Plon, 1997.

Jensen, Kimberly. *Mobilizing Minerva: American Women in the First World War.* Urbana: University of Illinois Press, 2007.

Kielsing, Eugenia. *Arming against Hitler: France and the Limits of Military Planning.* Lawrence: University of Kansas Press, 1996.

Lacour-Astol, Catherine. *Le genre de la Résistance. La Résistance féminine dans le Nord de la France.* Paris: Presses de Sciences Po, 2015.

Larkin, Maurice. *France since the Popular Front: Government and People, 1936–1996.* 2nd ed. New York: Oxford University Press, 1997.

Lynn, John A, II. Review of Thomas Cardoza, *Intrepid Women: Cantinières and Vivandières of the French Army. American Historical Review* 116, no. 3 (2011): 879–80.

———. *Women, Armies, and Warfare in Early Modern Europe.* New York: Cambridge University Press, 2008.

Marty, André. *La Révolte de la Mer Noire.* 4th ed. Paris: Éditions Sociales, 1949.

Noakes, Lucy. *Women in the British Army: War and the Gentler Sex, 1907–1948.* New York: Routledge, 2006.

Ralston, Dennis. *The Army of the Republic: The Place of the Military in the Political Evolution of France.* Cambridge, MA: MIT Press, 1997.

Read, Geoff. *The Republic of Men: Gender and the Political Parties in Interwar France.* Baton Rouge: Louisiana State University Press, 2014.

Régis, Antoine. *La Littérature Pacifiste et Internationaliste Française 1915–1935.* Paris: L'Harmattan, 2002.

Rolland, Denis. *La Grève des Tranchées: Les mutineries de 1917.* Paris: Imago, 2005.

Rupp, Leila. *Mobilizing Women for War: German and American Propaganda, 1939–1945.* Princeton, NJ: Princeton University Press, 1978.

Sarnoff, Daniella. "Interwar Fascism and the Franchise: Women's Suffrage and the *Ligues*." *Historical Reflections* 34, no. 2 (2008): 112–33.

Slavin, David. "The French Left and the Riff War, 1924–25: Racism and the Limits of Internationalism." *Journal of Contemporary History* 26 (1991): 5–32.

Smith, Bonnie G. *Confessions of a Concierge: Madam Lucie's History of Twentieth-Century France.* New Haven, CT: Yale University Press, 1985.

Smith, Paul. *Feminism and the Third Republic: Women's Political and Civil Rights in France, 1918–1945.* Oxford: Clarendon, 1996.

Travers, Susan, and Wendy Holden. *Tomorrow to Be Brave: A Memoir of the Only Woman Ever to Serve in the French Foreign Legion.* New York: Touchstone, 2007.

Virgili, Fabrice, and Danièle Voldman. *La Garçonne et l'assassin: Histoire de Louise et de Paul, déserteur travesti, dans le Paris des années folles.* Paris: Payot, 2011.

Wakeham, Sarah Rosetta. *An Uncommon Soldier: The Civil War Letters of Sarah Rosetta Wakeman, alias Pvt. Lyons Wakeman, 153rd Regiment, New York State Volunteers, 1862–1864.* Edited by Lauren Cook Burgess. New York: Oxford University Press, 1996.

Watson, Janet. *Fighting Different Wars: Experience, Memory, and the First World War in Britain.* New York: Cambridge University Press, 2004.

Weygand, Maxime. *Histoire de l'Armée Française.* Paris: Flammarion, 1961.

INDEX

192

INDEX

ANDREW ORR

is Assistant Professor of History at Kansas State University and a
member of its Security Studies Program. He earned his PhD
from the University of Notre Dame and his work focuses on the
French military and political history from 1870 to 1945. Orr lives
in Manhattan, Kansas.

CPSIA information can be obtained
at www.ICGtesting.com
Printed in the USA
LVHW041107140419
614129LV00003B/588